John Gabree writes regularly on urban problems for *Design & Environment, Fusion,* and several counter-culture newspapers. He also contributes a book review column to *Newsday,* moonlights as a carpenter, and devotes much of his free time to a vegetable and herb garden that graces his restored brownstone on Manhattan's Upper West Side. A New Yorker's New Yorker, his first wish for the city is to clear it of cars, restore its pleasures to bikers and pedestrians, refurbish the subways and replace diesel-powered buses with electric ones, have all truck deliveries made at night—and tear down the ugly and dangerous West Side Highway to create a magnificent park.

SURVIVING THE CITY

A Sourcebook of Papers on Urban Livability

Edited by
John Gabree

BALLANTINE BOOKS • NEW YORK

Copyright © 1973 by John Gabree

All rights reserved.

SBN 345-23616-5-195

First Printing: November, 1973

Printed in the United States of America

Cover photo by Mort Engel

BALLANTINE BOOKS, INC.
201 East 50th Street, New York, N.Y. 10022

To My Parents

Contents

Introduction	ix
The Ecological Approach to the Social Sciences F. Fraser Darling	1
Social Space in Interdisciplinary Perspective Anne Buttimer	15
City and Psyche A. E. Parr	30
Images of Urban Areas Derk de Jonge	45
Some Childhood Memories of the City Alvin Lukashok and Kevin Lynch	65
Architecture and Group Membership Leon Festinger	90
A City Is Not a Tree Christopher Alexander	106
The Social Effects of the Physical Environment Irving Rosow	137
The Human Implications of Current Redevelopment and Relocation Planning Herbert J. Gans	153
Mass Housing: Social Research and Design Brent C. Brolin and John Zeisel	180
Neighborhood Concepts in Sociological Perspective Suzanne Keller	190
Urban Design and Environmental Structuring Frank L. Elmer and Duncan B. Sutherland, Jr.	213
Improving the Design Process in Urban Renewal Roger Montgomery	219
Urban Sociology as an Aid to Urban Physical Development: Some Research Strategies William Michelson	240
Social Research and New Communities Peter Willmott	252

Introduction

Before we go any further, I should warn you what this book is not about. For the most part it is not about immediate answers to the problems of the city: it does not predict how the city will grow, it does not offer specific design solutions, it does not estimate the costs of capital outlays and maintenance, nor does it suggest how to maximize the use of the city's dwindling open space, how to face the approaching water shortage and energy, air, and noise pollution crises, how to dispose of the daily mountain of garbage, or how to short-circuit the communications overload. *Surviving The City* is aimed at one particular point: how the design professions—and the environments they produce—can be improved by the application of the insights, techniques and methods of the behavioral sciences.

The city, and latterly the metropolis, is the dominant form of human society. For 2,000 years, urban life and civilization have been virtually synonymous. Commerce, government and the arts have each roosted in the narrow alleyways or spanned the broad avenues of Athens, Rome, Paris, London and New York. The last 100 years have produced a new super city, the metropolis, probably already the home of most Westerners, soon to be home for a majority of the globe's inhabitants. Despite incredible obstacles—danger from crime, air and noise pollution, ever higher rents, inhuman transportation systems, unresponsive municipal governments and deteriorating services, most of us would prefer to live in a city.

People live in the city for many reasons: privacy, economic opportunity, ease of communication, proximity to cultural institutions, and so on. It is the planner's job to discover these motivations and to cater to them. It has been found, to take one example, that change has become the terrifying thing it is to many city dwellers because, in this century, it has led so often to the loss of a sense of security, an important element in an emotionally stable environment. This psychological insight should persuade a designer to find a new way to build a new neighborhood on the site of an old, established one. It is not perversity that leads, say, urban poor so often to prefer their old delapidated buildings to the sleek barren warrens of public housing. Clearly they miss something that made their lives in the slums richer. Planners must work with sociologists and psychologists to discover what that is.

The pieces in this volume, taken together, suggest ways in which interdisciplinary approaches to design can be achieved.

An anthology is a peculiar construction. It is shaped by its components the way a house might be if all you had was a hammer and some nails and whatever lengths of wood you could find. You might have an idea of the house you would like to build, but with your scraps of wood you would never manage more than an approximation. I had a pretty definite idea of the kind of book I wanted, but I discovered that, though the ideas I wanted to explore were generally in circulation, very few were set down in a manner useful to an anthologist. So *that* book remains to be written.

This book, full to bursting though it is with classic works of theory and practice, suffers from the fact that some of the pieces I originally wanted to include were too long. There are no chapters by Robert Sommer, for example, and only a short collaboration by Kevin Lynch, because the work of both men deserves to be studied in its entirety. Similarly, for variety's sake I have included only one piece by each author, even though there were other articles, especially by Christopher Alexander, Roger Montgomery, and A. E. Parr, that I would have liked to have included. Buckminster Fuller, Paul Goodman and Edward T. Hall, on the other hand, are too widely known to warrant inclusion of material that would be familiar to most readers. Most of the final choices were made from some combination of intrinsic value and relationship to the main theme.

As is usual, this book could not have been completed had I not been bailed out several times along the way by my friends. Besides the authors herein included, I owe thanks to Leonore Fleischer, my editor at Ballantine, who inspired this collection and then didn't pinch me too hard when the project sometimes seemed like a bad dream; E. R. Lendler, without whose copier, Nadja Tubelskaya, without whose files, and J. M. Vallely, without whose patience this volume never would have been completed; Ann Ferrebee of *Design & Environment* magazine, Paul Violi of *The Architectural Forum* magazine, and Robert Somma of *Fusion* magazine, who have helped and encouraged me at crucial moments; and my comrades at Dockery's Tavern (this time especially Eileen Palley and John Stickney) whose Thursday lunches have been for me an important part of surviving the city.

New York, January, 1973

Surviving the City

The Ecological Approach to the Social Sciences

F. Fraser Darling

Some years ago there was a great advance in Britain in the methods of growing grass, the basic food of livestock. We learned how to grow more grass, how to lay down new pastures, to select leafy strains, and to compound seed mixtures which would give early and late grazing. Indeed, such was the thrill of power, some agricultural scientists became grass fanciers and forgot the livestock in what should have been a cow's millenium.

Nobody asked the cow.

Nevertheless, the grass fanciers were sure they were in the position to supply the best of all possible cows' worlds and could point to results in increased stocking capacity, more beef, more milk. The problem of cows' lives was solved.

But was it? The cows had a habit of searching diligently in the hedge bottoms and some were so perverse as to break out of heaven and graze the roadside roughage. And lately, investigators have come upon a number of digestive disturbances and conditions, which can really only be called poisoning, occurring on these improved, artificial pastures.

Within the last five years, students of animal behavior have begun to study cows and record their observations. You can present the cow with a questionnaire, but she is inarticulate, like most human beings. Yet she has quite decided opinions and all sorts of little preferences, dislikes, and fussinesses which are important to the good life—of cows. We are learning more of how to keep cows in mental and physical health by watching them. When do they feed, when do they rest, what is it they seek in the hedge bottoms; and if they find it, how much of it do they want; what is the physical and chemical quality of the plant sought? Do cows like trees, and if so, what for—cover, browse, backscratchers, or what? What is the structure and nature of their community life? A cow's world, you will see, is becoming a complex one, and it is quite difficult to assess scientifically the various environmental factors which influence her well-being. Her life cannot be planned from the material end with such omniscience that she can be popped down in the environment which we are assured provides the greatest good for the greatest number—of cows. She has shown us that the environment should be planned around her as a sentient organism and a personality in a social group. She had forest-roaming ancestors.

So had we.

The much greater complexity of human communities and the more baffling mental and physical sicknesses we suffer as a result of having tried to create for ourselves a grass fancier's world, are the reasons for my choosing this title for my paper. You cannot turn a highly bred dairy cow back into the forest again, and it is quite certain that *we* are not going "back to nature." Yet we must go on learning something of the natural history of man.

I am merely a biologist whose main interest is ecology and animal behavior in relation to conservation, but during the last seventeen years I have been applying the methods of ecology to studying the life of the West Highland people among whom I have lived; the study was desultory for ten years or more, but has been intensive since then. The underlying principle in conservation today is to study the complexity of the habitat, the wholeness of the environment, and the relations and behavior of the animals within it in time as well as in space; and if you can keep the habitat going, in sufficient quantity that it is not dying on the fringes, there is no difficulty in conserving any particular animal within it. The social life of the animal is now recognized as being an important part of its environment. Conservation in this sense is closely associated with the pressures between human communities and their environment and between themselves. The study of these is human ecology.

At the end of these six years the conviction has grown

that the ecological approach to a study of human communities can be an illuminating one, but I would not be so bold as to say that I could now set down a sound statement of what human ecology is. Rather I have learned what a great deal we do not know, and the good idea of human ecology will need much hard thinking and careful discipline before it is good science. That is what many of us are seeking in our different ways: to make the social investigation of man into good science. Human ecology deals with the structure of animal communities which man dominates and their development through the ecological principle of succession. As Paul Sears says, "The social function of ecology is to provide a scientific basis whereby man may shape the environment and his relations to it as he expresses himself in and through his culture patterns." Perhaps in these early days of human ecology it would be better not to set it up as a science, but rather to say that human problems may be nearer solution if we tackle them ecologically.

I believe that human ecology and social science can be good science, but we should not confuse it with social service. If I may say so, the natural history of man and the emergent social sciences are not missionary endeavor. If, as scientists, we come upon an outbreak of wife-beating, the men's immortal souls and the women's suffering backs are not our primary concern, as investigators. We would seek causes for the phenomenon, and possibly find it in a hectoring foreman and the operation of peck-orders. Doormats among animals and men have a habit of being hard on their females and children.

There are different levels in what might be called the social management of man. These are exploration and fact-finding, research and the development of ideas, application, and maintenance. We should not confuse the first two of these strata with the second two.

I was once asked by a social anthropologist what human ecology was that social anthropology was not. This was a very right and proper question to which the reply should be that there is no difference. But I ventured to say that human ecology deals essentially with *process*. The value of the ecologist in society will be in his power and accuracy in elucidating causes and forecasting consequences.

The West Highland Problem

The relatively small West Highland and Hebridean populations live close to their physical elemental environment, and to the natural resources on which they have largely depended for their existence. It seemed to me, when I began the West Highland Survey seven years ago, that the problem of the Highlands should be investigated from the biological point of view, looking on the people—without the least disrespect—as members of the indigenous fauna and social animals, and inquiring what were the factors of change in the environment, or in them, which were rendering man a slowly failing species in that environment. This was an essay in human ecology, the approach of a naturalist in conservation as contrasted with the economic attitude of mind which tends to be that of the grass fancier toward the cow. The West Highland problem cannot be described here in detail, but will serve for illustration of what I consider to be the ecological approach to the study of social behavior.

Broadly, the Highland problem is that of a very old and in many ways primitive human culture existing in an administratively awkward and physically refractory terrain set on the fringe of a highly industrialized urban civilization, which itself is situated in one of the greenest, kindest lands on earth. Highlanders have been part and parcel of our national structure for only two hundred years, having until then lived a very different kind of life, in standards, laws, language, and techniques, than had the rest of Britain. Yet Highlanders are not New Hebrideans or Eskimos over whom, try as we may to the contrary, we feel some kind of mental superiority. Here is a race of people of probably greater average intelligence and intellect than the dominant group, indistinguishable from it in physical appearance. And as members of this race moved so smoothly and successfully in the dominant civilization, it was overlooked how different were the inner rhythm of life and the style of thought and tradition. The new centralized British government of that day merely extended its administrative, economic, and social regime to include the Highlands, and with some ameliorations and some encrustations this applies today.

The Ecological Approach to the Social Sciences

In human ecology we can never neglect history, for we are studying process; I would say, therefore, that a cross-sectional social survey is not ecological unless it studies origins and successions, in other words, process. We must always remember the significance of political action as an environmental factor. For example, the manipulation of the Salt Tax in the last part of the eighteenth and early nineteenth centuries had profound results on the lives of Highlanders, and the transposition of the English system of poor relief had some fantastic consequences. Again, imagine the island of Islay being immune from Spirit Duty, as it was in the late eighteenth century: distillers flocked in, the bread corn of the people was deflected to whisky, the distillers were soon making money advances (at their own rates) on the barley crops of small tenants; drunkenness was rife and the people were reduced to an appalling social state. The detailed research into population movement conducted by the West Highland Survey shows that this favored island has suffered more than any other part of the Highlands from excessive emigration.

Another historical factor at the root of the Highland problem of today, is the exploitation which the natural resources suffered in the past. The Tudor monarchs in England were already conscious that the supply of oak was dwindling, and there were prohibitions on the felling of English oak. This sent the shipbuilders northwards to the Scottish forests; and a hundred years later, when the iron districts of Surrey and Sussex had lost their trees, there was a determined attack on Highland forests to provide fuel and charcoal. The iron ore was shipped up there. The ultimate disappearance of the forests followed the introduction of sheep-farming on the extensive, extractive system in the second half of the eighteenth century.

The countryside was one of steep hills, initially poor rocks, and of high rainfall. The climax vegetation which conserved fertility was broken, and there was rapid deterioration of the habitat. That is the core of the problem today: the people are living in a devastated habitat. And now we come to another important ecological factor, the age of the culture. The Gael is living where he has lived for several thousand years and is tenacious of place and culture. How different from North Wisconsin, where settlers went in to still virgin forests in the 1920's, devastated their environment in a very short time, and left! "Ghost towns" remain. The administration which furthered the movement had forgotten the podsol conditions of the soil in relation to climate. A heterogeneous aggregation of people would not continue to inhabit a devastated terrain in the way an old culture hangs on to its place, even in decay.

Before leaving the historical aspect, we might consider briefly the effect of a change of food habits. Dr. Salaman of Cambridge has recently published his great book, *The History and Social Influence of the Potato;* it is a mine of wealth for the human ecologist. The acceptance of the potato as the staff of life allowed an immense increase in the number of mouths so long as a low standard of existence was accepted. The history of the west of Ireland and the West Highlands and islands of Scotland—both places where wheat was not grown and where the bread corn was relatively difficult to harvest—shows that the potato, coinciding with the practice of vaccination, did bring about a swarming of the population and a very marked depression in the standard of living. Potatoes and maize meal were staples of diet at the most chaotic period. Arthur Young tried to make the potato the food of the rural working class in England; Cobbett fought the potato school tooth and nail, and the English laborer stood firm by his wheaten loaf.

We may take it for granted that when a countryside begins to feed on much the same diet as its pigs, social problems are piling up ahead. And that is the right order; the change in diet precedes the social trouble. The human ecologist will never neglect the belly of the people. Professor Paul Sears has noted an interesting situation that occurred in Mexico. The government had prohibited the fermentation of a beer, pulque, from a plant called maguéy that is grown as a stiff hedge of spiky leaves. The result of the prohibition was a high incidence of diseases associated with deficiency of vitamin B, and only when the plant was ceasing to be grown was it discovered that it was one of the most efficient anti-erosion plants on the plateau.

To return to the Highlands: the destruction of the forests has meant the removal of cover, and this environmental factor is of great importance in human lives. Humanity needs cover for all sorts of things—shelter for crops and stock;

cover to enable a man to do a little experimentation which he dare not try if the eyes of every household in the township are upon him; and cover for courting and love-making. It is obvious what a social problem lack of cover imposes in certain types of urban communities. In the Highlands it has imposed a set of conventions almost the exact opposite of our own. Darkness is the only cover, but this is supplemented by a build-up of psychological cover. The Tiree crofter visits the Duke of Argyll's factor on the nights of no moon, though he could just as well go in the day. A fellow and a girl in the Hebrides will ignore each other in daytime should they meet on the road, but he will be calling at her home just about the time of night when in our culture we should have taken our leave. Good manners require that he be gone before it is light.

I have mentioned the value of cover in experimentation. We tend to forget how important it is in primitive communities that people should not be different, and the initial attempts to be different are the most dangerous ones. Think how in our own lives we like to experiment in private and avoid being different in the beginning. The Anglo-Saxon races have a firm belief in the power of demonstration in changing methods of doing things. This is a fallacy. The Gael or the Mexican is wiser. It does not matter that a changed practice will reap him a bigger material reward. That is not recompense for having to that extent placed himself outside his group. If the material reward is real, he will be envied by his fellows, and that is not a good state to be in. If the reward is illusory, he will be ridiculed, and that is not good either in a society where there is no privacy.

I have seen the sudden loss of cover depress a small community psychologically, because of the sudden cessation of the opportunity to grow flowers and fruit. Nor should we neglect an animate factor such as the rabbit as a creator of deserts, and as an animal weed of poor land. I have seen a community give up all effort at gardening because of rabbits, and looking forth on a deteriorating habitat fostered psychological ills of frustration and ultimate indifference. Village halls do not correct this kind of situation. The first requirement is a coordinated scheme of habitat rehabilitation. It is in this way that the Tennessee Valley Authority has been such a splendid ecological project.

Deterioration of the Habitat

The science of ecology deals with causes of observed biological phenomena, and it should be expected to lay bare multiple-factor causation, which is a very difficult field. But it is also concerned with consequences and ramifications. The practical value of ecology, as I have said, is the ability to forecast consequences of certain courses of action and of observable trends. The politician has to be very careful here, and I would suggest that the ecologist is as necessary a servant to the statesman as the economist. Let me take examples from the Highland problem. I have said that the destruction of the region's greatest natural wealth, its forests, was followed by the establishment of large-scale sheepfarming on the ranching, extractive system. The immediate social consequences of this were unfortunate, in that the people were pushed to the coast and suffered a forcible social break. This kind of sheepfarming meant a very heavy preponderance of sheep over cattle, and I have managed to discover in detail how this style of grazing destroys the habitat over a period of a century or so.

The soil is in general sour and peaty, and the roots of trees reaching down to the rock and possible glacial drift were an essential means of bringing mineral matter of a basic nature to the surface. First it went to the leaves, and as a proportion of the calcium-rich young leaves were eaten by caterpillars, there was a rain of their feces onto the surface of the ground, where they were consumed by earthworms, which are so necessary in the British terrain to the production of a porous, well-mixed soil. Removal of the trees has broken the circulatory system of basic salts and destroyed the continuum. Earthworms disappear if the calcium level of their medium is not maintained; the soil becomes a tough, peaty skin and loses its absorptive as well as its nutritive qualities. Sheep graze much more selectively than cattle and tend to remove the more palatable components of the herbage, especially the ameliorative legumes. Sheep also neglect tall and toughened herbage, so that burning of the terrain is necessary when the sheep-cattle ratio is wide. This practice in itself impoverishes the variety of the herbage, helps the spread of the bracken fern, and tends to produce a biotic climax of a few dominants of poor nutritive quality. Burning on peat slopes also tends to produce an impervious surface which accelerates lateral runoff. This runoff water, being heavily charged with carbonic acid as it runs over the acid peat, itself helps in souring the land in the glens. This is a story of impoverishment of habitat by imposing a foreign land use.

Where the sheep-cattle ratio is grossly disturbed, conditions for a peasantry become desperate. I have now reached the stage in the Highlands when I can say: "Tell me the cattle-sheep ratio in an area, and I shall know the social health of the people." If the ratio is wide, 30-50 or more sheep to one cattle-beast, there is serious trouble; if it is under 10, things are not so bad. One can also correlate the cattle-sheep ratio with the age-structure of the population. Another thing that becomes evident is that it is the children who keep milk cows on the land; when the age-structure gets top-heavy like that of Assynt in 1931, down goes the number of milk cows.

The descending spiral of fertility of the general habitat, as outlined above, is continued on the inbye land of the croft: when a man replaces his cattle with sheep, he finds he has no manure for his arable plot, and the yields go down so far that his capacity for winter cattle is decreased. He also finds that he must bring his ewes onto the inbye land to lamb, and there they stay, nibbling the heart out of the grass until the end of May. Such meadow land cannot be expected to yield a good crop of hay, and being relieved of grazing so late means that the hay crop is not ready to cut until a time when heavy rain is general. This means the hay will not be gotten well and its nutritive value will be poor, so that once more the ability to maintain a cattle stock and the fertility of the arable land is being assailed. It is quite definitely an ecological story, and to attempt to study social and economic problems apart from the biological background would be to blindfold oneself.

Now, where do the politician and economist conflict with the ecologist in the example just given? You may have heard that ten years ago hill sheepfarming was not paying, yet a supply of hill sheep was necessary for the stratification of crosses leading to the low-ground farms, which were paying.

The economist finds many good reasons for the discrepancy, though deterioration of the habitat by the hill sheep is not one of them. He says: "We must take some of the high profit from the fat-lamb end of the chain and put it back at the fountainhead." And this has been done by giving a substantial subsidy to hill ewes. The idea may have worked well in the Southern Uplands of Scotland, but in the poor terrain of the Highlands the ewe subsidy might have been specially designed for further deterioration of the habitat and for fostering social unhealth. The politician says we cannot start differentiating between one countryside and another in a measure of this kind. All he could do was to slap a still bigger subsidy on hill cattle and another new one on calves. The economists here will admit that this is a dangerous path to follow, and I as an ecologist will say, from close observation of this particular measure, that the ultimate good it can do is negligible unless it is linked with vigorous rehabilitation of habitat, which is the basis of social health.

Other Sources of Social Problems

Depopulation and distortion of the age-structure go together and bring a new set of social problems. People in and out of the Highlands have said often enough that industries should be established there, industries of the kind where wheels go round in an important way. But what do we find? Where such industry has been established, there has been even greater depopulation in the adjacent rural areas, yet the big problem is how to maintain dispersion. Fort William and Kinlochleven may have provided Britain with aluminum, but they have created new social problems and solved none.

The remoter areas of the Highlands need roads and better transport, and scarcely anyone can be found to question the benefit that might accrue. But again, this obvious measure of amelioration must be considered ecologically. For example, I happen to know well the townships on either side of a long sea loch, one side of which has a road and the other has not. The living conditions of the people either side are different. Those on the road buy Glasgow bread (untouched by hand) and packaged goods of all sorts, and I have seen tinned porridge sold from the vans. The communities are absolutely dependent on the vans, and their standard of husbandry is low. On the other side of the loch, more cows are kept; cheese and butter are made; homemade oatcakes and porridge are the cereal staple rather than bought bread; the men fish more, and the standard of husbandry is higher. So what has the road done? It has given those people the benefit of our well-known brands of this and that and a daily paper. But it has not so reorganized the habitat that the so-called higher standard of living can be paid for out of the greater amount of produce exported. Indeed, quite apart from the loss of social health and skills, these people are in a worse economic plight. On the roadless side there is still self-sufficiency, competence, and a realization that the croft must be well farmed. A road can be a benefit only if the environmental factors are closely studied and integrated. Here is seen clearly the effect on this small, old, subsistence culture, of being on the fringe of the most highly developed urban culture of its day. Had most of Britain been like the Highlands, the impact might have been less severe.

The ecologist asks that unquestioned beliefs should be questioned. Good communications is one of these; education is another. Consider, for example, the problem of educating the Reindeer Lapps in Scandinavia. How do you do it? The convenient way is to put the children in schools in the winter season when the Lapps are at the southernmost end of their pastoral migration. But if this is done the families and their reindeer are unduly immobilized, and the secret of pastoralism in poor terrain is to keep on the move. The winter range of the Reindeer Lapps is thus being overbrowsed, and as it is the amount of winter range which determines numbers of livestock, the damage to the birch and willow forests means that the high summer potential of the tundra is being less used. We can still believe in education, of course, but at least let us ponder methods of applying it, in terms of consequences on the habitat.

I have mentioned depopulation and the distortion of the age-group pyramids. The problems of human ecology arising from the phenomenon in small communities are manifold. In the first place, the old remain in power and so prevail that they can initiate an era of reaction in the life of a community, so that in a region of hard-shell Presbyterianism all gaiety for the young is frowned upon. And nowhere do the young show greater consideration for the old than in the Highlands. I know of townships where there are but few married couples now. Brothers and sisters have cared for their old folk, and now that they are gone they continue living in their parents' houses and cannot bring themselves to the considerable upset of getting married. The social urge and necessary gaiety are not there. This depression of the vivid social life of man is likely to lead to such undesirable consequences as burning of the hills in an excitement bordering on hysteria. The crass burnings of the heather are made ostensibly to further the growth of young grass; in actual fact they further the devastation of the habitat. The fires occur at Beltane, which was once the breeding season. Where the social life is in better order, burning is under control. That great American ecologist, Charles Adams, who has now turned his attention to mankind, told me recently of an almost identical phenomenon in one of the southern states, and of how the problem had solved itself with improvement in social conditions.

It is difficult to avoid the impression that religion is a considerable ecological factor, but it must always be related with other environmental characteristics. The areas of most pronounced depopulation in the Highlands have the harshest sects of Presbyterianism; but I do not want to overdo this idea or give a wrong impression, because the area of greatest congestion, Lewis, follows the same faith. What I would say is this: that in the Highlands a small, remote community with poor services would have more chance of survival if it were Catholic than if it were Free Presbyterian. This is because there is more sense of community to be found in the districts of the old, liberal—almost Columban —style of Catholicism. The culture is stronger altogether; music and folk tales have not been dimmed, and the status of women is higher. Birth rates are exactly the same. It is in these small, isolated communities, where the social pattern of humankind can scarcely be completed, that a factor which is associated with the old culture can be critical.

The human ecologist must always be on the lookout for these marginal factors, the comprehension of which may illuminate a much wider field where complexity defeats scientific investigation.

The Ecological Approach to the Social Sciences 13

There is one more illustration that I want to give from the Island of Lewis, which, as I have said, is a congested island. The terrain is poor, but the people have been there for 4,000 years or so, with various immigrant waves which have accepted the old culture and have not imposed their own. The old Celtic custom of subdivision of land, and the intense conviction that the land is theirs, have resulted in the island's being entirely held by crofters, all doing much the same thing. It is a one-class society worthy of very close study. Weaving has given prosperity, and though the land is tending to be neglected because it is more profitable to weave, the people cannot effect the social revolution of relinquishing at least lip service to subsistence husbandry, and thereby achieving division of labor and social stratification. There is an intense social life from house to house among the young in Lewis, who are numerous enough to maintain a fine gaiety in the face of religious proscription, but there is little knowledge of the constructive or artistic use of leisure. Nearly everybody is a peasant except for a handful of professional people in Stornoway. Prosperity has come as money—pound notes—but in rural Lewis there is nothing much to spend money on.* Social evolution would seem to have stuck, and needs a catalyst. Lewis will not allow itself to evolve, and the observer cannot help comparing the tremendous social vitality maintained by the good proportion of young folk, with the stricken life of the dying communities on the mainland shore. The right hand of Lewis reaches out for all that the world can offer, but her left hand holds fast to the croft in the unenclosed township, and she is anchored in time. The fact that the crofting townships are unenclosed, precludes differentiation of husbandry and agricultural improvement.

I want to close these remarks on the natural history of society by pointing the obvious: that tradition and accumulated experience are part of man's environment, and for all the importance of the physical and biological factors I have mentioned, the ethos is still the biggest ecological factor of all on the life of the individual. Here I would digress for a moment on methods of approach in gathering data. The

*At the moment of going to press, the export market for Harris tweed has suffered a relapse; there is depression in the weaving districts of Lewis.

ecologist must distrust the questionnaire so beloved of the sociologists, because it fails to take sufficient notice of the ethos of a people. The questionnaire will not necessarily give you scientific data. In the course of the West Highland Survey we compiled a punch-card Domesday of factual data about crofting townships and it is immensely valuable, but we never asked questions on personal household matters or questions of opinion. Had we done so we should either have come up against a brick wall or, with such a sensitive and penetrating people, we should have got the answers they thought we should like. Much the best way is observation and soaking in the culture. Ability to observe closely and interpret accurately, by way of a large grasp of the organism of a society in its habitat, is the essence of human ecology. It is an integrative science as much as an analytical one, with observation as its basis.

If the psychologists could devise courses in development of the power of observation as part of the training for a research career, we should at least be able to pick out at an early stage those graduates who are fitted to study man as a social animal. After that must come the faculty to use several disciplines. Teamwork in human ecology will be essential, but still each specialist will have to have the quality of delighting in another man's work and linking his own to it; and he cannot be the traditionally remote academic type, but must be inquisitive about what humankind is doing to itself.

Social Space in Interdisciplinary Perspective

Anne Buttimer
(Sister Mary Annette, O.P.)

Dramatic and exciting challenges confront geographers today. Revolutionary changes in empirical social patterns have spelled obsolescence for many traditional analytical procedures; radical transformations in the scholastic world have raised questions concerning the philosophical basis of social-science procedures. Behaviorists and existentialists pose the fundamental question: can science continue to serve a useful function by measuring and explaining the objective face and underlying mechanics of social reality, or must it also penetrate and incorporate its subjective dimensions?[1] As Edward T. Hall[2] so convincingly poses it: does time talk, does space speak? How does the silent language of time and space influence mankind's cultural variations? Geographers ask themselves: should we be satisfied with drafting an opaque, objective map of social patterns in space, or must we supplement this with the subjective or inside view?[3]

This problem is certainly not new. Jules Sion's 1908 study of Normandy showed how differences in the mentality of Norman and Picard peasants reflected and reinforced the contrasts between two physically similar regions.[4] Pierre Gourou's cleverly applied notion of *civilisation* proved how attitudes and skills influenced the evolution of landscape in the Far East.[5] Walter Firey's well-known Boston study[6] demonstrated how cultural variations and traditions have influenced land values in an urban area, and Renée Rochefort's Sicilian study[7] left little doubt concerning the predominant influence in social life on that island: the Mafia! In principle and in practice, then, substantive work demon-

Reprinted by permission from *Geographical Review*, Vol. 59, 1969, copyright by the American Geographical Society of New York.

strates the need for a penetrating analysis of this subjective component in geographical study. A recent article by Paul Claval[8] even suggests that the geographer's unique contribution might well be in comparative cross-cultural studies of group mentality. Few scholars, however, have given concrete and applicable research leads to this kind of analytical endeavor. Among those who have introduced some creative precedents along these lines are two French scholars, Maximilien Sorre and Paul-Henri Chombart de Lauwe, who developed the notion of social space. The present paper is an attempt to sketch certain dimensions of the social-space concept that developed through the dialogue between geographer and sociologist in France, and to discuss its application in urban research today.

Sorre, a traditional geographer with an eye to many new horizons, and Chombart de Lauwe, a sociologist-ethnologist with an equally ecumenical horizon, have many characteristics in common. Both can be considered, in a sense, as prophets unacceptable in their own country. French geographers have paid little overt tribute to Sorre: they have tended to regard him as unorthodox, verbose, and perhaps inclined to confuse science and philosophy. Sociologists of the Sorbonne vintage have sometimes dismissed Chombart de Lauwe's work as superficial, value laden, and marginal to the mainstream. However, if the French echo is faint, the international one is not; Sorre's ideas have claimed a wide audience in disciplines outside geography, and the precedents laid down by Chombart de Lauwe have been welcomed by many schools of sociology and regional planning.

Among Sorre's many contributions to geography are the liaisons that he forged with other disciplines, particularly with biology and sociology. Volume 1 of his chef d'oeuvre, *Les fondements de la géographie humaine*,[9] is permeated with an ecological theme, as its subtitle *Les fondements biologiques de la géographie humaine* indicates. Volume 2 has a more sociological, and sometimes psychological, theme —social groupings were placed within the context of their environment and treated as "techniques of social life"—and Volume 3 deals with settlement patterns as the visible inscription of group activity, attitude, and cultural tradition in the rural landscape. It was in the third volume of Sorre's *Fondements* that Chombart de Lauwe found inspiration for his now famous study of Paris,[10] in which he applied and extended the notion of "social space," loosely defined by Sorre.

From his younger colleague's research Sorre then drew conclusions and wrote during the 1950's on further applications of his social-space concept.[11] At the same time Chombart de Lauwe and his colleagues were advancing along new fronts, leaning more toward urban problems and related spatial planning.

The Concept of Social Space

The concept of social space was first articulated and applied in the 1890's by Émile Durkheim, whose approach to the study of social differentiation was somewhat innovative. Durkheim objected to the environmentalism of Friedrich Ratzel's *Anthropogeographie*, to the evolutionism implicit in Herbert Spencer's *Principles of Sociology*, and to the formalism of Georg Simmel's *Soziale Differenzierung*.[12] Durkheim saw social differentiation in purely social terms: sociology consisted of social morphology, which is the study of the *substrat social* (distribution of social forms) and of social physiology, which is the study of the segmentation, interaction, and "moral density" of society.[13] His definition of the substrat social was the social environment, or group framework, independent of the physical setting. Sorre considered Durkheim's definition of environment too narrow and cited many instances where physical conditions influenced social differentiation.[14] He believed the substrat social should incorporate both the physical and social environments, and for this twofold substrat he used Durkheim's term "social space," qualifying the original meaning to include the physical environment.

In the analysis of social space, the geographer's basic contribution would seem to consist primarily of mapping the distribution of various social groups (Durkheim's "social morphology"). However, the regional monographs of the Vidalian School also contributed to social physiology, showing, for example, the creative role of human groups in transforming their environment (substrat).[15] To place the concept of social space within Sorre's overall framework for human geography, we must recall a few general points laid out in the "Fondements." For Sorre, social life was an integral unity, and thus patterns of organization—from family and kinship groups to nation states and political blocs—were "techniques" of social life.[16] Consequently, he considered political space (the *Lebensraum* of a particular nation) or economic space (functional regions surrounding the *pôles de croissance*) to be constituent dimensions of social space. When he discussed the spaces of a more purely social nature (for example, religious, ethnic, or linguistic spaces), his language became confused and somewhat ambiguous.

On a global scale, then, Sorre envisioned social space as a mosaic of areas, each homogeneous in terms of the space perceptions of its inhabitants. Within each of the areas a network of points and lines radiating from certain *"points privilégié"* (theaters, schools, churches, and other foci of social movement) could be identified. Each group tended to have its own specific social space, which reflected its particular values, preferences, and aspirations. The density of social space reflected the complementarity, and consequently the degree of interaction, between groups.[17] This sounded unorthodox to Sorre's fellow geographers, but it inspired Chombart de Lauwe in sociology, who applied Sorre's ideas in empirical urban studies. Let us now examine some of these applications.

Perception of Habitat and Urban Social Space

Chombart de Lauwe's famous 1952 team study of Paris illustrated new dimensions of the social space concept. A distinction appeared, for example, between the objective and the subjective components of social space.[18] Objective social space was defined as "the spatial framework in which groups live; groups whose social structure and organization have been conditioned by ecological and cultural factors." Subjective social space was defined as "space as perceived by members of particular human groups."[19] Practically, then, urban spatial patterns were studied on two levels: each *arrondissement, quartier,* and *secteur* was described first in objective terms—that is, the spatial setting with its physical boundaries and communications network—and then in terms of the perceived dimensions and characteristics of that segment as these were subjectively identified by the occupants. In many cases objective and subjective "spaces" failed to coincide—subjective space reflecting values, aspirations, and cultural traditions that consciously or unconsciously distorted the objective dimensions of the environment.

The habitat-perception theme (*conceptions de l'habitation*) well illustrates the continuity between Sorre's original formula for social space and Chombart de Lauwe's subsequent research.[20] In Volume 3 of the *Fondements*, Sorre suggested that every life style (*genre de vie*) tended to inscribe itself in a typical habitat form. In the case of rural habitat, for example, he showed how work rhythms, agricultural regimes, social structure, and economic activities were related to house types and village patterns. He wrote at length on the "ecology of rural life," on the harmonious nexus binding society, economy, and geographical environment into a cohesive whole, which was reflected in a region's habitat forms. But in the urban context Sorre's ecological formula failed to explain or describe the habitat in functional terms. Like Vidal de la Blache, Sorre was a ruralite at heart, and though he paid homage to urbanization as a tremendous social feat, he consistently deplored the debilitating influence of smog, pollution, racial disharmony, and the rupture of his beloved "habitat ecology." It was Chombart de Lauwe who really explored the ecology of urban habitat.[21] Two cardinal concepts that permeate his work are social space on the one hand and social milieu on the other.

Social Space

For Chombart de Lauwe, urban social space connotes a hierarchy of spaces, within which groups live, move, and interact.[22] First there is "familial space," or the network of relationships characteristic of the domestic level of social interaction; then "neighborhood space," or the network that encompasses daily and local movement; "economic space," which embraces certain employment centers; and finally the "urban sector," or "urban regional" social space. The progressively larger and overlapping dimensions of these spatial horizons reflect daily, weekly, and occasional orbits of group social activity and constitute the normal spatial framework within which groups feel at ease.

Chombart de Lauwe has calculated thresholds in space beyond which certain groups cannot travel without experiencing frustrations, tensions, and feelings of anomie; such thresholds provide useful references for the urban planner and constitute critical indices of what a satisfactory housing or neighborhood unit might be.[23] An interesting complication arises, however, in that socioprofessional groups differ significantly from one another in their perceptions of space. For each socioprofessional group a general characteristic pyramid or hierarchy of spaces could be discerned, and numerous combinations of these hierarchies could be found within an urban region.[24] Viewed horizontally, then, social space comprises a network of roughly concentric bands or sectors that circumscribe the orbits of daily, weekly, and occasional circulation.[25]

Chombart de Lauwe has also explored the vertical dimension of social space. How many square feet per person constitute a desirable residential density? Few objective indices of satisfactory levels of residential density exist, though various density thresholds have been proposed for animals.[26] The effects of crowding and stress have been studied,[27] and the United States Office of Civil and Defense Mobilization has made specific recommendations concerning adequate space per person in shelters.[28] These indices, however, pertain to abnormal circumstances and provide tolerance thresholds under duress rather than optimal levels under normal conditions. When Chombart de Lauwe analyzed residential conditions among working-class families in Paris, he discovered that a density of 30-35 square yards of space per person per dwelling unit was optimal.[29] Where the density was less than 25-30 square yards per person, crime rates, anomie, and tension increased, probably because of overcrowding. Where the density was more than 45 square yards, other social and psychological problems arose, stemming from the patterns of parent-child relationships characteristic of an upwardly mobile socio-economic class.[30] As a result, a specific, objective index of residential density desirable for one socio-economic class was derived.

In retrospect, then, whereas Sorre's criteria for the delimitation of areas within social space were based on macroscopic and universal categories such as language and ethnic groups, nation states, and genres de vie, Chombart de Lauwe's criteria were microscopic and more sociological (for example, socio-economic and special-interest groups). The contrast between them is not only in the approach, but also in the scale: one applies to the world in general and to rural settlement in particular; the other is strictly oriented to the urban environment.

Social Milieu

In the urban context also, a complementary notion occurs in Chombart de Lauwe's work, namely the concept of social milieu. What is meant by social milieu? Every schoolboy knows that life in the Quartier Latin is not the same as life on Montmartre, nor is Montparnasse comparable to the XXe arrondissement, but what definition or formula could specify the actual ingredients that make up the social milieu of these places? Chombart de Lauwe identified three distinct levels: *milieu géographique*, or time-space framework; *milieu technique*, or level of technological equipment; and *milieu culturel*, or the traditional atmosphere perceived by the inhabitants or ascribed by others.[31] All three levels, in vital combination, constitute the effective social milieu, in the context of which all social behavior should be placed.

But how are these three levels to be separated for systematic analysis, while simultaneously maintaining a holistic conception of social milieu? Chombart de Lauwe criticizes the factor-analytic approach evident in American sociology; he refuses to employ such terms as "factors" and "elements," or to use other concepts that imply a unidirectional pattern of relationships. He regards it as more important to decipher the intricate and complex fiber that holds a milieu together than to deal with the actual mechanics of specific parts. Thus he speaks of variables that pattern themselves around certain recognizable *ensembles*. In practice, however, his own methodological procedure could be regarded as simply a carefully designed factor analysis of five major groups of phenomena: 1) population patterns within a time-space framework; 2) economic-activity patterns; 3) social groupings, relationships, behavior, and attitudes; 4) communications and cultural and spiritual life; and 5) educational level.[32] Each of these ensembles, then, constitutes a system, or organic whole, vitally linked with other ensembles by the value system, attitudes, and needs of its component groups. We see again the relationship between social milieu and the emergence of social-space hierarchies for particular groups. It is in fact the combined contrasts of social-milieu and social-space hierarchies that constitute the basic differences between eastern, western, and central Paris.[33]

Sorre's Résumé: Avenues for Cooperative Research

By the late 1950's Sorre could recapitulate his original ideas and could modify, contradict, and refine some of his original suggestions. He no doubt rejoiced to see empirical evidence that space assumed different meanings in the life patterns of different groups and that these differences influenced the geography of Paris. But did this apparent success also threaten obsolescence? Were these findings proof that physical "geographical" space was of little significance in urban study? On the contrary, Sorre cautioned that the problem for an urban geographer was not so much one of slicing up social space into a series of component "spaces," as of examining how these were harmonized in the concrete life situations of particular urban regions.[34] From the Paris study, there was some evidence, for example, that when a group's aspirations transcended their attainable horizons, or when spatially juxtaposed groups held widely contrasting ideas about space, tensions arose, which influenced spatial movements, thus affecting the geography of that sector of the city.

The Paris findings reinforced some of Sorre's original hunches (for example, that the social rift which persisted in the dormitory village of Petit-Clamart was entirely due to differences of *genre de vie*[35]) and dispelled others (for example, the necessary relationship between habitation form and *genre de vie* in the urban context). Ecological principles governing rural habitat could not be applied in the urban context where functional relations between work and home were entirely different, and there was no obvious harmony of social structure, lifestyle, and settlement type such as that found in the Breton hamlet or in the Lorraine village.

One of the most valuable conclusions Sorre drew was that geographer and sociologist could cooperate in the study of such complex questions as social mobility and migrations.[36] Only through such collaboration could one discover how social mobility relates to spatial mobility or unravel the psychological ties that make certain settlement forms forces that stabilize and others forces that stimulate migration of rural and urban groups. Resistance to change—for instance, the inertia of the *vignoble* in Bas-Languedoc, of the mining communities of Lorraine, of the textile workers of Lancashire—provided suitable subjects for interdisciplinary work. Thus throughout the late 1950's—and especially in his *nunc dimittis* volume, *L'homme sur la terre*—Sorre repeatedly advocated collaboration between geographers and sociologists.[37]

Chombart de Lauwe and Spatial Preferences

Since the early 1960's Chombart de Lauwe and his team have advanced along many new fronts.[38] "L'intégration du citadin à sa ville et à son quartier,"[39] for example, approached the study of social space on three levels: on the behavioral level (where and how people live and move), on the level of knowledge (where people know that alternative opportunities are available), and on the aspirational level (where people would like to go if they had the opportunity). The whole tone of their research has thus taken on a behavioral orientation, which again affords a potential link with current research in geography, the *géographie volontaire*,[40] so popular among French scholars at the present time.

Three questions, then, are posed. Where do Parisians live? Where would they like to live? And what prevents them from living where they wish? Parisians evidently would like to live outside the metropolitan area, and would migrate if their employer would move. But there are marked differences in the attitudes of socio-economic groups regarding a choice of locale. Working-class families on the whole, if their housing conditions are reasonably good, do not want to leave Paris; but most other groups believe that the ideal place to live would be *"en province."* The three major poles of attraction are the Alps, the Midi, and Brittany, and the optimum size of the receiving town is in the neighborhood of 100,000 to 400,000 population.

Analysis of the internal spatial preferences yield more clear-cut differences among socio-professional groups.[41] 1) The flight to the suburbs is made primarily by the liberal professionals and the more wealthy executives. If industrial workers' families move at all, it is to the "inner suburbs," where they still have access to public transportation facilities. Persons employed in service activities tend to remain near the center, close to their clientele. 2) For most occupational groups the ideal place to live is in a neighborhood that has some kind of identity. This identity can be defined by clear-cut physical boundaries, by a traditional reputation, by a commercial atmosphere, or by other special earmarks that people attach to that environment. 3) Tendencies toward spatial segregation for social reasons are most marked among the clerks and office workers, are less marked among industrial workers, and are scarcely evident at all among the service-occupation group. Residential segregation and spatial mobility go hand in hand in most cases. 4) Among the most highly prized characteristics of an ideal place to live are privacy, space, and the freedom to choose either participation or no involvement in local life.

These generalizations offer interesting points of comparison with patterns evident in other countries. The evolving spatial order of metropolitan suburbs in the United States follows less definite lines, but also reveals a response to socially held values and attitudes. Recent literature suggests an increasing social consciousness in the design and selection of residential areas, and a correlative decline in the importance of economic forces.[42] Thus whatever the social or political context, we find a widespread acceptance of planning for social preferences rather than individual responses to the laws of a market economy, as a major determinant of spatial form today.

Practical Applications

On the basis of these French precedents one may speculate on the practical utility of the social-space concept in urban analysis today. On the whole, its primary value perhaps is in the connections postulated between the internal subjective order (attitudes, traditions, and aspirations) and the external spatial order, within an urban milieu. Research on these connections parallels recent work in other fields.

Notions akin to social space (for example, ethnic domain, biotope, and so on) can be found in anthropology, but for the most part they are approached from an ecological or psychological point of view. A biotope is defined in social psychology as the "habitat or locale to which an organism is attracted through some combination of learning, imprinting, and instinct."[43] An ecological approach to the study of such biotopes is demonstrated in Barth's study of ethnic communities in North Pakistan,[44] and Hall's "science of proxemics" applies similar concepts to urban analysis.[45] Chombart de Lauwe's work would suggest, in these terms, that every biotope has an internal hierarchical structure composed of personal, familial, neighborhood, and regional spaces, and second, that this structure varies from one socio-economic group to another. This raises the question of whether individuals within particular professional groups have a consistent pattern of biotope preferences with respect to housing design and location, to recreational needs, and to the propensity to move. Is there, for instance, any consistent relationship between workaday ("proximate") space facilities —for example, in office, classroom, or factory—and the weekend recreational preferences? Is there a relationship between the lack of sensory stimulation in routine urban occupations and the quest for sensory stimulation in outdoor recreational activities during vacations? Again, how is adjustment to biotope (defined in ecological and psychological terms) related to turnover rates in suburban housing developments? The spatial order of metropolitan fringe areas provides a fascinating field of research when viewed from this perspective.

Another possibility for the cooperative work between geographer and sociologist suggested by Sorre lies in the realm of mobility and migrations. It is a cliché that spatial mobility is closely associated with social mobility among middle-class Americans; however, the class differentials in propensity to move within metropolitan suburbs are less well defined than was previously imagined.[46] Chombart de

Lauwe has unraveled some of the motivations behind changes of residence in the Parisian context and has shown that failure to attain the ideal leads to psychotic disorders and social tensions.[47] The notion of social space has thus served as a heuristic and seminal concept, producing a number of distinct research orientations, each of which could be analyzed more incisively by specialists in different disciplines. It may serve in the future as a coordinating framework for interdisciplinary research on the subjective dimensions of human behavior in space. Like so many other rich ideas in the history of social science, the disintegration and demise of social space as a single unified analytical concept is simply the necessary prelude to a new harvest of research endeavors.

Sorre and Chombart de Lauwe in Perspective

Despite their common philosophical and methodological ideas, Sorre and Chombart de Lauwe differed radically in one respect; Sorre could never reconcile himself to the idea of planning, whereas Chombart de Lauwe's work is almost entirely directed toward practical goals. This perhaps reflects a difference of generation, Sorre representing the prewar bourgeois "knowledge for knowledge's sake" tradition, and Chombart de Lauwe the postwar avant garde style of nonacademic applied knowledge. Because of their fundamental difference in outlook, their writings must be evaluated from a different perspective. Sorre's work is essentially a kind of armchair conceptualization, which can serve as a preamble to, and an organizational framework for, empirical research. Chombart de Lauwe, on the other hand, seemingly so anxious to arrive at quick solutions to urgent social problems, often appears to slide too rapidly through the analytical part to arrive at readily applicable results.

In retrospect, what these two scholars have given us is a set of conceptual guidelines rather than readily usable research formulas. Sorre, the great humanist, has bequeathed excellent textbooks for teaching social geography, but he did not establish a research school; he had few students who, overtly at least, followed up his proposed leads. Chombart de Lauwe could in many ways be considered as the first great internationalist among French sociologists since the time of Marcel Mauss and Maurice Halbwachs. He has simplified and integrated many conceptual lines developed in American, German, and British schools of social science, and thus has helped to stimulate dialogue among the various traditions as well as among the specialists within particular schools. He calls for a common language that will enable sociologists to communicate with architects and engineers and that will permit citizens and planners to collaborate in the creation of the new social environment.

Notes

1. Martin G. Plattel, *Social Philosophy* (Pittsburgh: Duquesne, 1965); A.C. de Waehlens, *L'existentialisme de Merleau-Ponty* (Brussels, 1963).

2. Edward T. Hall, *The Silent Language* (New York: Premier Books, 1965). See also idem, *The Hidden Dimension* (New York: Garden City, 1966).

3. Paul Claval, "Géographie et psychologie des peuples," *Revue de Psychologie des Peuples*, Vol. 21 (1966), pp. 386-401; idem, *Essai sur l'évolution de la géographie humaine* (Paris, 1964). See also R.W. Kates and J.F. Wohlwill, eds., "Man's Response to the Physical Environment," *Journal of Social Issues*, Vol. 22, No. 4 (1966).

4. Jules Sion, *Les paysans de la Normandie orientale: Pays de Caux, Bray, Vexin Norman, Vallée de la Seine: Étude géographique* (Paris 1909). See also the review of this work by Paul Vidal de la Blache in the *Annales de Géographie*, Vol. 18 (1909), pp. 177-181.

5. Pierre Gourou, "Étude du monde tropical," *L'Annuaire du Collège de France*, Vol. 63 (1962-1963), pp. 261-275; idem, "Changes in Civilization and Their Influence on Landscape," *Impact*, Vol. 14 (1964), pp. 57-71.

6. Walter Firey, *Land Use in Central Boston* (Cambridge, Mass: Harvard University Press, 1947).

7. Renée Rochefort, *Le travail en Sicile* (Paris, 1961).

8. Claval, "Géographie et psychologie des peuples."

9. Maximilien Sorre, *Les fondements de la géographie humaine* (3 vols., Paris, 1943-1952). For a summary of Sorre's publications, see Françoise Grivot, "Bibliographie des oeuvres de Maximilien Sorre," *Annales de Géographie*, Vol. 72 (1963), pp. 186-191.

10. See the introductory statement by Paul-Henri Chombart de Lauwe in *Paris et l'agglomération parisienne* by Chombart de Lauwe and others, 2 vols. (Paris, 1952), Vol. 1, pp. 19-26.

11. Sorre, *Les migrations des peuples: Essai sur la mobilité géographique* (Paris, 1955); *Rencontres de la géographie et de la sociologie* (Paris, 1957); and "La géographie psychologique: L'adaptation au milieu climatique et biosocial," in *Traité de psychologie appliquée* (Paris, 1958), Vol. 6, Chap. 3, pp. 1343-1393.

12. Émile Durkheim, *De la division du travail social* (Paris, 1893; 5th edit., 1926). See also *idem, Les règles de la méthode sociologique* (Paris, 1895); Friedrich Ratzel, *Anthropogéographie* (2 vols, Stuttgart, 1882 and 1891); Herbert Spencer, *Principles of Sociology* (London, 1876); and Georg Simmel, *Soziale Differenzierung* (Berlin, 1890).

13. Durkheim, *De la division du travail social.*

14. Sorre, *Rencontres de la géographie et de la sociologie*, Chap. 1.

15. *Ibid.*

16. Sorre, *L'homme sur la terre* (Paris, 1961).

17. Sorre, "L'espace du géographe et du sociologue," *Rencontres de la géographie*, pp. 87-114.

18. Chombart de Lauwe and others, *Paris et l'agglomération parisienne.* See also Chombart de Lauwe, *Paris: Essais de sociologie* (Paris, 1966.)

19. Chombart de Lauwe and others, *Paris et l'agglomération.* Also Chombart de Lauwe, *Essais de sociologie*, pp. 96-101.

20. Chombart de Lauwe, *Famille et habitation*, Vol. 1, *La vie quotidienne des familles ouvrieres* (Paris, 1956), and Vol. 2, *Science humaines et conceptions de l'habitation* (Paris, 1959).

21. Chombart de Lauwe's ecological and integrative tone is best illustrated in his lectures and articles, for example, in his lecture on "Sociologie, sciences humaines et transformations sociales," delivered at Louvain in November, 1966, and published in *Revue de l'Enseignement Superieur*, Nos. 1-2, (1965), pp. 11-19. See also his *Des Hommes et des villes* (Paris, 1965).

22. Chombart de Lauwe, "L'évolution des besoins et la conception dynamique de la famille," *Revue Française de Sociologie.* Vol. 1 (1960), pp. 403-425; and *idem*, "Le milieu social et l'étude sociologique des cas individuels," *Information Sociales*, No. 2, (February, 1959), pp. 41-55.

23. Chombart de Lauwe, *Famille et habitation*, Vol. 1; *idem, Des hommes et des villes.* For the pathological consequences of unattained horizons, see *idem*, "Hypotheses pour une psychosociologie de la fatigue," *Revue de Médecine Psychosomatique et de Psychologie Médicale*, Vol. 3 (1966), pp. 275-286.

24. Chombart de Lauwe, *Des hommes et des villes.*

25. Chombart de Lauwe and others, *Paris et l'agglomération.*

26. Neal M. Burns, R.M. Chambers, and E. Hendler, *Unusual Environments and Human Behavior* (New York: Free Press, 1963).

27. John B. Calhoun, "Population Density and Social Pathology," *Scientific American*, Vol. 206, No. 2 (1962) pp. 139-148, W. Craig, "Why Do Animals Fight?" *International Journal of Ethics*, Vol. 31 (1921), pp. 264-278.

28. *Guide for Executives*, (Battle Creek, Mich.: Office of Civil and Defense Mobilization, 1959 [OCDM NP-10-1]); *Guide for Architects and Engineers*, (ibid., 1960 [OCDM NP-10-2]). See also *Procedures for Managing Large Fallout Shelters*, (Stanford, Calif.; Dunlap and Associates, 1959).

29. Chombart de Lauwe, *Famille et habitation*, Vol. 2.

30. Hall, *The Hidden Dimension*, pp. 161-162.

31. This is emphasized particularly in "Le rôle de l'obsérvation en sociologie," *Revue de l'Institut de Sociologie* [Université Libre de Bruxelles], Vol. 1, No. 1 (1960), pp. 27-43.

32. *Ibid.* See also Chombart de Lauwe, "Le milieu social et l'étude sociologique des cas individuels."

33. Chombart de Lauwe and others, *Paris et l'agglomération*, Vol. 1, pp. 68 ff.

34. Sorre, *Rencontres de la géographie et de la sociologie.*

35. Chombart de Lauwe and others, *Paris et l'agglomération*, Vol. 1, p. 243.

36. Sorre, *Rencontres de la géographie*, pp. 53-86.

37. *Ibid.* See also *idem, L'homme sur la terre*, pp. 96-101.

38. The headquarters of the main group, the Centre d'Ethnologie Sociale, is at Montrouge. There one finds interdisciplinary research on the general theme, "evolution of social life," subsidized by the Centre National de Recherche Scientifique. An interesting offshoot, the Centre d'Études des Groupes Sociaux, works on practical problems relating to urban planning, for example, work on the decentralization policy now being implemented in Paris.

39. Chombart de Lauwe and others, *L'intégration du citadin à sa ville et à son quartier*, 4 vols. (Paris, 1962-1965). See also *idem, Logement et vie familiale: Étude sociologique des quartiers nouveaux* (Paris: Centre d'Etudes des Groupes Sociaux, 1965) and *L'attraction de Paris sur sa banlieue* (Paris, 1965).

40. Jean Labasse's work is probably most illustrative of this new trend among French geographers; see his *L'organisation de l'espace: Éléments de géographie volontaire* (Paris, 1966). See also Jean Gottmann, *Essais sur l'amenagement de l'espace habité* (Paris, 1966).

41. These are some of the general results of the work of Chombart de Lauwe and others, *L'intégration du citadin à sa ville.*

42. Donald J. Bogue, *The Structure of the Metropolitan Community* (New York: Russell & Russell, reprint of 1949 ed.); William M. Dobriner, *Class in Suburbia* (Englewood Cliffs, N.J.: Prentice-Hall, 1963); Amos H. Hawley, *The Changing Shape of Metropolitan America* (Glencoe, Ill.: Free Press, 1956); Herbert J. Gans, *The Levittowners* (New York: Pantheon, 1967); Gerardus Antonius Wissink, *American Cities in Perspective, with Special Reference to the Development of Their Fringe Areas* (Assen, Neth., 1962).

43. Robert Sommer, "Man's Proximate Environment," *Journal of Social Issues*, Vol. 22, No. 4 (1966), pp. 59-70. Reference on p. 62.

44. Fredrik Barth, "Ecologic Relationships of Ethnic Groups in Swat, North Pakistan," *American Anthropologist*, Vol. 58, (1956), pp. 1079-1089.

45. Hall, *The Hidden Dimension.*

46. See, for example, Walter T. Martin, *The Rural-Urban Fringe* (Eugene, Ore., U. of Ore. Press, 1953); Amos H. Hawley, *The Changing Shape of Metropolitan America* (Glencoe, Ill.: Free Press, 1956); R. E. Pahl, "Urbs in Rure: The Metropolitan Fringe in Hertfordshire," *London School of Economics and Political Science Geographical Papers*, No. 2, (1965).

47. Chombart de Lauwe and others, *L'attraction de Paris sur sa banlieue.*

City and Psyche

A. E. Parr

The creeping blight of monotony in our surroundings, particularly as they present themselves to our sense of vision, has been bewailed by people of so many different talents, interests, vocations, and avocations that their criticism must express a widely felt sense of want. Even such an ardent advocate of "show-the-bones" constructivism in architecture as Ada Louise Huxtable often joins the chorus. And who among us has not felt a gradual nibbling away of incentives for a stroll in our streets as the richly varied revelations of individual tastes in small buildings give way to the endlessly repeated unadorned forms of modern architecture? Who can fail to share William H. Whyte's appreciation of "at least one hideous house to relieve the good taste"?

Actually nobody is even trying to deny the progressive elimination of visual complexity and copious detail. On the contrary, our designers take great pride in having condemned and discarded all "applied ornamentation" in order to frame our lives in endless vistas of "clean façades," as pure as laundered sheets drying in the sun, but less lively. In this stern environment we walk when we feel in need of the exercise, or when the dog has to go, but we do not promenade for the visual pleasures of varied experience.

James Marston Fitch has summed up the stylistic criteria of modern architecture as "simplicity, economy, and efficiency" but finds it "apparent that above and beyond physical performance, laymen ask something more of buildings, some quality which they have found in the traditional design and miss in the modern one." Fitch identifies the missing quality as "sentiment" but expresses no suspicion that the

Reprinted by permission from *Yale Review*, 1965, copyright by Yale University.

popular demand may spring from a true organic need for perceptual stimulation, and not merely from the mental and sentimental habits of mind that determine only the particular form of our sensory appetites in a certain age and tradition. Sullivan's "Autobiography of an Idea" offers a moving ode of gratitude for the wonders and values of varied experience in his early life, even when he speaks with a touch of asperity about some particular recollection of his past.

But unless we can show that diversity is actually good for us, perhaps even essential, and not merely gratifying to our senses and sentiments, our wishes will never alter the dictates of society's arbiters of taste, or prevail against them. This is easy to understand, for several reasons. Unless our critics are merely going to echo the commonplace, a prime prerequisite for membership in their exalted circle must obviously be a hearty dislike for anything that a majority of their fellow men relish and enjoy—at least until the object of attention disappears from daily life and becomes a relic of the past, which our experts may then have the pleasure of rediscovering without having to peer over the shoulders of the crowd. In the meantime those who seek satisfaction for their visual hunger beyond the precincts defined by current esthetic doctrine are harshly denounced for the "consummate vulgarity" of their "parvenu love of the novel, the flashy, and the bizarre." It is enlightening to examine how consistent defenders of the faith are in interpreting and applying esthetic dogma. According to Miss Huxtable "architecture is properly the expression of structural techniques," and Frank Lloyd Wright has ruled that "all ornament if not developed within the nature of architecture and as an organic part of such expression, vitiates the whole fabric no matter how clever or beautiful it may be as something in itself." It would be very difficult for any unprejudiced person to see the risers, wastelines, traps, and fixtures of our bathrooms as expressions of the "structural truth" of architecture, and not as applied features added for the despised purposes of convenience, if not outright luxury. But applied plumbing for the comfort of our bowels is splendid, while applied ornamentation to ease the hunger of our minds is beneath contempt and "treason to modern architecture." It is amusing to see a critical exponent of modernity become more lyrical about the Seagram executives' men's room than about almost anything else he comments upon. Evidently the room is a little gem of ornamentation that probably has little to do with its functions, and even less to do with the expression of the building's structural technique.

Conceding a battle they are only rarely able to win, many architects try to avoid artistic conflict by recognizing interior decoration as a field apart, not governed by the rules that apply to building-design, but generously set aside for the individual self-expression of owner, user, or decorator, with applied ornamentation and other "extraneous" garniture entirely permissible. But the tactical expedient of such an arbitrary division of esthetic domains has lost all semblance of logical justification in the urban communities of our megalopolitan age. In the open space of the countryside, a farmhouse, a mansion, or a castle are only scattered objects in the broader vista of the landscape. In an urban environment all spaces are enclosed, and the exterior aspects of the buildings form the interiors of the cityscape. Life in our cities is an inside life in the womb of urban architecture both indoors and out. The conflicts or uneasy compromises between architectural design and interior decoration that we see all around us bear wistful evidence of frustrated yearnings for a visually more abundant mode of existence.

A psychological want need not be consciously felt and verbally articulated to have organic reality. Neither is the strongest and most volubly expressed desire necessarily proof that something of genuine value is lacking. We must look in other directions for objective evidence of the demands actually placed upon our environment by our minds and bodies. Since it would not be permissible to use human beings for experiments with conditions that might have permanently detrimental effects upon the mind, the confirmation or refutation of any working hypothesis that seems reasonable in its premises will have to come chiefly from the study of our nearest relatives of the animal kingdom, with ex post facto observations of the human condition serving to verify the validity of the observations for our own species.

It would seem logical to assume that just as our bodies need food and exercise to grow strong and healthy, so does our brain need an adequate sensory intake and stimulation for its optimum development. And the measure of our perceptual diet is obviously not how much we perceive, but how many significantly different images our senses transmit to our minds—in other words, the diversity rather than the repetitive quantity of our experiences. These common-sense expectations are amply confirmed by experiments with mammals other than man. Donald W. Fiske and Salvatore R. Maddi, and their many collaborators in *Functions of Varied Experience*, have assembled and abstracted much of the pertinent evidence, including the results of their own research, and conclude that "there is certainly evidence that the more variable of two early environments produces an adult organism that is perceptually and behaviorally more alert, flexible, and able to cope with change." D. O. Hebb puts it even more succinctly when he states that "perceptual restriction in infancy certainly produces a low level of intelligence."

The problems of the space age have caused man to experiment upon himself with the effects of environmental conditions that are much more drastic than most of those tested upon other species, but also of shorter duration relative to total life span. The most widely dramatized of these investigations examine the impact of what is as nearly as possible complete "sensory deprivation," that is, the exclusion of all sensory stimuli. Of more interest to our subject is probably the work of Woodburn Heron and others which did not have for its purpose to "cut individuals off from any sensory stimulation whatsoever, but to remove all pattern of perceptual information," or, in other words, to expose the subject to complete monotony. In these circumstances Heron found a definite impairment of thinking, among other results that we will come back to later.

Many of the investigators also point out that, beyond a certain maximum, varied experience may itself become overwhelming and deleterious. This, however, scarcely needs to concern us much for the next hundred years insofar as our visual environment is concerned, when we note the direction in which urban architecture and environmental design are now pushing us.

There are, then, rather abundant indications of a possible relationship between diversity of milieu and mental capacity, at least under experimental conditions. But alertness and level of intelligence do not uniquely determine pattern of behavior. Heron has found that "the higher organisms actively avoid a completely monotonous environment." When Jane Jacobs asks why it is that "office workers on Park Avenue turn off to Lexington or Madison Avenue at the first corner they reach," and why short blocks are apt to be busier than long ones, her queries actually corroborate Heron's general assertion. The questions also suggest some very interesting examples of the manner in which Heron's principle of avoidance of monotony may affect urban life and economy.

Welker (in Fiske and Maddi) assigns a somewhat more positive role to the responding organism when he expresses "no doubt that animals tend to produce or seek certain levels of stimulation." Rolling along on a particularly monotonous stretch of highway we are quite likely to find ourselves unintentionally driving much faster than we realize, until we take a look at the speedometer, and this inadvertent haste may simply be the manifestation of a subconscious effort to compensate for lack of variety in the environmental image by increasing the rate of change of scenery, or, in other words, by substituting diversity in time when the diversity in space proves inadequate. Boutourline also noticed among pedestrian spectators at the Seattle World's Fair a tendency to walk faster when the contents of the surroundings decreased in the direction of travel. If empty space actually speeds the visitors on their way, it occurred to me that the theories generally followed in attempting to create "restful" intervals between museum exhibits may well be totally wrong, and this suspicion has also been reinforced by new information.

But the guise in which the pursuit of stimulation becomes most important to our main theme is best revealed in the aspects of behavior that we associate with the spirit of adventure. The craving for adventure, which generally finds its strongest expression in the younger generation, is actually a demand for experiences that cannot be entirely foreseen. In the old days when each block had a dozen façades, and one street did not show you what the next street would look like as well, this youthful hunger for the unexpected could be satisfied by simple exploration of the surroundings, which seems to be the natural outlet for the urge, turning its promptings into an asset in the struggle for existence. From his studies of monkeys Robert A. Butler concluded that they, and presumably all primates, have a strong motive toward visual exploration of their environment. As we make our cities more and more uniform by design and regulations, we rob exploration of its rewards, till we force the young to seek the stimulus of the unexpected in their own unpredictable behavior rather than in a too predictable milieu. On the basis of this reasoning I have already postulated elsewhere that there may quite possibly be some contributory positive connection between modern architecture and juvenile delinquency. A similar thought is expressed by Roul Tunley, when he "wonders how many of our restless, energetic pioneer heroes would have been juvenile delinquents if compelled to live today in our towns and cities."

In his interviews with authorities and experts and his search of the literature, Tunley found wide general agreement that a thirst for adventure, rather than a basically antisocial attitude, is at the bottom of most delinquent behavior. He also encountered frequent spontaneous expressions of the opinion voiced by the New York City gangwork supervisor who told him that "as far as the kids are concerned, the old houses were far better than the new ones." These findings on the nature of juvenile delinquency are not merely subjective illustrations of wishful thinking. The Gluecks, for example, in *Unraveling Juvenile Delinquency* can report that 47.9 percent of delinquents compared with only 9.5 percent of non-delinquents studied by them "expressed a preference for adventurous activities." All of these observations and conclusions point toward a need to restore to the cityscape a degree of diversity that will again establish a natural and beneficial outlet for the spirit of adventure in exploration rather than unpremeditated behavior which so often turns out to be misbehavior. But in order to accomplish this task we need a far greater and more precise knowledge of the relationship between diversity and curiosity than anyone can offer today, and we need the information in terms that our environmental designers can apply to their tasks. Again we find a vast and urgent need for research in environmental psychology.

Before we continue it may be well to attempt to correct a frequent misunderstanding. The planning of a small village, or even of group housing for agricultural labor, is often discussed as if it were a small-scale example of urban design, or, at least, a pilot experiment. But it is not. When we are merely creating a shelter for intermittent temporary withdrawals from the natural surroundings, mostly at night, we can rely upon nature to continue to provide the diet of diversity demanded by our mental appetites. Urban design does not begin to face its real tasks until community development passes the point where the man-made milieu becomes a replacement of the natural setting and not only a protection against some of its elements. The critical dimension might be looked for in the extent to which the average radius of action of a child in its formative years is contained within, or extends beyond the cityscape, or in some other criterion similarly related to psychological needs.

The method of dealing separately with different aspects of our outward behavior and our psychological reactions must in no way be taken to suggest that these are in fact independent phenomena. The thirst for adventure and the behavior to which it leads obviously play a tremendous role in the process of learning and the development of our intelligence, which we considered first, but the emotional factors that may lead to delinquency are inextricably involved with the elements of intellectual curiosity that govern the individual in his explorations or his misbehavior.

We seem to have been happily reassured that delinquency in most cases springs primarily from a healthy, but misdirected spirit of adventure, which might easily have been turned to better uses. Nevertheless, there can be no disputing that emotions are always involved, and may, in situations for which they are badly adjusted, become the primary cause rather than a minor corollary of objectionable and harmful behavior. In exploring our affective responses to the environment it is convenient to make a distinction between diffuse emotional tones, or moods, and feelings that are oriented toward a definite focal point. We may simply be in an angry mood, or we may be angry at something or somebody. That our perceptual environment continually influences and can sometimes dominate both our moods and our specific feelings is hardly open to debate. Our language and literature are full of expressions attesting to our common knowledge of such relationships between mind and milieu. We speak of threatening mountains, blissful valleys, depressing city canyons, cheerful gardens, and so on. The entire art

City and Psyche

of stage design is based upon the assumption that our emotional state is directly influenced by our visual surroundings, and theatrical experience abundantly proves the validity of its premise. It is interesting to note that stagecraft commonly uses architectural motifs for the strongest impact. For these reasons it might seem logical to expect that there would be a great deal of knowledge at hand concerning the relationship between environment and emotions. But in this expectation we are badly disappointed. Everybody knows that the field is there, and many have tried to describe what it looks like as seen across the fences of other disciplines, particularly through the eyes of artistic intuition. But nobody seems to have made the field his own and subjected it to the rigorous scientific examination so urgently needed to direct the steps of our progress.

In all this welter of ignorance and guesswork there is one phenomenon on which everybody, from mystery writer to social commentator, is in such universal agreement that it becomes impossible to doubt the presence of some reality behind the words. Described in an infinite variety of ways, the observations assign to the physical environment itself the power of inducing or enhancing a sense of frustration and insecurity among its inmates. That these states of mind and emotion may also spring from numerous other causes is not the point, but that the nonhuman milieu may function as an independent cause among the others. Harrison Salisbury has spoken of "the crushing anonymity, loneliness and ugliness of high-rise apartments." John D. MacDonald refers to "disposable cubicles for dispensable people," and "bright boxes which diminish the people who (have) to live and work in them." We could go on quoting at length from those who might perhaps be listed as unfriendly witnesses against the developing cityscape. Probably more effective confirmation can be obtained from the utterances and assertions of the leaders and apostles of modern architecture.

According to Walter Gropius *"Functionalism was not considered a rationalistic process merely. It embraced psychological problems as well . . . . We realized that emotional needs are just as imperative as any utilitarian ones and demand to be satisfied."* In the pursuit of this ideal, functionalism has subjected all the statics of structure and all the properties of materials to the most rigorous and objective study. But it seems impossible to find any evidence of similarly exacting and impersonal research directed toward the discovery of the environmental configurations and conditions most conducive to intellectual vigor and emotional satisfaction. One gathers the impression that it was considered superfluous to explore the actual needs of the psyche, since artistic intuition clearly reveals what the needs ought to be, whether that is what they are or not. Giedion tells us that the architect "like all real artists, has to realize in advance the main emotional needs of his fellow citizens, long before they themselves are aware of them." In the circumstances one should perhaps not be too surprised by the reappraisal of the functionalist movement offered some twenty years later by one of its ardent admirers, Nikolaus Pevsner, who states that "it is the creative energy of this world in which we live and work and which we want to master, a world of science and technology, of speed and danger, of hard struggles and *no personal security*, that is glorified in Gropius' architecture, and as long as this is the world and these are its ambitions and problems, the style of Gropius and the other pioneers will be valid." (Italics added.)

From the day a man first laid one stone upon another the purpose of building has been to shelter us against the weather, protect us against enemies and dangers, and shield us from the terrors that dwell in the anonymous darkness and distance beyond. According to Pevsner, functionalism has put an end to much of this. To calm our fears and make us feel secure in our surroundings is no longer a purpose of architecture. The proper aim should be to glorify, and thereby reinforce, our anxieties, instead of trying to ease our tensions by the design of our milieu. This attempted justification by complete perversion of the natural and logical reasons for building is actually the strongest possible condemnation of what it would defend.

There are today many brilliant defectors from the narrow creed of rigid functionalism. But the goal of their rebellion has generally been the achievement of individual self-expression, which demands inquiry only into the artist's own esthetic reactions and his creative ability to fit an expression of his personal taste to the material functions and purposes that must be served by his design. The need to investigate the general relationship between mind and milieu that the functionalists ought to have felt can obviously not have as much meaning to the true believers in polymorphous architectural individualism. We must be deeply grateful to the rebels for having retarded our descent toward monotony, but it has not been within their aims to advance the kind of research that might change the clearly esthetic aspects of design from a pure to an applied art. It is, therefore, still timely for others to reaffirm that it is one of the first responsibilities of architecture not to express, but to alleviate, the pressures that burden our minds and dampen our pleasures. We can no longer leave it to the architects to divine our needs in a Delphic daze. There are better ways of discovering what our actual wants are. Giedion has revealed the problem very clearly in his statement that "aesthetic impacts influence us at all moments. Consciously, or in most cases subconsciously, they provoke friendly or hostile reactions." And Yamasaki (according to von Eckardt) has pointed to the solution we must seek in the creation of buildings that can give us a sense of happiness, peace, and security. But the search itself lies in the field of psychology, and its success can only be insured by using the rigorous methods of scientific inquiry to determine the needs, which artistic genius may then be able to meet.

If we could find a way to bring about the personal happiness of every member of the human species, any distinction between private feelings and emotional responses of broader social concern would lose all meaning. But while we are still trying to reach the millennium through our vale of tears, it is useful to recognize that there are some sentiments such as the joys of accomplishment, the pleasures of a beautiful sight, and even the love between a man and a woman, which seriously influence only a narrow and intimate circle, while other emotional states may have consequences quickly involving human relations on a wide scale. With the tensions that plague the world today one of the problems that must concern us most is the unanswered question of whether or not a state of increased irritability can be directly induced by the environment.

It was reported by Anitra Karsten as long ago as 1928 that the effects upon human beings of prolonged repetition of the same activity included a growing nervous tension and an increase in emotional outbursts. Under more extreme conditions of isolation in a completely monotonous environment Heron also found that the subjects became "markedly irritable" and developed "childish emotional responses." There has so far been nothing to suggest that urban monotony and experimental monotony should differ in anything but degree. Is it not, therefore, within the realm of possibility that lack of diversity in the one may have effects quite similar to those resulting from uniformity in the other? If such a contingency is even conceivable, does it not become a compelling moral obligation for those concerned with the design of our environment to see to it that the possibilities are fully and competently investigated? Perhaps the intuition of a mystery writer is not too far wrong when John D. MacDonald wonders if "the hideous new, tax-shelter buildings" have not "played some significant part in creating New York's ever-increasing flavor of surly and savage bitterness." In the broader and more positive terms of B. V. Doshi and Christopher Alexander "mass-produced, mass-design-regimented houses and offices stunt (man's) spiritual and esthetic development and eventually destroy his mental well being."

We are not here concerned with the qualities and impact of outstanding single masterpieces of modern architecture, but with the changing total composition of cityscapes in which "less able architects have been released from the imperatives of originality" as remarked by von Eckardt, who feels that "architecture is better for it." But what about the people? In the absence of verifiable facts there can, of course, not be any agreement about specific relationships between environmental configurations and emotional states, but there is an impressive consensus of opinion that such relationships do exist and are, in fact, omnipresent.

Every thought and feeling we experience leaves its traces on our personality. If enduring features of our surroundings provoke steadily predominant moods or frequently repeated emotional responses, the conclusion seems inescapable that the environment itself may be a major determinant of personality. Both folklore and literature make numerous allusions to the molding of character by the encompassing features of country and community. The plainsman is molded by the plains, as naturally as a tumble-weed. The sailor reflects the temper of the seas in every thought and feeling passing through his mind. Mountain people living in the ominous shadows of looming precipices become introvert and coercive in their attitudes toward others, while the inhabitants of the wide and pleasant valleys are extrovert, gay, and tolerant. There are almost certainly many important kernels of truth hidden in the substance of these legends, impressions, and subjective beliefs, which receive a kind of lefthanded confirmation in the authoritative voice of Harold F. Searles, who concludes that the maturation throughout life of the individual personality needs to be seen as "inextricably a part of . . . a matrix comprised not only of other human beings but . . . of predominantly nonhuman elements —trees, clouds, stars, landscapes, buildings and so on *ad infinitum*." But impersonally tested evidence is, again, almost totally lacking, although it should not be very hard to obtain if our anthropologists and social psychologists would apply to the study of human behavior the method of multiple correlations that has proved so fruitful in animal ecology.

From the subjective testimony of numerous articulate and sensitive witnesses to the human condition, through introspection, and by extrapolation from facts gathered more objectively in the observation of other species, there seems to emerge a strong suggestion of important cause and effect relationships between our perceptual environment and our mental development, our rational or senseless behavior, our amiable or irritable tempers, our emotional responses in general, and our total personalities. And through it all runs a clear intimation that perceptual diversity beyond the confining limitations of any currently fashionable esthetic doctrine may be an essential need of the human psyche. If these are factors of importance today, will their importance become greater or less in the future now being shaped by the population explosion? Again we must turn to the study of animal populations for analogous information that may help us to devise a working hypothesis for human psychology under the pressure of increasing numbers. The investigations on rats conducted by John B. Calhoun seem particularly enlightening and pertinent to our inquiry.

As the population pressure increased Calhoun noted the appearance of several groups of deviant individuals with patterns of behavior that are not normally present in the hierarchy of a rat community. Below the dominant males both in status and in level of activity the homosexuals or pansexuals make their entry into rat society. Another new group, called the "probers," have given up all dreams of social prestige. They take no part in the fight for status, but are otherwise hyperactive both sexually and in other respects. They seek locations where they can stare in upon the females in the brood pens, but flee, only to return later, if a dominant male so much as looks at them. When opportunity presents itself to attack an unprotected female they dispense completely with the courtship ritual observed by all decent rats, and will not tolerate a short wait. All of which adds up to a very good description of the Peeping Tom-rapists who plague our own over-concentrated communities. The worst thing about rats is that they act so human. In high density rat populations there also appears a third new type of animal, which Calhoun politely calls the somnambulists and others more rudely refer to as zombies. The zombies take no interest in either sex, and social status leaves them totally indifferent, but they like to eat, especially when the others are not feeding and fighting them for the food. The zombies are the fattest of the rats, with the sleekest fur. I have an uneasy feeling that I should recognize these unfortunate characters in our own society too.

These deviationists among the rats may help us to understand better the aberrant members of our own species and the circumstances that lead to their presence in significant numbers. But of more immediate interest to our discussion is Calhoun's report that even the dominant males that retained the most normal behavior also in the overcrowded population exhibit occasional signs of pathology by "going berserk," attacking females, juveniles, and others toward whom they would normally act in a peaceful manner. Such observations suggest the terrible possibility that the population explosion by itself alone may bring about behavioral and emotional instability at the very time when the need for calmness and constancy of attitude and action reaches a maximum.

The relatively phlegmatic way of life in rural solitude is accepted as a fact of human experience everywhere. It is a trait that has been featured in stories and jokes as long as there have been cities to compare with the rustic condition.

By reverse implication on this also ascribes a more choleric temper to the crowded multitude of the urban centers. Man seems to follow the example of the rats in this, as in so many other things having to do with behavior.

At this point we may seem to be preparing a case for the control of population growth, and the evidence certainly points very strongly toward the need for such action. But this important topic is not the subject of these comments, which have merely been building up to the almost casual remark by Calhoun, confirmed by other investigators, that "space requirements may be restricted with appropriate structural configurations." In other words, environmental design may ameliorate or, at least, defer the psychopathological effects "directly attributable to overcrowding" (Hudson Hoagland), thereby, perhaps, giving the world time to ward off the even more drastic consequences that might flow from the untimely development of mass irritability and pugnacity.

In the life of man, and probably also in the life of the rats, we shall undoubtedly find that among the most important factors in the spatial pattern that makes population pressures less intolerable and exasperating, are the chances the environment offers for privacy. It is hardly a coincidence that the nation particularly noted for its ability to maintain privacy in congestion is also rightly famous for its capacity to remain calm under stress.

At the human level, at least, the need for privacy is a complex desire which cannot be satisfactorily fulfilled by simple isolation in the anonymity of featureless cubicles. It also demands opportunity to identify with a distinctive personal domain, which, in turn, puts a premium on diversity. Wherever we pry we seem to uncover some good reason to suspect that diversity may, indeed, be a great virtue in itself, and should, perhaps, be made one of the crucial tests of true functionalism. However this may be, it is time to recognize that design is a communication from mind to mind, not from mind to body. Functionalism of structure and physical purpose is essential, but only as the inert matrix on which the higher values and utilities serving our mental needs must be impressed.

The challenge to environmental design is obvious in the statement by Searles that "whether in surroundings that are largely natural or largely manmade . . . this environment, far from being of little or no account to human personality development, constitutes one of the most basically important ingredients of human psychological existence". The psychologists can not design our surroundings. That is not the field in which their talents and training lie. Nor do they, as yet, have very much to contribute of concrete and applicable information concerning specifically human demands upon the structural configuration of space. But, with a little incentive and more support, a usable body of knowledge could be rapidly developed, so that factual psychological information can begin to replace fatuous esthetic doctrine as a tool of the designer's art.

If we wish to achieve a lasting peace among all people, safe against the emotional epidemics of a crowded planet, we must learn to design our environment for mental health and peace of mind. Summit conferences may not be enough.

Images of Urban Areas
Their Structure and
Psychological Foundations

Derk de Jonge

The ideal of city planning is the arrangement of human artifacts in urban space to ensure optimum conditions for the development of social life and human happiness. We can achieve this object only to a limited extent, as we do not have sufficient knowledge of the means to attain this goal. But we may assume that one of the conditions for an effective use of urban space is that residents and visitors should be able to find their way about with ease, or at least without a great effort.

A fascinating study of the images of a city that exist in people's minds, and which enable them to orient themselves in urban areas has been made by Kevin Lynch.[1] He has found that people consistently use and organize sensory clues from the environment, relying on a selection of impressions to simplify the over-all structure. One urban environment lends itself better to this process than another. A city is most likely to evoke a strong image in any given observer if it can be apprehended as a pattern of high continuity, with a number of distinctive parts clearly interconnected. Lynch has called this quality "imageability."

In order to test the idea of imageability, he made analyses of the central areas of Boston, Jersey City, and Los Angeles. A systematic field reconnaissance of each area, made by a trained observer, was compared with the images

Reprinted by permission from *Journal of the American Institute of Planners*, Vol. XXVIII, No. 4, Nov. 1962, copyright by The American Institute of Planners.

of a small sample of residents. In a lengthy interview, each informant was requested to give descriptions, indicate locations, and make sketches of the area in question. He was also asked to perform a number of imaginary trips. Lynch found there were distinct differences in the imageability of the three cities studied and that the images were generally composed of five kinds of elements: paths, nodes, landmarks, districts, and edges. If a city is to have a satisfying form, these elements must be patterned together in a legible structure. Paths may form a network (a grid, for example) in which repetition makes relationships sufficiently regular and predictable. It is also necessary that the parts have "identity"—that is, those qualities by which one object can be distinguished from another and recognized as a separate entity.

In a review in the *Journal of the American Institute of Planners*, the work of Lynch has rightly been called "one of the most important contributions to large-scale design theory."[2] It has further been pointed out that the sample of informants was too small and too specialized to allow generalization of the findings. This will be possible only after further systematic empirical study, for which the methods and concepts contributed by Lynch's pioneer research can serve as starting-points.

The Scope of This Inquiry

The following account describes an attempt to make a contribution in this field. The purpose of this piece of research was to find answers to the following questions:

a) Can the research methods and techniques developed by Lynch be used, in a simplified form, for studies that are less elaborate, but that can cover a wider variety of urban areas and of informants?

b) If this is so, are the conclusions formulated by Lynch about the formation and nature of city images confirmed by such studies, and can any further relations be established between "urban form" and "city image"?

c) At what level can the results be generalized?

This investigation was made at the Housing and

City Planning Research Section in the Department of Architecture of the Technical University of Delft (Holland).

In the first phase of the inquiry some 20 staff members of the Department of Architecture in Delft were interviewed to see what their images were of the central areas of Amsterdam, Rotterdam, The Hague, Utrecht, Leyden, and Delft. The structures of these cities are entirely different from those of the American cities studied by Lynch; further, there are also considerable variations in pattern from one Dutch city to another. The character of these central areas has been determined largely by topographic and historic factors. In Rotterdam, however, there was extensive reconstruction on more modern lines after the large-scale destruction during the last war.

In the second phase the investigation was extended to about one hundred people, selected at random, living in a number of urban residential neighborhoods in South Holland. In each area 20 to 40 people, predominantly wives of skilled workers and white-collar employees, were interviewed. For most of the areas studied, the images of a number of laymen were compared with those of the professional city planners working in Delft; in some cases, further comparisons were made with maps drawn by professionals in other fields. For the downtown areas, a systematic comparison of the cities was made both for each individual informant and for all the informants together.

The main questions asked were:

1) *To what extent are you familiar with this area?*

2) *Will you draw a rough map of the area such as you imagine it for yourself? Can you also indicate the boundaries of the area?*

3) *What are, in your opinion, the most striking elements and buildings in this area?*

4) *Are there any places, here or elsewhere, where you find orientation difficult?*

In recording the statements of the informants, attention was given to the order of the elements in the sketch maps, remarks as to ease or difficulty in orientation, and the relation of the imaged area to the surrounding parts of the city. Each interview took about a quarter of an hour to half an hour.

The planners were asked to approach the subject in a non-technical way—to think of the everyday use they make of the area, rather than of their professional views. Under these conditions, their reactions did not differ significantly from those of other people of the same educational level. Many housewives, however, found it difficult, if not impossible, to draw sketch maps of their neighborhood. In these cases, the interview was focused on routes and problems of orientation, without direct reference to maps.

In the registration and presentation of the map images a technique was adopted that is somewhat different from the one used by Lynch. In comparing the map images of his subjects and of trained observers, Lynch transferred elements from sketch maps to accurate base maps. Thus the objective structure of urban space (represented on his base maps) as well as the subjective perception of this structure entered into the picture. To a certain extent, subjective and objective data were mixed on every map.

As a social scientist, I have first of all aimed at studying the relations between objective data (rendered on accurate maps and recorded by means of aerial photos) and subjective images (appearing in the form of sketch maps). I have kept the two kinds of maps apart, so that they are given in "pure" form. Thus, any resemblance between an accurate map (or aerial photo) and the image map will be inherent in them, and not a result of the method of recording or presentation. The sketch maps chosen for illustration here are typical ones, showing features which appear on most of the sketches of a particular area.

Results

The reactions of the informants showed a high degree of uniformity and consistency so far as the main points of image formation and image structure were concerned. In general, the quality of the sketch maps produced paralleled orientation in the field. Where most people had difficulties in sketching a rough map of an area, orientation was also difficult, for casual visitors if not for residents. Where people generally found it easy to draw a sketch map that was both simple and adequate, orientation was also easy, provided that the identity of the separate elements of the area was clear enough.

On the whole the methods and techniques described by Lynch were found to be useful instruments for the investigation of people's images of urban areas. This is also true if they are simplified for use in extensive investigations, including the comparison of several urban areas and their respective images. So the question formulated under a) can be answered in the affirmative. Additional data must be presented in order to answer the questions posed under b) and c). In doing this I shall focus on the most interesting areas: Amsterdam, Rotterdam, The Hague, and three residential neighborhoods.

Amsterdam

Objective Structure: Three key elements in the structure of the old town are closely related to the river: the Mint Square, the Dam, and the Central Station. The Mint Square, with its notable Mint Tower, is located where the river first enters the ancient city. Where the mouth of the Amstel used to be, the Central Station has been built on an artificial island in the estuary. Midway between the Mint Square and the Central Station is the Dam, a great square that marks the site of the original dam on the river, and is now the location of the Royal Palace. As a public meeting place for important occasions, the Dam has a national and civic importance comparable to that of Trafalgar Square in London. Two parallel streets connect the Mint Square to the Central Station, passing through the Dam at mid-point. One is a major traffic route, called Damrak on one side of the Dam, Rokin on the other. The other route is a narrow shopping street called Nieuwendijk north of the Dam and Kalverstraat to the south.

Around this old linear core, the city laid out a major extension in the seventeenth century. Its dominant element consists of three major concentric canals, which, together with a number of radial streets and canals, form a spider web pattern. The major canals are further distinguished by rows of impressive homes built by prosperous merchants in the

Sketch Maps of Central Amsterdam

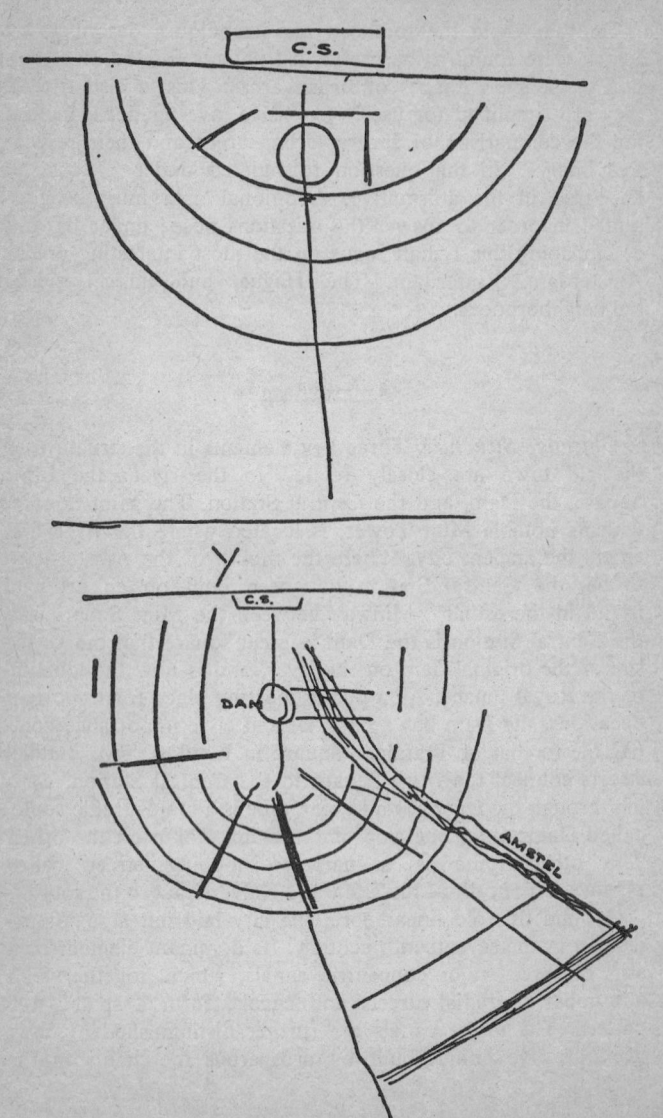

Images of Urban Areas

seventeenth century. A large number of the one-time patricians' homes are now used as offices, but there are still many artists and bohemians whose ideal is to live in an old house along one of the fine old canals. The present-day central shopping area of Amsterdam is situated partly within the old linear city and partly along some of the radial streets intersecting the belt of canals.

*General Characteristics of the Image: A*s Lynch had conjectured, the map structure of Amsterdam produces a very strong image. Every informant indicates as the central path the main route along the river bank from the Central Station via the Dam Square to the Mint. This route is visualized as an axis placed in the middle of a series of concentric semicircles, representing the major canals. The shopping streets (Nieuwendijk and Kalverstraat) form a secondary element accompanying the main route, although in fact this narrow path, with its attractive shop windows, is the route that most people take when they walk. The Central Station Square, the Dam Square, and the Mint are seen as nodes marked by unique landmarks (the railroad station, the Royal Palace and the Mint Tower respectively).

Irregularities in the actual plan are smoothed out in the image. The central main route is seen as a straight line, although in reality there are some bends. The semi-circles of the image are more abstract than the spiderweb of the actual plan. This simplified pattern is accurate enough for general orientation. Since the main structure of the city is essentially regular, minor irregularities are not troublesome.

It should be noted that the bends in the major canals can be seen from any point along them. This feature gives a sense of direction, since the city center is on the inner side of the curve. The spiderweb structure also gives great prominence to the most central spaces: the Central Station and the Dam, either of which can be regarded as the center of the semi-circle. Further, the series of canals make the whole central area of Amsterdam stand out clearly from the surrounding nineteenth-century neighborhoods.

The strong predominance of the main elements in the spatial structure should also be noted: informants give comparatively little attention to separate buildings. At the same time, many elements have a clear identity, so that there is no tedious repetition. The main difficulty for strangers seems to be in distinguishing the three major canals from one another. According to the police, people sometimes think their parked car has been stolen because they have returned to the wrong canal.

Rotterdam

Objective Structure: The ancient city took the form of a triangle, situated on a bend in the river Meuse (Maas). What is now the wide Coolsingel artery was once a canal at the western boundary of the old city. Gradually the central business and shopping district has been shifting westward—a process accelerated by the postwar reconstruction that was necessary after the devastation of much of the center by the bombardment of 1940.

Those elements of the city whose function is most central are now largely located near the Coolsingel, and the Central Station is even farther to the west. Thus the situation is quite different from that in Amsterdam. The triangle of the old city is intersected by an elevated railway. The Central Station is near a second traffic artery, the Weena, which runs at a right angle to the Coolsingel. The two arteries come together at the Hofplein traffic circle.

Hardly any old houses or other buildings that were worthwhile from an aesthetic or historic point of view have survived the blitz and the reconstruction. The Coolsingel is characterized by a great number of big, modern buildings (including Breuer's Bijenkorf Department Store) along this wide artery. A new shopping mall, the Lijnbaan, runs partly parallel and partly at right angles to the Coolsingel. Large scale building activities are constantly going on in the center of Rotterdam, such as the construction of new buildings and a tunnel works for the new subway.

The Image: Those informants who have the clearest image visualize this central area as an L-shaped configuration of the Weena and Coolsingel—plus—Lijnbaan. The link between these two parts of the L is the Hofplein node, with its characteristic form and its fountains. The Coolsingel is the major path mentioned by about 90 percent of the informants.

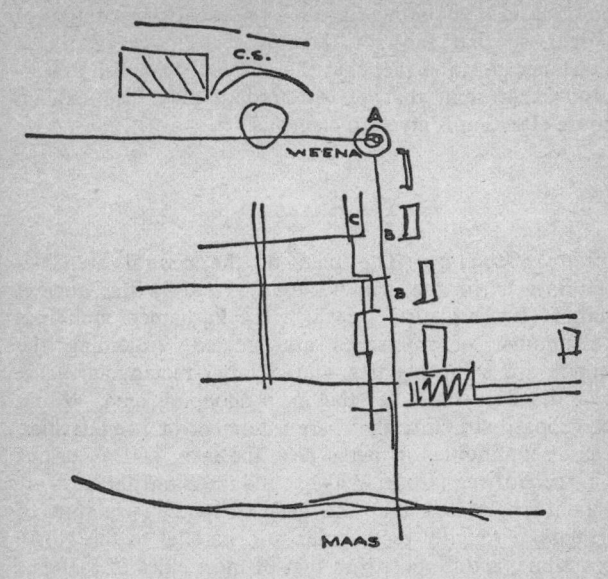

Sketch Map of Central Rotterdam

A. *Hofplein Traffic Circle*
B. *Coolsingel*
C. *Lijnbaan*

The Lijnbaan is indicated on the sketch maps by approximately the same number. Eighty percent draw the Central Station, 70 percent indicate the Weena as a major path, and 60 percent show the Hofplein node.

Most informants have no clear picture of the boundaries between the central area and surrounding parts of the city. Thus in five sketches the elevated railway is indicated as the edge of the central area, while in five others it is there, but not as a boundary line. There is also a lack of clarity in the relation of the central area to other elements, such as the harbor and the district on the other side of the elevated railroad.

Individual buildings and other objects are mentioned to a greater extent than in Amsterdam. This may be due in part to the fact that buildings are more widely separated in Rotterdam, so that each of them is seen more clearly at some distance. But the fact that the over-all image of Rotterdam is weaker than that of Amsterdam may also explain why more attention is given to elements.

The Hague

Objective Structure: The plan of the central area developed largely in the Middle Ages. Here is the ancient Binnenhof (Earl's Court) in which the Parliament buildings and a number of ministries are located. Adjoining the Binnenhof are some squares and a large rectangular lake. West of the Binnenhof lies the main shopping area. Within this chessboard structure there are a number of irregularities, such as discontinuities in paths near the lake, and a curious bend in the Hofweg (Court Way) round the Binnenhof.

It should be noted that the general spatial structure of The Hague, a roughly rectangular grid parallel to the North Sea coast line, is different from that of most cities in the west of the Netherlands. The Hague traditionally lacked independent status, and the city has never been strongly fortified. In most other Dutch cities, fortifications have promoted a more concentric structure. According to an old saying, The Hague is "the finest village of Europe," and this phrase is still used jocularly to distinguish The Hague from Amsterdam and Rotterdam.

The Image: The method of composing most sketch maps of The Hague differs fundamentally from the methods used for the other two cities. In Amsterdam and Rotterdam, the paths and nodes that are important for transportation tend to be the primary elements of the pattern. In The Hague the dominant element is the Court with the adjoining lake. These two objects are taken as the starting-point for the majority of the sketch maps, and then other nearby elements are placed in relation to them. In doing this, many people move outward in a spiral; but on the whole they do not go very far.

The old canals (*singels*) round the 18th-century city do not play any part in the images recorded. They seem to disappear into the chessboard pattern of which they form

Sketch Map of Earl's Court And Surroundings, The Hague

A. Earl's Court
B. Lake

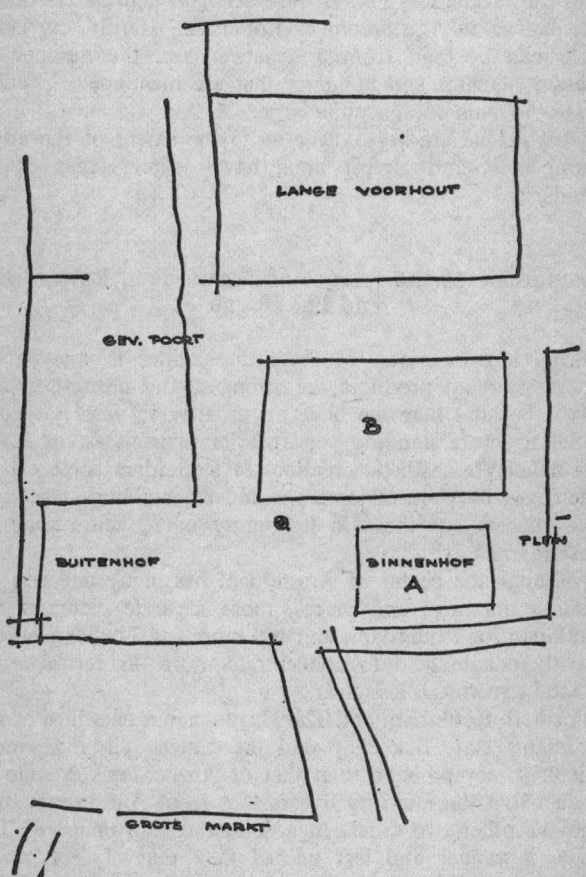

part. It should also be noted that in the field these canals are not at all conspicuous elements. On the other hand, the bend in the Hofweg path is sketched by 18 out of 19 informants drawing this route. This can be explained by the fact that here is a striking departure from the general structure, clearly visible at a point just before the central open space.

In The Hague there is no wide, straight, and clearly dominant path as in Amsterdam or Rotterdam. Hardly any landmarks can be seen from a distance. Yet, the number of separate elements and buildings that are mentioned, in addition to the main ones, is quite large.

Most people are very vague as to the extent of the city's central area, and almost none have definite ideas of its boundaries.

Comparison of the Images of Amsterdam, Rotterdam, and The Hague

From a comparison of these three cities it is apparent that Amsterdam produces the strongest and clearest image. This is because here we have an urban area with a unique spatial structure standing out from its environs as the result of a deliberate aesthetic creation. In Rotterdam some clarity is achieved by wide major paths and big buildings placed in large spaces, but there is less unity of structure than in Amsterdam.

Although the center of Amsterdam has many fine and interesting buildings and places, more separate elements are mentioned for Rotterdam, and still more for The Hague. Apparently people tend to concentrate more on details when the total structure is less clear.

For both Rotterdam and The Hague, about one-third of the informants state that they find the pattern (if any) more difficult to comprehend than that of Amsterdam, in spite of the fact that the majority live farther from Amsterdam than from the other two cities. In general the map image of The Hague is vaguer and less unified than that of Rotterdam. Almost no one has been able to relate the central area of The Hague to the over-all grid of this city in his sketch.

Amsterdam is loved by many people, both residents and

Images of Urban Areas

City Elements Included on Sketch Maps	Number of Informants Identifying Each Element
Amsterdam: Total Number of Informants, 25	
PATHS:	
Main path, Central Station to Mint	22
Drawn as a straight line	15
Semi-circle of canals	20
Other paths, secondary	17
NODES:	
Central Station Square	18
Dam Square	17
Mint Circus	9
Other nodes	10
ROTTERDAM: Total Number of Informants, 22	
PATHS:	
Coolsingel	19
Coolsingel plus Lijnbaan	18
Weena	15
Other paths	24
NODES:	
Station Square	17
Hofplein	13
BUILDINGS:	
Town Hall	10
Wholesale Trade Building	6
Bijenkorf Department Store	6
Exchange	6
OTHER ELEMENTS:	7
The Hague: Total Number of Informants, 25	
PATHS	
Hofweg	19
Bend indicated in sketch	18
Grote Markstraat	15
Spui	12
Kneuterdijk	11
Poten	9
OTHER ELEMENTS:	
Lake near Earl's Court	21
Earl's Court	19
Outer Court	15
All others, combined	60

strangers. There are many reasons for this love, but one among them may be the beautiful structure of the central area, with both a clear over-all pattern and many identifiable parts.

Two Residential Neighborhoods in Delft

Objective Structure: A comparative study was made of two residential neighborhoods built in Delft in recent years. One of them, the Bomenbuurt, has a very simple structure. It numbers about 635 dwellings on an area of 900 x 1,000 feet. There is a mixed development of row-houses and apartment buildings of two or three stories. Generally, row-houses have been built on one side of a street and an apartment block on the other. All the dwellings have concrete outer walls, and all have been built according to a new, non-traditional method.

The street pattern is a rectangular grid, with one diagonal line leading from the edge of the neighborhood to a community building and a small square with a few shops. Near this square there are also a number of semi-detached houses. This is a comparatively small area with a regular street plan, showing irregularity only near the core.

The Voordijkhoornsepolder is about twice as large (about 2,500 x 925 feet), and numbers some 1200 dwellings: one-family houses, apartments, maisonettes, and seven high-rise blocks, three of which had been completed when the study was made.

The street pattern is roughly rectangular, with a number of small deviations from the right angle and the straight line. A broad road, the van Foreestweg, divides the neighborhood into two halves. On this road are some 25 shops, a small canal, and a sizeable square. There are some supermarkets that are used also by people from the adjacent parts of Delft. One large, central, green area is situated on both sides of the square, and within the neighborhood there are four other green spaces, with apartment blocks and houses around them. Thus each street is situated in a characteristic way in relation to the edge of the neighborhood, the center of the neighborhood, or one of the squares.

The Image: The interviews showed that in the Bomenbuurt visitors, and even some absent-minded residents, often took the wrong street in consequence of the great uniformity in layout and architecture. This was especially true of the central streets when approached from the north. From the southern entrance—the diagonal line along the shops— it was much easier to find the right street. When coming from the North, some people even relied on minor details, such as the window curtains of the apartments or houses. A succession of more than three similar elements seems to impede spontaneous recognition and consequent choice of the right street.

Thus, in the most monotonous part of the Bomenbuurt there was regularity of structure, but lack of identity of the parts. Informants also had a number of complaints about the uniform appearance of the housing blocks and the "ugly" appearance of the concrete outer walls.

In the Voordijkhoornsepolder the situation was quite different. As each street and each housing block had its own distinctive orientation and architecture, identity was established more or less automatically by residents and visitors. Here there were many fewer complaints of monotonous blocks or streets. Variety among the elements was greatly increased by the different types of dwellings and by the presence of open spaces of various dimensions.

This comparison demonstrates that present-day planning can avoid monotony even in modern housing developments, and create a pattern that makes orientation easy.

The Leeuwendaal Neighborhood

As an example of a difficult area to be oriented properly in, several informants mentioned the Leeuwendaal neighborhood in Rijswijk (a suburb of The Hague). This area was rebuilt about the turn of the century, and the street plan reveals *Art Nouveau* influences. The streets run mostly in gentle curves, the interrelations of which (if any) cannot be comprehended in the field.

Interviews with some 30 residents showed that many cas-

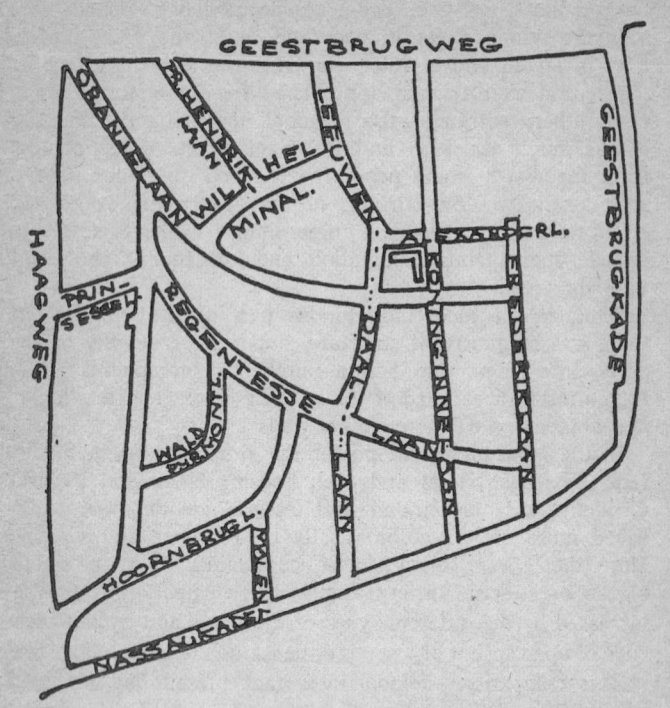

MAP OF LEEUWENDAAL NEIGHBORHOOD

ual visitors lose their way, and that even people who have lived here for decades find it difficult to draw an adequate sketch map. The one reproduced here shows an attempt that failed. The curves of the longest streets that are basic to the total pattern were not imaged adequately; thus it became impossible to link them up correctly with other streets.

Most inhabitants were able to find their way in the area not because they comprehended the total pattern (which was too complicated for them to remember), but because they knew each path separately. Those who only visited the area

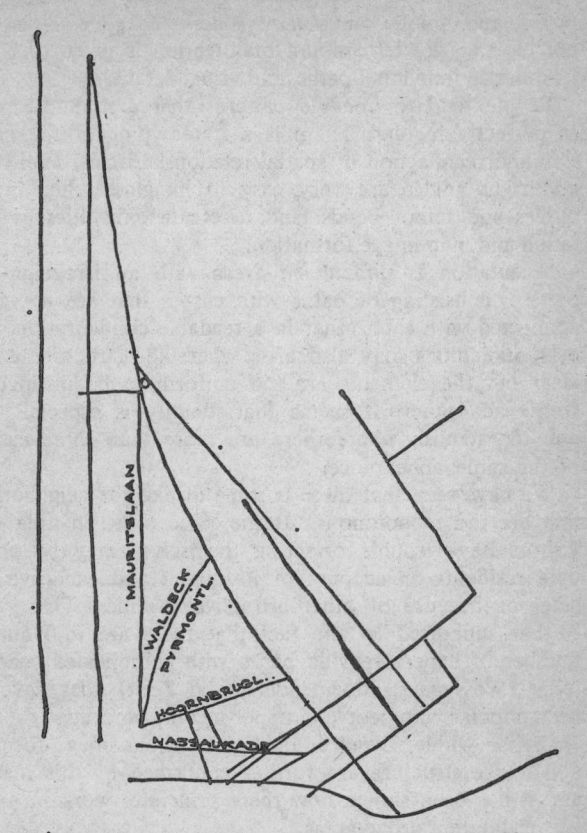

Sketch Map of Leeuwendaal Neighborhood

occasionally knew just a few isolated routes, which is what one tends to do in an area where orientation is difficult.

Conclusions

The following conclusions can be drawn. Formation of a map image is easiest where there is a street plan with a regular pattern, and a single dominant path, characteristic nodes, and unique landmarks. Where the general pattern is not clear, a greater amount of attention is given to isolated landmarks, individual paths, and visual details.

People tend to imagine patterns that are almost regular as perfectly regular. There is a stereotyping of the perception and recollection of spatial relations. Circles, semi-circles, and right angles are very easy to imagine, while quarter-circles and minor bends tend to create difficulties in orientation and map image formation.

Orientation is difficult in areas with an irregular street pattern, consisting of paths with curves that are not clearly connected with each other in a readable configuration. However, difficulties may also arise where the structure is quite clear but the elements are too uniform to be distinguished from each other. It seems that identity is especially difficult to establish where there are more than three elements of the same appearance.

We have seen that there is some dislike for neighborhoods that are too monotonous. At the same time, an area where visitors have trouble orienting themselves may be popular with residents on account of its quaint and exclusive character or because of other attractive qualities. This view is further supported by the fact that there are in Holland a number of expensive villa parks with complicated road patterns (Wassenaar, Bloemendaal, and Zeist) that have long been popular with people in upper-income brackets.

On the whole, Lynch's conclusions about image formation and image structure are further confirmed by this material; and it has been shown how these principles work in a number of different urban areas.

The fact that research in Holland has led to much the same conclusions as those of Lynch's is in itself an indication that his findings are not limited to the comparatively small sample he used. Further indications of the validity of the above conclusions on map image formation are to be found in two kinds of data: 1) orientation maps, and 2) the "laws" of Gestalt psychology.

1) Simple maps for rapid and easy orientation in given areas are issued by tourist offices, transit companies, and such institutions. In this connection, Lynch mentions the pocket map of subway lines of the London Transport Cor-

poration. This map has also been commented upon by Arnheim,[3] who says: (It) "gives the needed information with the utmost clarity and at the same time delights the eye through the harmony of its design. This is achieved by renouncing all geographic detail except for the pertinent topological properties—that is, sequence of stops and interconnections. All roads are reduced to straight lines; all angles to the two simplest: ninety degrees and forty-five degrees. The map leaves out and distorts a great deal, and just because of this it is the best possible picture of what it wants to show." Arnheim has also noted that more than three or four similar elements are "visually undistinguished."[4]

The orientation maps show the same kind of selection of details and simplification of pattern as the sketch maps drawn by our informants. In addition, landmarks are often indicated on these maps in the form of small drawings showing the objects in perspective. Most readers will remember such maps from their own experience.

2) A basic problem for Gestalt psychology has been to identify factors that organize the visual field into independent units. Many experiments have been made with figures composed of points and lines, in which subjects were asked to indicate what configurations they recognized. A number of conditions were thus found to play an important, if not exclusive, part in producing visual form: proximity, similarity, closed form, "good contour," common movement, and experience.[5] The perception of separate elements as one visual form is further promoted by such characteristics as regularity, symmetry, inclusiveness, harmony, maximal simplicity, and conciseness.

A number of dots arranged in an approximately circular fashion are seen as if they were really a circle, angles of 87 degrees or 93 degrees look like right angles. Drawings with gaps tend to be seen as closed, figures which are not quite symmetrical tend to be perceived as symmetrical. Thus, much the same process of selection, simplification, and predilection for "pure" forms (such as the right angle and the circle) were observed in the Gestalt experiments as were observed in the map images of urban areas studied here. So our research can be said to have shown that people's perceptions of the main pattern of urban space tend to follow the same "laws" Gestalt psychologists have found in their laboratory experiments.

We may therefore conclude that the results with regard to map images can be generalized, at any rate for literate man in Western society. Of course it still remains to be seen to what extent and in what way insight into image structure can be used to increase the liveability of cities and towns. This problem cannot be solved by social scientists alone; it calls for study by designers and social psychologists working jointly to investigate this important aspect of design.

Notes

1. Kevin Lynch, *The Image of the City* (Cambridge, Mass.: The Technology Press and Harvard University Press, 1960).

2. David A. Crane, Review in *Journal of the American Institute of Planners*, XXVII (May, 1961), 152.

3. Rudolph Arnheim, *Art and Visual Perception: A Psychology of the Creative Eye* (Berkeley: University of California Press, 1954).

4. *Ibid.*, p. 4.

5. David Katz, *Gestalt Psychology, its Nature and Significance*, trans. Robert Tyson (London: Methuen, 1951), pp. 24-28 and 40-41.

Some Childhood Memories of the City

Alvin Lukashok and Kevin Lynch

What does a child notice in his city? What elements of the physical environment leave the deepest impression? A class of architects and planners at M.I.T. wrote short papers on their memories of the environment in which they lived as children. Their homes were dispersed from Bangkok to Brooklyn, their play spaces from country lawns to slum pavements, and yet there were striking similarities in the reports. They spoke of trees, or the lack thereof; the ground under their feet, or what had been substituted for it. They made mention of hills and water and streetcars, of space and of the physical marks of social status. Many other elements, such as buildings and traffic, schools and playgrounds, took a distinctly secondary place if they appeared at all. Some interesting light was also thrown on a child's idea of the neighborhood and of the city as a whole.

All of this was tempting enough to suggest a somewhat more methodical study of childhood memories, with the objective of answering two questions: first and primarily, to what does the child pay attention in his outdoor physical world; and, secondly, how does he respond emotionally to these features?

In the summer of 1955, forty subjects were interviewed for their memories, and their responses tape recorded. Twenty-two were M.I.T. students, eighteen were nonstudents, with occupations ranging from sociologist to cab driver. Seven were women. None were professionally involved in urbanism or design. The ages ranged from eighteen to thir-

Reprinted by permission from *Journal of the American Institute of Planners*, Vol. XXII, No. 3, Summer, 1956, copyright by The American Institute of Planners.

ty-two, and all but four or five were middle class. The majority were born and raised in Boston, but there was a sprinkling of outlanders from New York or even more distant cities such as Lisbon, Riga, Warsaw, Berlin, and Vienna.

The basic assumption was that present adult memories reflect actual childhood preoccupations, i.e., that items which persist over such a long time span are records of the real, salient, emotionally important experiences of youth. There are, of course, at least four other possibilities:

a. The memory is of an actual but not important experience; it is an accidental retention. This seemed unlikely, particularly where the memory is supported by vivid detail.

b. It is a false memory, a product of what others have said, or otherwise the result of experience *after* childhood. This probably occurs, and is difficult to detect.

c. Consciously or not, the memories are employed to cover something else, or are selected and marshalled to impress the interviewer. Some attempts to impress the interviewer did, in fact, occur and in the analysis this distortion of emphasis has been taken into account as much as possible.

d. Finally, while retained memories may indicate important experiences, nevertheless many other truly important events may have been forgotten.

Features in the landscape may be important for many reasons, of course: because the experience occurs frequently; because of strong emotional ties; because of the relation to the child's needs. In any case, these items are worth the attention of the city builder.

Method

Each interview began with a question concerning the person's home and street, encouraging him to continue from this, telling his memories as he pleased, so long as he did not wander too far afield from perceptual material. Then direct questions were asked on such subjects as traffic, the neighborhood, and attitude to the city as a whole, or on other questions growing out of preceding answers. These questions might deal with strong likes and dislikes that the person expressed concerning any part of the city scene. Preferences in downtown areas were discussed, or the kind of street on which the subject would live if he could. Elementary and naive as these direct questions may seem, yet by experience it was found that they produced the most satisfactory, honest and exhaustive answers. Very little has been done previously to apply this simple method to urban design.

As a first step in the analysis, these interviews were broken down into arbitrary topics, ranked in their frequency of spontaneous or especially vivid mention, depending upon the judgment of the experimenter:

Frequency of mention of various topics
(out of a total of 40 interviews)

Lawns	27	Ground Surface in general, 36
Other ground surfaces	25	
Topography	24	
Wall materials	23	
Trees	21	
Mass transport	21	
Color	20	
Families per house	19	
Sense of space	17	
Water	15	
Cleanliness	15	
Crowdedness	13	
Awareness of a neighborhood	12	
Play in "waste" areas	12	
Order and maintenance	11	
Traffic	9	
Shopping	8	
Historical association	7	
Orientation to the city: through		
High school	14	
Wandering	8	
Parent's occupation	7	
Transportation lines	7	
After-school occupation	5	
Play	4	

The City "Floor"

Among the items mentioned most often are the lawns. A lawn is associated with spaciousness and a sense of freedom.

The positive effect associated with this was expressed, for example, in the following:

> "I was very happy. I remember the first day we got there I was running over the lawns, up the slopes because it was so much of a change."

The size of the lawn and its upkeep indicates the status of an area. For instance:

> "After you ride along Cleary Square the houses become nicer, they have lawns, some are set up on a hill, a little off the street."

In one interview on Scarsdale, two neighborhoods are compared in terms of house set-back and what the subject calls the "estate" quality of some properties. Even small front lawns are mentioned and when the subject has lived in a house with no yard or lawn around it, he is still aware of the lawn as being a status indicator in other, presumably better, neighborhoods. The lawn provides play space, and for many subjects the front or back yard is their earliest play area, and, as will become more and more evident, a child remembers what he can play on or with.

Not only just the lawns, but the entire "floor" of his environment is of great importance to the child. Very few things are so close to him for play. Of all the various types of floor coverings mentioned, grass is the best liked, then dirt that can be dug or molded, and after that any smooth surface that allows roller skating or bicycling. Driveways are occasionally mentioned in this regard.

The floor surfaces that a child seems to dislike are asphalt on open spaces that otherwise would remain grassy, and brick, gravel and cobblestones placed where he can suffer a fall. Of the few people who mention brick-paved surfaces, none talk about the visual qualities of such surfaces, all dislike the uneven texture it provides. A typical attitude is expressed by a girl who said when describing a street:

> "It had a hill and a brick sidewalk, which is not good for roller skating."

Another subject refers to Beacon Hill:

> "I remember distinctly the brick sidewalks. I didn't like that at all. I was strictly for cement sidewalks, didn't like brick; they jibbled and jabbled all ways."

The child is sensitive to the floor and its various coverings because it is the prime condition of his main activity—play. This surface, rarely the conscious concern of the designer, so often left to surveyor, contractor or sheer custom, thus turns out to be the most important sensuous element of all.

Texture and Color

The city floor is the textured surface which has the most powerful impact on the child. While another type of surface, the material of the building walls, was also often mentioned, it is nevertheless clear that it had a totally different significance. Comments on wall materials almost always convey the impression that they are one of the standard and expected ingredients of the description of a region and rarely seem to carry much emotional significance. In a few cases they are used to convey a sense of shabbiness, or of darkness and thus of gloominess. "The usual red brick" is also an epithet of dislike applied to schoolhouses.

Color, which was brought up in some twenty of the interviews, is almost invariably an inseparable part of the descriptive term for the wall material, and seems to have little life of its own in memory. Occasionally "green" is used as a synonym for foliage or grass, in a purely conceptual way. Only in a few cases did color seem to have much impact, usually by characterizing the tone of a dreary area, as "gray." Another remembers being disgusted by "yellow" grass in Franklin Park.

Foliage

Trees are mentioned with great frequency. With few minor exceptions trees and foliage are remembered with great warmth. When describing an ideal street these are usually included, and they are mentioned in the preferred downtown sections. Children like trees and foliage for many reasons. They provide the ideal environment for play. Offering shade in the summer, they can be climbed, they can be carved, they are hiding places. They are places where children can create their own fantasies. Here is a memory that expresses this:

> "We had a big oak tree in front of our house which was sort of a favorite. Then they were planting these small ones which were supposed to grow into these big ones someday but never got a chance because we'd hang on them or try to climb them and break them off. During the latter part of the spring, when they used to get real bushy, they almost covered the street in sort of a tunnel. It gave a nice feeling of security. You could walk on the outside of the trees and be blocked off from the road. Yet it wasn't the same thing as barriers you encountered in Brookline, it was sort of a friendly thing. We carved our initials in them. You could do a lot of things with them, climb them, hit them, hide behind them . . . you could see out between the trees but none could see in, and we used to hide in there and watch people . . . I always liked to watch people."

There are those who remember the pleasure of being shaded by trees.

> "I can remember in the summertime it was beautiful along Saratoga and Bennington Streets because it was shaded. We used to play on the front stoop of somebody's house, and it was so nice to get under the trees for shade."

Of course, not everybody feels this way, especially if their experience living among trees is limited. Here is a comment of a New Yorker:

> "There were very few trees, occasionally thin trees . . . I remember wondering when I was young why they bothered, because it seemed obvious that the trees had absolutely nothing to do. I really didn't miss them. What little foliage there was in the city would seem to interfere."

But the majority are so at ease in their love of trees and green that there is hardly an interview that in some way does not take them into account. Trees are alive, they move but are always there. They regularly change their form in step with the great seasons. For some subjects the trees are the dominant impression of their childhood:

> "There were maple trees along our street . . . It's about the only tree I've ever been conscious of; it's the first tree I remember the name of, I've thought of it all my life. White birch trees, too, have a special meaning . . . But when I think of Scarsdale, I think of maple trees."

Play Areas

One of the interesting things coming out of the interviews is that children seem to prefer to play anywhere but the playground. Some of the following comments will illustrate the feelings of many children. A boy from Jersey City played in the park

> "near the bushes to get away from the playgrounds."

A girl remembers:

> "We would rather play in the foliage. I think it represented a certain amount of mystery and imagination. You could invent things. Bushes sort of formed a clump surrounding an open space, and this can begin to mean something to you, such as a house."

Another person:

> "Our idea, when I was 9 or 10 years old, was not to play on the playground but to find some place where there were rocks and broken bottles . . . a lot of trees and holes to fall into."

In commenting on the extensive program of playground construction that took place in Manhattan under the direction of Robert Moses, one person said:

> "I remember Riverside Park before it turned into . . . developed areas . . . I remember there being a lot more space to play in. The big change, the big spurt of playground building had gone up. I was sort of pleased with having

all these nice places to play in, the nice things that moved and worked, etc., but there simply wasn't enough space just to go and play in and do idiotic things in. You couldn't dig, for example; I like to dig. There weren't many places to dig because of the hard asphalt on the playground."

Another, in referring to where he used to play, said:

"Out in back was a big field where the grass was over your head. They have cut that down now and made a playground out of it so it isn't as romantic.

Referring to some empty land, one person said:

"The land surrounding the school was sort of jungle—trees and brush growing up, very unkempt . . . It wasn't much outside but I remember we used to play there a lot and have a great time there."

One girl remembers:

"I really liked to play most of all in the back alleys. It was interesting. There were all kinds of doorways to go under. Very colorful place. I'd feel like an adventurer. That seemed to be the main place of activity for children . . . It was a wonderful place to hide, you see, because of all kinds of doors and passageways."

The garage and garage area, so often the insoluble part of many architectural design problems, is usually remembered by the child with great affection. Children remember garage roofs as places to climb to and jump off from. Garages seem to have the importance of enclosed spaces without the accompanying authority of adult organization.

These are positive statements and nowhere do we find them contradicted. A child's play is most satisfactory when it allows him the greatest opportunity to manipulate his environment according to his needs: to imagine, create, and hide. A well-differentiated world, and one that is plastic to his hands and mind, is his desire. That is perhaps why so many people remember with pleasure the overgrown lot, thick brush and woods. It is sufficient to give us pause in our treatment of "waste" or "untidy" areas, or in the design of play spaces. Naturally, as the child grows older, the type of organized activity he wants demands a different type of open space. In some of the interviews we find the conventional open playground, mentioned without any negative effect, but again not with any positive effect either. Most often it is in reference to the organized games of adolescence.

Hills

The majority of the interviews mention the local topography in one way or another. The hilliness or flatness of an area is noted in the basic descriptions, and, on the whole, people remember keenly and with pleasure the hills that were in the vicinity. A typical example is the person from Scarsdale who makes comparisons of her hills in Westchester to the disliked flatness of Long Island. There are some who include hilliness as part of their requirement for an ideal location of their home. More usually, the memory of a hill is part of the play area, lending itself to many types of activity such as coasting. Because so often a hill is not the best site for building, it is the last part of the area developed, allowing it to remain wild and therefore attractive to children. If there is any negative affect toward hills it is in terms of their inconvenience—the difficulties of getting up them in winter and the number of accidents which take place because of them. But on the whole this variation in topography is strongly desired. And yet, although the child is sensitive to hills, it is surprising how little the *general* hilliness of such a place as Chelsea affected the memories. The subjects mentioned that certain places were on hills or that they played on certain hills but nowhere were we given any indication that the central characteristic of Chelsea is its hills.

Transport and Traffic

Frequently mentioned were the mass transport vehicles. This includes trolleys, buses, trains, or even ships. It is here distinguished from traffic. The flow of vehicles as a total pattern. In the interviews there is a strong but ambivalent feeling toward mass transport vehicles. The delight of watching trains, buses or trolleys is usually paired with impressions of dirt and noise. One person, describing with pleasure his memories of watching trains in the Jersey City station, still remarks that:

> ". . . it seemed very dirty and black."

The excitement that this type of experience affords is illustrated by the following memories:

> "One thing I can remember very clearly is going to the subway and being very impressed by subway trains. I remember that it was rather dingy and rather filthy, and the big cold tracks were very interesting, always the signs . . . 'Danger—Third Rail'."

And:

> ". . . the elevated, that was miserable. When you stand at the corner of the street, even with your father, with all these cars honking, darkness from the buildings and the elevated cutting it off, and then one of these things would come roaring down the tracks, clattering and clashing."

The last impression is undeniably negative in effect, yet there is that tension and excitement in the description that reflects the child's closely held interest.

Impressions and memories of trolleys and trains are often associated with the noise they make. These are the noises children often hear, especially at night.

> "Talbot Street, I can remember, had these streetcars on it. It was cobblestone, a pretty noisy street; if a car went down you heard the car. I used to live on the top floor and could hear the streetcars ten blocks away, and after a while you can tell exactly where they were, what stop, just by the sound."

It may be that we sometimes make mistakes in isolating our railroads or burying our transit vehicles. For a child at least, these seem to be a very adventurous part of city life.

As far as traffic in general is concerned, it is mentioned much less often. Most of the people remember being warned by their parents about its dangers, but there is no evidence that they had or retained strong feelings about it. Traffic seems to be taken for granted in childhood. It may be, of course, that in the last ten or fifteen years traffic has increased from the stage of mild discomfort to one of near crisis for some of our major cities. But in these memories, traffic is remembered as a mild interference with play rather than a more serious threat. It is also, like mass transport, a source of pleasure to the child. It was for the one who said:

> "I got over the hill and went down the square, and maybe I liked the increased activity that I came upon—the streetcars, all the people and everything."

Or the girl from Berlin:

> "Part of our apartment was facing the street, and the balcony and my room was facing the street. I remember looking out before bedtime at night and watching the traffic. I liked that very much. Our street was leading into a main street where they had a trolley car and I even could see that."

It is of some interest that the two interviews that deal with Manhattan never mention traffic. In answer to a direct question about traffic, one person said:

> "I don't remember noticing traffic; there wasn't that much."

This, about uptown Manhattan! Is the great volume of traffic on Manhattan streets such an ordinary part of the environment that it goes unnoticed?

Space and the Sense of Crowdedness

The sense of space is put in strong terms, and with positive effect, in at least seventeen of the forty interviews. This consideration, often felt to be restricted to technical conversations among professional architects and planners, is keenly felt, and often articulated as such, by people who rarely think of these problems technically. At times the word might not be used, but the sense is expressed, as in the following comment:

> "Take Franklin Field especially. It was quite a big field, being wide open there. Now when I look at it, it's closing in on you."

Often it is one of the earliest impressions mentioned. Here are a number of examples, the first referring to a park:

> ". . . It was a very nice place to walk around; it was larger; it gave you the impression of having more space and more green."

Another from Vienna:

> "The first thing I remember about Vienna physically? There are two things—one is the wide spaces, wide airy squares . . ."

A girl from Scarsdale:

> "I remember having the great big playground with space to move and play. I remember no feeling of closeness, which I have noticed later on in my life as I have moved into cities."

Referring to Lisbon:

> "But you don't get the confined feeling that you do in New York, for example, because none of the buildings were that high. Most of the streets in residential areas were wide, or they seemed wide anyway."

Or to Baltimore:

> "The downtown area was not very pretty to me at all and I didn't like it very well, except for one street which is the longest street . . . in Baltimore. It runs from the suburbs all the way downtown, very broad . . . I tend to like broad streets, the one where I first lived and this one."

Some Childhood Memories of the City

This is indeed a common theme:

> "The upper Concourse had no shops on it, was very much wider, and could be seen to stretch for greater distance, and I liked this very much."

Occasionally spaces of a different quality are remarked upon:

> "Boston was almost like a maze. You felt you were at the bottom of a maze with high walls, noisy with echoes from cars beeping their horns."

> "One street was interlocked with another so that you would climb stairs or step down and move around in a labyrinth of little streets, and one house almost embracing or sitting on the other house so that you never get the feeling of separate units, but one continuum of little streets which was moving like a path. All of these were descending toward the Vistula." (of old Warsaw)

Crowdedness has an overwhelming effect on the impression formed of the physical environment. The fact that it occurs only thirteen times out of forty does not give a strong enough indication of how widely this feeling pervades the memory. It is the obverse of space, but its more pressing and immediate aspect. As in the case of space, it is one of the earliest things mentioned and there is little mistaking the effect. In the first paragraph of one interview:

> "The district I lived in was notably apartment and tenement houses, usually crowded."

Another interview, after the question, "What's the first thing you remember?", begins:

> "Very crowded. Everybody knows everybody."

It is interesting to note that in no interview does the subject complain about too much space. Rarely is there even a reference to the emptiness or the loneliness of great spaces, and although it is generally felt by designers that public squares can be too large to be comfortable and by their excessive dimensions destroy just those qualities for which they are designed, yet in none of these interviews do we see any reaction remotely echoing this objection—with perhaps the exception of the Warsaw interview where one might infer that some of the courtyards in the wealthier parts of Warsaw had a deserted and empty feeling or again in the following:

> "Both Berkeley and Arlington used to run down to the Charles. This was a bit larger sensation than the Public Gardens because the river is very broad. You feel a bit more lonely there."

If one might hazard a generalization, it is that there is so little open space left in our cities that, in their hunger for it, most people cannot afford to be concerned with the quality of the space, they are grateful that it is there. This feeling of gratitude, and complementary feelings of resentment toward any elimination of open space, was expressed by a cab driver whose last sentiment during the interview was:

> "Boston Common is one of the best parks in all New England. They'll never get that."

Marks of Social Status

An aspect of the city environment that is constantly mentioned is the number of families per dwelling. When describing a street or a neighborhood this is one of the first things to which a person will refer. Whether there is one family, two families or three families per house is of great importance and is closely related to feelings of crowdedness. The number of families per house is the usual indicator of social boundaries. It is fundamental in describing the differences between one neighborhood and another, or between one street and another. Closely allied to this is the feeling of cleanliness, as well as the order and maintenance apparent in the neighborhood.

The emotions lying behind the adjectives of "clean" and "dirty" were universal among the subjects and perhaps only

Some Childhood Memories of the City

surprising in their frequency of mention and in the strength of the feelings that go with them.

"I remember the section of our city was rather nice. It was clean. I never saw any accumulated dirt. They had a man clean the streets every morning and empty garbage. Everything was done, there was nothing left, and it was always clean looking."

"The buildings were sort of old, not in the sense that they were built a long while ago but that they were actually beginning to fall down; they were dirty; some of the structure was breaking down and falling away. The streets were bad, as I recall. They had pavement on them but were broken down and needed repairs, and the sidewalks in the same fashion. It gave me the appearance of being all cluttered up, dirty."

"Around this neighborhood were the best residential areas in the city. They were centrally located. Streets were extremely clean, with trees, and houses were well kept." (of Riga)

"The most clear memory I have of it was that it was confusing—everything seemed to be big and dirty and ugly. I was afraid, I think, of this house."

"We'd go into Franklin Park which was right across the street, which I didn't like very much because it was a grubby park, not well kept. Sometimes you like dirt when you're out in the woods—it's good and clean. But in Franklin Park it looked as if the earth was laid there by some contractor, and the grass was yellow, spotted, and the ground was hard, and it was really dirty."

"Just a straight street . . . but clean. It was a nice clean street."

"What part of Boston?"

"The dirty part! Big four-decker house. There was an ash heap in the back and I used to climb on it. It was a dirty street, long street . . . In Somerville we lived in a three-decker, nice house—nice because it was so different from the other one. It was clean . . ."

It is only to be expected that judgments as to crowdedness, cleanliness, upkeep of areas be expressed in social terms.

There is nothing subtle about this; the people who express themselves so are quite aware of what they mean and are at pains to let you know it. For instance:

> "All around that area, up the hill to the Chelsea border going into Everett, the homes are far better, the people are much richer or more well-to-do. I don't think you'll find any three-family houses, more one-family houses, and the two-family houses are very nice . . . The exteriors might possibly be newly shingled or freshly painted. The grass is well kept. All the homes in this area have at least small plots in front of the house with grass and bushes. The cleanliness of the houses makes them look decent, and the fact that you know the people do have a certain amount of money probably will produce a psychological effect . . . . When I say 'nice' I think it may have to do with the psychological aspect of it, because you know the people there are very nice, their kids go to college, and to varying degrees their houses are well kept on the insides as well as painted on the outside every now and then."

Another person, in reference to Huntington, Long Island:

> "I thought and think that the Village is a lot prettier than the Station because the type of person that lives in the Village is more of the business capacity, whereas the person that lives in the Station is more of the working type of person, and consequently there is a great deal of difference in the homes."

Here is a comment that brings together a number of the above considerations:

> "Orient Heights seemed nicer in the sense that the houses were nicer, newer houses. There were more brick houses—very attractive looking. In our neighborhood, for example, the street would go down, right off the street you would have two or three-story tenement houses. There would be no grass in the front yard, and in the back yard there used to be just dozens of clotheslines. When I was a kid, I often wondered how the people in Orient Heights ever got their clothes washed because we used to have these clotheslines, and you go through Orient Heights where the people own their own homes, they didn't have any clotheslines, and it was always in my mind how they got their clothes washed and dried. They never seemed to hang them out. This

was quite a contrast, the absence of dozens and dozens of clotheslines. In front of the house they would have a plot of grass. Instead of just walking along the street and falling into the house, you would go up five or six stairs, you'd have grass in the front and flowers around. Many people would have flagpoles in front of the houses. We didn't have those things. The clothesline question stuck in my mind. The houses were smaller, that is, single-family homes; two-family homes were kept up much nicer."

He also says:

"The people in Orient Heights, a much nicer section, with nicer homes, more grass—there was a feeling of resentment for those people."

It is of interest to contrast the above account of this section of Boston with that of another person who was interviewed:

"Then there was the Orient Heights section. That's still East Boston. That's definitely way out of our class. That's where the rich people would be living. That's where you would have your home with trees, yards and gardens. I used to go up there as a kid and steal apples off the trees. I never felt any envy about that section a bit. I used to enjoy going up there and stealing apples and peaches, but as far as wanting to live there it never occurred to me. I used to remark about the fact as how they could just live and sit and do nothing. Too quiet, that's what I always said. I thought I'd never want to live in a place like that, too quiet for me."

All three of the comments show how strongly the sense of space is reflected in lawns and yards. They also reflect the sense of upkeep and neatness. Two out of the three comments stress the number of families per house as an index of crowdedness or its lack. But all three cannot describe the differences in neighborhood without bringing in the term of social comparison. It would be interesting to know how much of what is perceived about a neighborhood is based on preconceived notions of the habits of the class that lives there. This is a whole area which is largely outside the control of city planners, which cannot help but make its effect on their designs.

The interaction of social status and perception is a part

of the interview material that deserves further study. One suspects that for many people no area, no matter how delightfully planned, can ever compete aesthetically with other areas of higher status. For architects and planners who are increasingly called upon to design housing projects, which by their very nature have class labels, this type of information is critical. So far, the results in income-limited housing are far from reassuring architecturally. The relative segregation and scale of housing projects—whether they should be scattered in such a way as to minimize their presence—is immediately brought into focus by these considerations, even though superficially such reasoning seems to surrender to what some people might call an unattractive snobbery.

Associations

This leads us to consideration of the role of historical and cultural associations in the city scene. An obvious example where these are strong is Beacon Hill in Boston, an area that is enjoyed by many who consider it beautiful mainly because of its associations. Although there were not many who talked of the physical environment in those terms, this type of perception played a large part in the most imaginative interviews, especially those about European cities. Many people, because of such linkages, will enjoy or remark upon elements that they otherwise think unpleasant or insignificant. Here are two examples:

"There were individual things in the city which started to acquire a great deal of emotional values for me. I can't say it was really the things in themselves that did it. It was also the literary associations which would make me want to think they were good—such things as Brooklyn Bridge . . . But Brooklyn Bridge was always very, very strange and somewhat foreboding . . . I started to walk across it myself more than once or twice, and I really did get interested in it, knowing a little bit about the history of it. I came to think of it as beautiful, whereas I hadn't before."

"Louisburg Square—I like the square itself, the history of it. It was up there a couple of times . . ."

Some Childhood Memories of the City

Of course, for many, such as the person who commented on the brick sidewalk on Beacon Hill, such knowledge is merely another reason why the building or neighborhood should be torn down. To them it is proof of its age and therefore of its obsolescence.

The theme of *wandering,* though not mentioned often and then always linked to adolescence, is yet of great interest because it reflects a certain fascination in the city for its own sake. It is often stimulated by an interest in historical monuments, or in the appearance of different class areas, or in the literary associations of certain neighborhoods like Beacon Hill in Boston or Greenwich Village in New York. Sometimes there are those who will wander for pleasures of curiosity alone. The comments which follow will illustrate some of these delights:

"A lot of my sense of the city came from looking at it at night, especially later on in high school. My friends and I used to walk through the city when it was still . . . even so far as to go down, on weekends, to the Battery and walk all the way uptown to 86th Street . . . .

"It was actually from this part of the city (Lafayette Street) I would explore, walking westward and wind up in the Village . . . My first sense of the Village (was) . . . simply looking at it itself and noticing how marvelous it was to find a place like this . . . The crookedness and apparent randomness of the path of the street, an escape from the gridiron pattern, fascinated me very much."

"At about the age of 12 or 11 I started the custom of spending Saturday mornings walking from the West End through Scollay Square along Tremont and the Common and down to the Boston Public Library which I began to know. I liked the city and it was a walk that had so many different experiences in it—to go from the slums of the West End, very picturesque ones they were. Then to walk through the business district and go around the Common and down to the quieter and a little bit more Bostonian business district of Boylston Street to the Library where I'd spend the afternoon."

The American subjects who indulged in this type of activity were in the minority and often, as children, in some way unhappy with their home environment, using this as a form of play. In the interviews with the subjects from Riga, and Warsaw and Vienna, however, this activity was more frequently mentioned and seemed more directly stimulated by interest in the excitement of the urban areas themselves.

Most of the people interviewed do not express such feelings about the city, except for the early reactions to the downtown area. If the children go downtown it usually is for some specific purpose such as a job or entertainment, taking in a movie or a ball game. They do not express a feeling of enjoying the city for its own sake.

The desire to wander and take pleasure in the city presumes that there is a city worth wandering about. The absence of pleasure in the city for itself, the pleasure we have seen in the above comments and which comes through the interviews pertaining to Riga, Warsaw and Vienna, suggests that there may be a diffuseness in the American city that makes this difficult. It suggests that greater satisfactions in this direction might be possible with a more concentrated or differentiated urban enviroment. Incidentally, the majority of persons interviewed were engineering students, and their reaction to such satisfactions might be somewhat more negative than what would be shown by a wider sampling of the population.

Orientation

We were interested in finding out how people think of their city as a whole, how they gain a conception of its overall pattern. The majority of the people interviewed oriented themselves to the city, not by wandering, but through the more ordinary processes of going to high school or having after-school jobs that sent them to various sections. Here are comments that illustrate these two ways in which children get to know the larger city:

> "I had a job in Boston. My father was a tailor . . . and he got me a job with another tailor . . . who wanted someone to carry coats to different places in town. That's how I learned how to get from one spot to another. Then, of course, you're always looking for something new or adventure and

Some Childhood Memories of the City

you try going around a different block to get there and in that way you know different parts of town."

"I went to Boston Trade High School and I would leave East Boston to go to Roxbury to school. That would more or less make me aware of other sections of the city. For example, I never had any occasion to go to Dorchester; I still don't know anything about Dorchester; I'm not aware of it and I feel nothing towards it or against it . . . Trade School made me aware of certain sections of Roxbury. I would meet people there, fellows from high school, and I would go to their homes. If we had common interests we would get to know each others' districts that way."

As can be seen from the table on page 67, going to high school is the most common way by which people start to grasp the city in its completeness.

In general, the people interviewed who came from the Boston area showed a lack of appreciation of the city as a whole. If any one attitude comes out, it is a hatred for and desire to avoid the downtown areas. Under questioning they will admit that certain areas are not too bad, usually the Common and the Commonwealth Avenue or the Beacon Street area, but their desires run to the suburbs.

Occasionally there are hints of how the parts of a city seem to "fit together," or on the contrary to take on a confusing pattern:

"I remember it had a sort of square with two or three streets running into it, except the square was not in the center of things but off to one side. That was really confusing. You got to one spot and you were afraid to move because you were afraid you'd get lost."

"You could locate yourself by landmarks. There was a series of hotels so you knew you were here, and on the other side you would be near a certain park. The landmarks in the city . . . were historical buildings or historical sites, natural kinds of locations like parks or hills, and in the downtown area there were, of course, movies, theater, opera . . . . If you remember the locality you can locate yourself quickly . . . Sections that I knew I knew well, and the rest sort of fit in."

"It was pretty massive and confusing when I was a youngster, very difficult to find my way around."

Neighborhoods

It is also interesting to see that the sense of neighborhood, although fairly well developed, does not seem to follow lines that many planners refer to as "the neighborhood." To begin with, the conception of the neighborhood in any given physical area seems to differ according to the age and personality of the child perceiving it. The twelve-year-old's neighborhood does not coincide with that of the high school student nor with the adult's. The employment of unique and fixed physical boundaries to define the neighborhood for all groups may be of doubtful validity. Secondly, it becomes clear how small and sharply limited is the "neighborhood" of a child; how it is sometimes determined by minor physical irregularities:

"There wasn't any other kid my age on the street; they were all older, two or three years older, or younger. A couple of streets away there were a lot of kids my age. Occasionally I'd go over there, but I sort of had the feeling that they were different; they lived on that street. I don't know why. There might have been a reason because my street was the only street in the area with all single-family houses, and everyone knows each other. On these other streets they were longer in the first place and are all three- to six-family houses."

"We more or less considered the neighborhood constituted a block. Your gang constituted a block and then there was a group down in the other block ... Within our block we were the ones. Everybody in their own block within that area, five or six blocks, felt that way. Another sort of feeling of a neighborhood was that in our block there was a drug store, a First National, two or three candy stores, and that constituted a sort of cohesiveness; we were a unit. Each block, come to think of it, had a store—a grocery store, maybe not a drug store, a gasoline station, which added a little bit of unity to the group. These trading areas seemed to more or less unify people."

"I had a friend way down the other end of the street. That was sort of no-man's land. By the time you got there you were in a different neighborhood altogether. The whole—all the surroundings seemed to be chopped up into little bits, so that as soon as you went any distance at all you were somewhere else altogether. Maybe it was because I was so young that it seemed such a long distance. But you rounded sort of a bend and your house was out. Although the houses looked somewhat the same, they just weren't."

Other Topics

Water is brought up in a quarter of the interviews and always with an expression of pleasure. The pleasure seems to be associated with the potentialities for play and physical activity:

"Around lunch time I'd go out to the Public Gardens which also became very important to me. I loved going there. I liked to watch the swan boats. I'd follow a whole string of ducks along the bank, go fishing for guppies or pick up snails along the retaining wall . . . "

"I loved the ocean. I used to do a lot of swimming. When I started swimming. Wood Island Park was really the big place."

Commercial activity is mentioned in a few of the interviews, usually either in a purely descriptive way or with conflicting emotions of excitement or exhaustion. It is clear, however, that "going downtown" is an event of some importance in a child's life:

"There was another big area, a big thing, a very big area. There's a movie there—Coolidge Corner. I went there before I went downtown."

"In other parts, which served as market places, they were colorful with all the things sold, and the noise and variety of people—I liked them because I liked to move around in the large crowds and get lost."

"It seemed like there was a million people there, pushcarts and what-have-you . . . It was pretty run-down, very dirty . . . I hated to go there. I hated it because it was crowded and I was usually tired at the end of the day."

"I remember taking the train to Boston a few times with my father to go into his office, a big building. Buildings sort of awed you at that age. You stand at the corner and look up and you wonder why they built them so tall."

Caveat

The limitations of this material must be obvious to the reader: the small size and unbalanced nature of the sample, the use of memories lying at the "surface" of the subject's mind, the fact that they refer to conditions ten or fifteen years ago. One would not conclude, for example, that cities should be built of trees, floor textures, spaces and streetcars, leaving out telephone poles or buildings because they are rarely mentioned in the interviews. Nor, to be somewhat less ridiculous, should we stop building playgrounds because children "do not like them." This material, rather, particularly if more broadly and firmly based on extensive and systematic research, might become one part of the background against which design decisions are reached: in the detailed layout of a playground, for instance, or in the attitude toward "waste" spaces in the city plan. The reliance on memories, used here, should now be checked by direct interviews with children.

It is equally clear that these interviews have dealt with memories of certain years of childhood, and thus speak only of the way in which a rather restricted age group views its city. That cities cannot be built only for children is obvious enough. It would be most interesting to extend this method to the memories of years spent as adults in various urban settings.

Summary

Knowledge of how people react to their physical environment, and how they invest it with emotional qualities, is quite as important as knowing the technical or economic or sociological resultants of a given form. It may be extremely useful, simply to know something of the features which seem to be most significant to people, so that these features may receive special design attention.

The feelings and key elements that run through all the

interviews on childhood memories have strong similarities. The remembered children were sharply aware of lawns and floor surfaces; they delighted in foliage, woods and green. There is a strong and pleasant memory for hills and for water in the landscape. A somewhat ambiguous fascination with the big transportation vehicles is equally clear. There was conscious alertness to spatial qualities, a definite preference for openness and spaciousness, and distaste for crowdedness. Even in childhood, perception is strongly colored by associations of social status: by "niceness," by cleanliness, by upkeep, and by money.

All of these must be connected with more spontaneous aspects to be satisfying. The child wants variety with a chance for some adventure; he has a strong need to act upon the physical environment, to be stimulated by it, and to realize his imaginative fantasies through it.

The majority of people interviewed preferred suburban living. They hate "the city," but when pressed express a fondness for a few central areas that have some of the virtues put forth above. For most people, the sense of the urban area as a total pattern is largely undeveloped, and they rarely conceive of the city as something that might give pleasure in itself. They hardly expect to have an *enjoyable* city environment, as if a mild civic nausea were a normal burden of man's existence.

Architecture and Group Membership

Leon Festinger

The architect and planner have traditionally concerned themselves with supplying physical convenience and satisfying physical needs. They have, for example, been able to specify minimum standards for things like the number of square feet of floor space necessary for a given size family. They have acquired a great deal of knowledge concerning arrangements of rooms for maximum convenience, arrangement of streets for easy accessibility and the like. They must now, or in the very near future, also concern themselves with supplying *social* convenience and satisfying social needs. This growing emphasis on the social consequences of architecture and city planning results from two parallel developments:

1. New housing is more and more being built in planned developments. That is, communities are being built rather than homes. The architect under these circumstances assumes the responsibility for planning much that is important for the social as well as the physical life of people.

2. Basic research on social processes, the behavior of persons in groups, and the effects of group membership has proceded far enough to show the great importance of these things in the lives of people. The problems have begun to be clearly formulated and facts have begun to emerge which can be used by the architect.

These two independent developments must be brought together. In the face of the new problems with which the architect must cope and the new responsibilities he has assumed, he cannot afford to ignore the facts, present and

Reprinted by permission from *Journal of Social Issues*, Vol. 17, Nos. 1 and 2, 1951, copyright by the Society for the Psychological Study of Social Issues.

Architecture and Group Membership 91

potential, which offer help in carrying out his task. Let us examine in detail some of the points at which the research of the social scientist on group processes has bearing on what the architect does.

The Importance of Group Membership

A significant aspect of our society is that persons desire membership in groups. It is extremely rare to find a person who does not seek such membership and is content to live with a minimum of social contact with other people. It is more common to find people with membership in a wide variety of different kinds of groups, both formal and informal.

The process of entering and leaving groups is a continuing one for most people. The small informal social groups to which they belong change their membership; some friends drift away and new ones are made; a person will leave a club and, perhaps, join a different one.

To understand the significance of acquiring group memberships and of belonging to groups, it is first necessary to understand why people seek membership in groups and how groups acquire power over their members.

Sources of Attraction to Groups

Social life, interpersonal relationships, and membership in groups are important aspects of persons' lives because so many goals and satisfactions are attainable most easily in groups, and in some cases, only through association with other people. The multitude of attractions which draw people into groups and into associations with others may be conveniently summarized under three general headings:

Groups frequently mediate the attainment of important individual goals. This source of attraction is recognized by groups and used to attract members. Along these lines, a club will offer different facilities for use only by recognized members. While the overt use of such attractions is generally available only to organized, formal groups, informal groups also frequently attract members because of the goals which they mediate. Thus a person who seeks to be regarded as "upper class," for example, will be strongly attracted to associations whose members are regarded as having such status. By establishing such associations he then may achieve the goal of being himself included in this category.

It is, of course, unlikely that any social group has the mediation of goals as its sole attraction. Yet the mediation of goals should be separated from the other attractions for a number of reasons. First, the attraction of group membership is not so much in sheer belonging, but rather in attaining something by means of this membership. With some types of goals the attraction to the group may cease once the goal is attained. Secondly, with respect to such sources of attraction, a specific group is rarely indispensable. There will generally be other, perhaps more difficult, means of attaining these goals. Thus the group, on both these counts, holds its members on a rather tenuous basis to the extent that the mediation of personal goals is the source of attraction.

The activities in which the group engages are frequently attractive to the member. Many groups form simply on the basis of a common activity which the members like to engage in, and the attraction to this activity may remain one of the major sources of attraction to the group. Thus both formal and informal groups will form to play bridge, tennis, poker, to discuss books or political issues, to have parties and dances, and so on. Here again, it is rare to find a group where this would be the sole source of attraction. Other sources of attraction will also be present, but it seems worth while to distinguish this one from the others on a theoretical basis.

Generally, no single group to which a person may belong has relevance for every aspect of his life. A group such as the family has a relatively wide realm of relevance. At the other extreme, groups with exceptionally narrow realms of relevance depend primarily on the activities in which they engage to attract and hold their members. In general, the realms of relevance of such groups are identical with the activities which are the source of attraction to the group. To the extent that this is true, the group may have relatively little importance in the lives of its members.

Architecture and Group Membership

Almost all groups are, at least in part, attractive because people have needs that can be satisfied only by personal relationships with other people. Some of these needs are friendship, approval and support from other persons, respect and prestige from those with whom one associates, and the like. We are undoubtedly not yet aware of all the personal needs that fall into this general category, nor are we aware of why such needs exist and why they are as powerful as they seem to be. There is no question, however, that they are powerful motivators of human behavior. Since satisfaction of these needs can only occur in the course of personal associations with others, belonging to groups which offer the possibility of satisfying them is virtually a necessity for most humans. Indeed, the state of loneliness, of not knowing other people and having no close personal relationships, is a state of extreme psychological hardship.

The Process of Entering and Leaving Groups

Having examined the attractions to groups, we may now look at the process by which people enter and leave groups and the circumstances under which such movement takes place. It is obvious that a person will attempt to move into groups which offer the possibility of satisfying his particular needs. It is also clear that persons will attempt to move out of groups which no longer satisfy their needs or whose negative aspects outweigh the positive satisfactions of belonging to the group. Disapproval by other members, low status in the group, and other such states of affairs can produce pressure to leave the group.

Moving out of one group and into some other one is, however, not an entirely unrestricted matter. While there are some groups out of which one may move at will and some groups into which one may move with relatively little difficulty, most groups exert some restraints against their members' leaving and many groups exert greater restraints against new members' entering. Formal, organized groups frequently have rules governing the admission of new members. Informal groups also have such rules which, although not formalized, are frequently even more restrictive. An additional difficulty in entering some informal groups is the lack of an easy way of making contact with the group.

We have then the simultaneous existence of forces tending to move people in and out of groups and forces restraining such movement. Groups differ in their attraction for members, and members differ in how satisfying the group membership is for them.

Groups can influence the attitudes, opinions, and behavior patterns of their members. The manner in which these influences are exerted is most often informal and subtle. The expression of some opinion receives approval or disapproval; a certain manner of behaving gains acceptance; a certain way of looking at things becomes the normal and "correct" way. When pressures for uniformity arise among the members, the group may bring about such uniformity. Since we shall elaborate some of these powers of the group in the specific context of housing, we content ourselves here with summarizing some of the conditions under which they are effective.

The extent to which the group can produce lasting change in opinions, attitudes, and behavior in its members depends on the strength of the attraction to the group, that is, on the extent to which the group satisfies the needs of its members. The force on a member to remain in the group is the force which, in a sense, he applies upon himself to accept the opinions, and behaviors of others in the group as correct.

The areas where the group most easily exerts influence correspond to those areas relevant to the functioning of the group and to those needs which the group can and does satisfy in its members. If the exertion of influence becomes an overt, formalized process, the group can extend its influence to a broader area, but as long as the influence process remains subtle, informal, and unrecognized, influence will only be exerted within the group's realm of relevance.

Groups which are difficult for the member to leave, either because the group itself erects restraints against leaving or because outsiders do not easily permit members to leave the group, can exert power over memebrs by threats of punishment. Such power is exercised in overt and recognized manner and is effective in producing overt change in members; it may not necessarily be effective in producing changes in opinions or attitudes which are not open to public examination.

The Social Importance of Architecture

In our discussion of entering and leaving groups we have omitted one major aspect, namely, involuntary membership in groups. Many group memberships are involuntary. One is born into a certain family and ethnic group, and, be it satisfactory or not, one remains a member.

Living in a house also means involuntary membership in a group. The decisions of the architect in designing the house, in laying out the site plan for a group of houses, and in deciding who will live in the houses determine to a large extent the nature of the group memberships which will be imposed upon the residents of the houses. When a person moves into a house, his social life and the group membership that will be attributed to him by outsiders will already have been determined to some extent by these decisions.

Even within the general community in which he lives and with which he is identified by other people, the specific site plan of the group of houses in which his own is located further affects the amount and nature of his social contacts. To illustrate these effects, let us refer to a number of empirical studies.

A study of group formation[3]* was conducted in a housing project built by the Massachusetts Institute of Technology for occupancy by married veteran students. The development consisted of 100 single or semi-attached small houses arranged in courts consisting of from eight to thirteen houses. Each court was a U-shaped affair with the houses facing into a grassy area; the open end of each U faced onto a street which bisected the housing project. The project was rather unusual in that a great degree of homogeneity existed among the residents, who were all married veteran students at M.I.T. There was no freedom of choice of dwelling unit within the project, since all were assigned to houses in

---

*Numbers refer to references listed at the end of this article.

the order in which their names appeared on the waiting list. The study in question began soon after the project was fully occupied and, consequently, was able to trace the development of friendships and informal social groups quite thoroughly.

It is a fair summary to say that two major factors affecting the friendships which developed were 1) sheer distance between houses and 2) the direction in which a house faced. Friendships developed more frequently between next-door neighbors, less frequently between people whose houses were separated by another house, and so on. As the distance between houses increased, the number of friendships fell off so rapidly that it was rare to find a friendship between persons who lived in houses that were separated by more than four or five other houses. People also tended to make friends with those whose houses faced their own. Because of the arrangement of the courts in the housing project, these two factors combined to make it easy for social groups to develop within the court and difficult for social groups to develop on any other basis. Each court in the project became a more or less cohesive group with a social life of its own. The relatively little social contact that did exist between one court and another, was almost entirely limited to contact between adjacent courts. Because of the design of the project the social groups which developed were determined by the order in which the names happened to appear on the waiting list.

There were instances in which the site plan of the project had more profound effects than merely to determine with whom one associated. Indeed, on occasion the arrangement of the houses severely limited the social life of their occupants. It will be recalled that the open end of the U of each court faced a street which bisected the project. In order to have the street appear "lived on," ten of the houses near the street had been turned so that they faced the street rather than the court area like the other houses. This apparently small change in the direction in which a house faced had a considerable effect on the lives of the people who, by accident, happened to occupy these end houses. They had less than half as many friends in the project as did those whose houses faced the court area. The consistency of this finding

Architecture and Group Membership

left no doubt that the turning of these houses toward the street had made involuntary social isolates out of the persons who lived in them.

The same study investigated the development of social groups in an adjoining project that was also maintained for married veteran students of the same school. This project consisted of thirteen apartment buildings with ten apartments in each building. Each building had two floors with five apartments in a row on each floor. The same types of effects of architecture on friendship formation were found here. Once more, sheer physical distance between apartments within the same building was a major factor determining which friendships developed. Needless to say, there were relatively few friendships between residents of different floors of the same building and even fewer between residents of different buildings. Even along the same floor of the same building, the number of friendships decreased rapidly as one went from adjoining apartments to apartments separated by one, two, or three others.

Again, slight architectural features had important effects on the social life of the apartment residents. The positions of the stairways leading to the second floor enabled the residents of some apartments to make more friends, while leaving other apartments in relative social isolation. The position of the mailboxes in each building added to the social life of the residents of the apartment near which they were located. The social activity of some residents and the relative social isolation of others could largely be traced to such minor architectural features.

Results like these have been confirmed in other kinds of communities.[1,4] Living in a certain house in a certain neighborhood determines many of a person's group memberships, not only as others see them, but also as they are actually lived. Since such group memberships have much to do with how people behave toward each other, and since these group memberships are potential sources of satisfaction for many important needs, it is important that groups formed on a relatively involuntary basis be satisfying ones. If a group which one can easily leave is unsatisfying, one may find another group which provides more satisfaction, if such a group is easily accessible. But one can not easily avoid the group memberships that come with residence in a specific location unless one is prepared to suffer relative social isolation. Social isolation or continued group membership of an unsatisfying sort can seriously affect the total context within which the person lives. We shall discuss below two studies of general housing satisfaction and social functioning as examples of the wider effects of satisfactory and unsatisfactory involuntary group memberships occasioned by living in particular housing projects.

Effects of Involuntary Group Membership in a Housing Project

An Example of Satisfying Group Membership

The previously mentioned study by Festinger, Schachter and Back, in addition to investigating the determinants of group formation, concerned itself with the social life of the residents. It was clear that the group memberships provided in the housing community were satisfying ones for the residents. This may have been because of the homogeneity and common interests of the residents; it may have been affected by the temporary nature of residence in the project and perhaps by other factors. Whatever the basis for this satisfactory group life, we have here an example of involuntary group membership which does provide the satisfactions generally desired of group membership. Let us examine the results of this state of affairs.

Social and emotional aspects of living in the project. One of the most prominent aspects of life in Westgate was the ease with which friendships formed. Most people remarked about it in the interviews, emphasizing that it was one of the most satisfactory aspects of living there. On the whole, they felt it was easy to make friends, that the friendships they had made would probably be lasting ones, and that the resulting social life was satisfactory. The following comments from Westgate residents are typical:

> There are wonderful people in this court. We have a lot of social life and do almost everything together.

Architecture and Group Membership

We don't very often go out of Westgate for amusements. Almost all of our friends are here, and there is really so much to do here.

About two thirds of the residents reported that their social life was entirely or primarily within the Westgate community. More than 90 percent of the residents felt that they had enough friends in Westgate and had as much social life as they wanted.

There were several general consequences of this. The most prominent was a general satisfaction with the homes and with living in the community. Only one or two residents expressed any desire to leave Westgate and live elsewhere. More than half of the residents were vigorous in their statements that they would not consider leaving Westgate at all.

This general satisfaction existed in spite of, and seemed to compensate for, many physical inadequacies of the houses. At the time of our study there were many physical nuisances in the houses. Some were incompletely equipped, the grounds were muddy and had not yet been landscaped, they were difficult to heat in the winter, and the like. One example of the reaction to such physical inadequacies will suffice, however, to illustrate the point. At the time of the investigation many of the houses had trouble with the roofs. The houses were prefabricated, and many of the roofs had not been assembled properly. All the roofs have since been fixed, but in the interviews about one third of the residents reported that the roofs leaked. Any rain accompanied by a moderately strong wind would apparently raise the roof slightly, and water would pour down the walls. One family reported that in a particular strong rain the roof had started to blow off; the husband had to go outside and hold the roof down until the wind subsided.

It is remarkable, however, that even such serious physical inconvenience did not create a strong impression on the residents. Typically the reaction was, "Oh yes, there are many things wrong with these houses, but we love it here and wouldn't want to move."

The adequate and satisfying social life was sufficient to override many inconveniences. The result was a rather happy social and psychological existence. The phenomenon may perhaps best be summed up by the expression which many of the people in Westgate used: "We're all in the same boat."

Group action and group standards in the community. There are grounds for believing that successful community action is possible only under conditions like those found in Westgate where there is considerable identification with the community, where people find satisfying social life and want to continue to belong to the community.

One late afternoon an unoccupied building adjoining Westgate caught fire and burned down. Sparks fell on some of the closer Westgate houses, and there was much concern about the fire spreading to the project. That evening a group of tenants made plans for starting a tenant organization which would try to obtain more adequate fire protection. Once started, the tenant organization also dealt with many other aspects of life in the project, including social activities. A tenant council of representatives from each of the courts in Westgate was established, and this council continued to function fairly successfully. This spontaneous beginning of a community organization which received enough active support in the community to enable its continued successful functioning in a number of activities is rather unusual, considering the difficulty of starting such community activities in other situations.

The attitudes of the tenants toward the community organization and its activities, and their active participation in the tenant organization were to a major extent determined by their small-group memberships within a Westgate project. It will be recalled that the physical structure of the project was such that small social groups tended to form along court lines. Each court became a more or less cohesive social group, somewhat separated from the other groups in the project. Each of these small court groups within the project tended to react to the tenant organization as a unit. In one court all but two or three of the residents might be favorably inclined to the organization and active in its affairs. In another court all but two or three of the residents would be quite hostile to the tenant organization and would be entirely inactive with respect to its activities.

Architecture and Group Membership

The reactions of individual residents to the tenant organization were so influenced by the small informal groups to which they belonged as to produce relative uniformity within each of these groups. Within each group the degree of uniformity depended on how attractive the group was for its members. Those groups which were very attractive to their members showed high uniformity of opinion and behavior with respect to the tenant organization. Those groups which were relatively less attractive to their members showed correspondingly less uniformity. In other words, the degree to which a group was able to influence the attitudes, opinions, and behavior of its members depended on how much the members wanted to remain in the group. These small social groups, whose specific composition derived from the architectural design of the project, were a major influence on the thinking and behavior of the residents and were important in determining the structure of the community as a whole.

With this close relationship between social life and opinions about community-wide affairs, one might also expect that persons whose opinions and behavior differed from those prevailing around them would feel the effects of this divergence in their social life within the project. This was found to be the case. Those persons within each court who could be called deviates—that is, whose attitudes toward the tenant organization or whose behavior with respect to it, differed substantially from the norm of their social group—were relatively rejected by the other members. The deviates were infrequently mentioned as close friends.

Let us summarize the results of this study. There was a good deal of social life and a resultant satisfaction with living in the project. The social groups which formed exerted influences on the relationships of members to the total community, and social relationships within the project were affected by the similarity or difference of attitudes among the residents. Some of these effects, namely, the satisfying emotional life and the power of the group to influence its members, are results that we would expect from the general considerations about group membership which were discussed earlier in the paper. Where group membership is satisfying, it tends to lose its character of involuntary membership. But whether or not group memberships in Westgate were satisfying, it would have been difficult or impossible for most residents to escape from the memberships thrust upon them as a result of living in Westgate. The fact that the memberships were satisfying was fortuitous.

A government housing project built for shipyard workers in 1942 was studied by Festinger and Kelley.[2] It illustrates the effect of involuntary group membership that is not satisfying. The project consisted of 100 single and semi-attached permanent housing units. It was built in the middle of a residential area of a town about fifteen miles from a large city. At the time of the study, 1947, about 40 percent of the population of Regent Hill were older residents who had once worked in the shipyards and had remained in the project after the end of the war. The others were persons who had moved in later during the period of acute housing shortages. The great majority of the residents keenly felt that they had been forced to live in the project by circumstances beyond their control. For those who had moved in during the war, it was the shipyards and war exigencies that had forced them to live there. For the others, it was the acute housing shortage and impossibility of finding other places to live that had made them come to Regent Hill.

The group memberships forced upon them by living in the project were resented, and attempts were made to avoid them. Many residents stated that they had not expected to like the type of person who lived in a government housing project. They expected to find the other residents rather low-class people and did not want to be forced to associate with them. Thus, irrespective of the actual potentialities which these group memberships may have had, they were unsatisfying because the residents never encouraged the development of any group life and indeed tried to dissociate themselves from the community in which they were forced to live. Let us examine the consequences of this state of affairs.

The social and emotional aspects of membership in the Regent Hill project. The residents of the project had on the whole an inadequate social life. Indeed, for many residents the state of affairs might be described as self-imposed social

Architecture and Group Membership

isolation. Most residents reported only one or two friends in the community, and about one-fourth did not have any friends there.

There was, in addition, a surprisingly great amount of hostility expressed toward neighbors in the project. In one interview survey more than 60 percent of those interviewed expressed belief that their neighbors were low-class people with whom it was undesirable to associate. In other words, the residents had come to the project expecting to find undesirable neighbors in "a government housing project." They feared the group memberships forced upon them; choosing between such undesirable and unsatisfying group membership and no membership at all, they tended to choose the latter.

One might expect from such a state of affairs that the residents of the project would have tended to make friends and belong to groups in the surrounding community. This, however, was not the case. While they may have desired such group membership in the surrounding community, there were a number of factors which prevented their achieving it. Since they looked down on the project and its residents, they imagined that outsiders would also have the same attitudes toward people from the project. Thus, in any contact which they had with the people in the surrounding community they strove to detach themselves from the project. This, of course, placed severe limitations on the kinds of contacts they could have with the surrounding community and severely limited the number of channels available to them for making such contacts. The result was that the project residents were also rather isolated from the surrounding town. Only about 20 percent of the project residents were members of any town clubs or organizations. There were relatively few friendships between project residents and townspeople. Compared to residents of the surrounding community who had been living there the same length of time, the project residents were clearly in a state of relative social isolation.

We thus have practically the opposite state of affairs from that of Westgate. Instead of a full and satisfying social life there was here a very unsatisfactory state of little social life and great difficulty in achieving group memberships which had the possibility of being satisfying. As one might expect, this state of affairs generalized into attitudes toward their homes and toward the community. Most residents were dissatisfied with living in the Regent Hill project. Many wanted to leave and expressed the intention of doing so as soon as they could find a suitable place elsewhere. The physical inconveniences which did exist in the project became very important and were major sources of irritation to the residents.

Group standards and group action. The investigators in this study, after assessing and attempting to diagnose the state of affairs in the Regent Hill project, tried experimentally to change the pattern of social life within the project and to change the seemingly dominant pattern of hostility among neighbors. The experiment tried to stimulate contacts among the residents by getting them to cooperate on a program of community activities. In contrast to the spontaneity and ease with which a community organization and community activities had arisen in Westgate, such a program in Regent Hill, even with the help of skilled community workers, was by no means an easy affair. Feelings of non-cooperation, hostility, threatened status and prestige, and reluctance to enter into contact with other project residents all made such a program difficult to start and carry on. We do not need to dwell here on the success of the program and the changes of various kinds that were created. The point we wish to make is that, in the absence of real need-satisfaction from the group memberships, the whole context of social and personal life was adversely affected.

In the preceding pages we have done little more than indicate in general the contribution which present and potential knowledge in the area of group membership and group life can make to the field of housing. It is clear that group membership has a very important place in the lives of people. It is also clear that the decisions of the architect, planner, or housing administrator will affect group memberships and, directly or indirectly, the total context of the lives of the people. We have described an instance in which the design of the houses and the physical and spatial relations among houses had an important influence on the formation of social groups. We have also described instances in which these involuntary group memberships were satisfying and others in which they were not satisfying. This difference in satisfaction affected the social life within the community and the satisfaction with living in the houses.

With the aid of a vigorous program of research we can learn much more about these phenomena. Before the social psychologist can materially affect the decisions of the architect and the planner, it is necessary to accumulate this additional knowledge. How do architectural design and site planning variations affect social intercourse among people? What kinds of social interactions exist among neighbors in a community? How does the nature of the group memberships affect family living patterns and other aspects of the functioning of individuals? How do the characteristics of the residents—their interests, backgrounds, anticipations of permanency, and the like—affect the formation and functioning of community groups? And how do community facilities interact with these other factors?

Many more questions like these can be asked, and they can be phrased specifically enough so that answers can be obtained. The more of these questions we answer, the more we will be able to build houses and communities which provide for people the satisfactory social and private lives we would like to see.

References

1. Caplow, Theodore, and Forman, R. "Neighborhood interaction in a homogeneous community," *American Sociological Review*, 1950, *15*, 357-366.

2. Festinger, Leon, and Kelley, Harold H. *Changing Attitudes through Social Contact: An Experimental Study of a Housing Project* (to be published).

3. Festinger, Leon, Schachter, Stanley, anl Back, Kurt. *Social Pressures in Informal Groups.* New York: Harper and Brothers, 1950.

4. Merton, Robert K. "The social psychology of housing," in Dennis, W. (ed.), *Current Trends in Social Psychology.* Pittsburgh: University of Pittsburgh Press, 1948.

A City Is Not a Tree

Christopher Alexander

The tree of my title is not a green tree with leaves. It is the name for a pattern of thought. The semi-lattice is the name for another, more complex, pattern of thought.

In order to relate these abstract patterns to the nature of the city, I must first make a simple distinction. I want to call those cities which have arisen more or less spontaneously over many, many years *natural cities*. And I shall call those cities and parts of cities which have been deliberately created by designers and planners *artificial cities*. Siena, Liverpool, Kyoto, Manhattan are examples of natural cities. Levittown, Chandigarh, and the British New Towns are examples of artificial cities.

It is more and more widely recognized today that there is some essential ingredient missing from artificial cities. When compared with ancient cities that have acquired the patina of life, our modern attempts to create cities artificially are, from a human point of view, entirely unsuccessful.

Architects themselves admit more and more freely that they really like living in old buildings more than new ones. The non-art-loving public at large, instead of being grateful to architects for what they do, regards the onset of modern buildings and modern cities everywhere as an inevitable, rather sad piece of the larger fact that the world is going to the dogs.

It is much too easy to say that these opinions represent only people's unwillingness to forget the past, and their determination to be traditional. For myself, I trust this conservatism. Americans are usually willing to move with the times. Their growing reluctance to accept the modern city evidently expresses a longing for some real thing, something which for the moment escapes our grasp.

The prospect that we may be turning the world into a place peopled only by little glass and concrete boxes has alarmed many architects too. To combat the glass box future, many valiant protests and designs have been put forward, all hoping to recreate in modern form the various characteristics of the natural city which seem to give it life. But so far these designs have only remade the old. They have not been able to create the new.

"Outrage," the *Architectural Review's* campaign against the way in which new construction and telegraph poles are wrecking the English town, based its remedies, essentially, on the idea that the spatial sequence of buildings and open spaces must be controlled if scale is to be preserved—an idea that really derives from Camillo Sitte's book about ancient squares and piazzas.

Another kind of remedy, in protest against the monotony of Levittown, tries to recapture the richness of shape found in the houses of a natural old town. Llewelyn Davies' village at Rushbrooke in England is an example—each cottage is slightly different from its neighbor, the roofs jut in and out at picturesque angles.

A third suggested remedy is to get high density back into the city. The idea seems to be that if the whole metropolis could only be like Grand Central Station, with lots and lots of layers and tunnels all over the place, and enough people milling around in them, maybe it would be human again.

Another very brilliant critic of the deadness which is everywhere is Jane Jacobs. Her criticisms are excellent. But when you read her concrete proposals for what we should do instead, you get the idea that she wants the great modern city to be a sort of mixture between Greenwich village and some Italian hill town, full of short blocks and people sitting in the street.

The problem these designers have tried to face is real. It is vital that we discover the property of old towns which gave them life and get it back into our own artificial cities. But we cannot do this merely by remaking English villages,

Italian piazzas, and Grand Central Stations. Too many designers today seem to be yearning for the physical and plastic characteristics of the past, instead of searching for the abstract ordering principle which the towns of the past happened to have, and which our modern conceptions of the city have not yet found.

What is the inner nature, the ordering principle, which distinguishes the artificial city from the natural city?

You will have guessed from my title what I believe this ordering principle to be. I believe that a natural city has the organization of a semi-lattice; but that when we organize a city artificially, we organize it as a tree.

Both the tree and the semi-lattice are ways of thinking about how a large collection of many small systems goes to make up a large and complex system. More generally, they are both names for structures of sets.

In order to define such structures, let me first define the concept of a set. A set is a collection of elements which for some reason we think of as belonging together. Since, as designers, we are concerned with the physical living city and its physical backbone, we most naturally restrict ourselves to considering sets which are collections of material elements such as people, blades of grass, cars, bricks, molecules, houses, gardens, water pipes, the water molecules that run in them, etc.

When the elements of a set belong together because they cooperate or work together somehow, we call the set of elements a system.

For example, in Berkeley at the corner of Hearst and Euclid, there is a drug store, and outside the drug store a traffic light. In the entrance to the drug store there is a newsrack where the day's papers are displayed. When the light is red, people who are waiting to cross the street stand idly by the light; and since they have nothing to do, they look at the papers displayed on the newsrack which they can see from where they stand. Some of them just read the headlines, others actually buy a paper while they wait.

This effect makes the newsrack and the traffic light interdependent; the newsrack, the newspapers on it, the money going from people's pockets to the dime slot, the people who stop at the light and read papers, the traffic light, the elec-

A City Is Not a Tree

tric impulses which make the lights change, and the sidewalk which the people stand on form a system—they all work together.

From the designer's point of view, the physically unchanging part of this system is of special interest. The newsrack, the traffic light, and the sidewalk between them, related as they are, form the fixed part of the system. It is the unchanging receptacle in which the changing parts of the system—people, newspapers, money, and electrical impulses—can work together. I define this fixed part as a unit of the city. It derives its coherence as a unit both from the forces which hold its own elements together, and from the dynamic coherence of the larger living system which includes it as a fixed invariant part.

Of the many, many fixed concrete subsets of the city which are the receptacles for its systems, and can therefore be thought of as significant physical units, we usually single out a few for special consideration. In fact, I claim that whatever picture of the city someone has is defined precisely by the subsets he sees as units.

Now, a collection of subsets which goes to make up such a picture is not merely an amorphous collection. Automatically, merely because relationships are established among the subsets once the subsets are chosen, the collection has a definite structure.

To understand this structure, let us think abstractly for a moment, using numbers as symbols. Instead of talking about the real sets of millions of real particles which occur in the city, let us consider a simpler structure made of just half a dozen elements. Label these elements 1, 2, 3, 4, 5, 6. Not including the full set [1, 2, 3, 4, 5, 6], the empty set [-], and the one element sets [1], [2], [3], [4], [5], [6], there are 56 different subsets we can pick from six elements.

Suppose we now pick out certain of these 56 sets (just as we pick out certain sets and call them units when we form our picture of the city). Let us say, for example, that we pick the following subsets: [123], [34], [45], [234], [345], [12345], [3456].

What are the possible relationships among these sets? Some sets will be entirely part of larger sets, as [34] is part of [345] and [3456]. Some of the sets will overlap, like [123] and

A

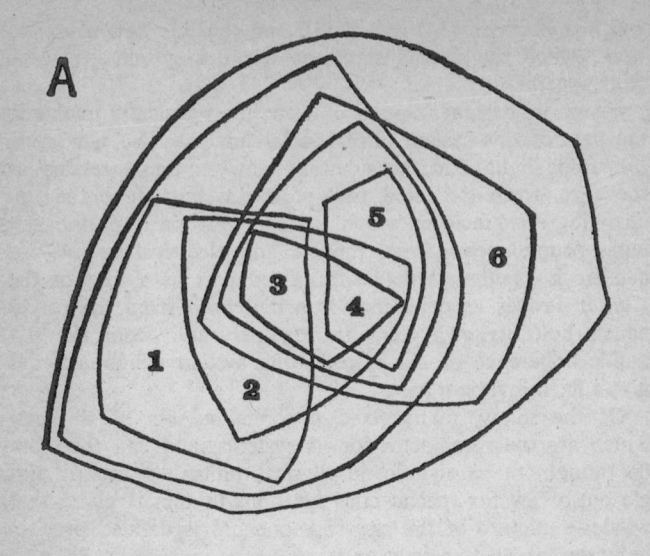

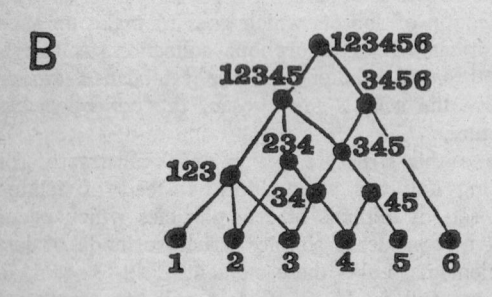

B

[234]. Some of the sets will be disjoint—that is, contain no elements in common, like [123] and [45].

We can see these relationships displayed in two ways. In diagram A each set chosen to be a unit has a line drawn round it. In diagram B the chosen sets are arranged in order of ascending magnitude, so that whenever one set contains another (as [345] contains [34]), there is a vertical path leading from one to the other. For the sake of clarity and visual economy, it is usual to draw lines only between sets which have no further sets and lines between them; thus the line between [34] and [345], and the line between [345] and [3456], make it unnecessary to draw a line between [34] and [3456].

As we see from these two representations, the choice of subsets alone endows the collection of subsets as a whole with an overall structure. This is the structure which we are concerned with here. When the structure meets certain conditions it is called a semi-lattice. When it meets other more restrictive conditions, it is called a tree.

The semi-lattice axiom goes like this:

A collection of sets forms a semi-lattice if and only if, when two overlapping sets belong to the collection, then the set of elements common to both also belongs to the collection.

The structure illustrated in diagrams A and B is a semi-lattice. It satisfies the axiom since, for instance, [234] and [345] both belong to the collection and their common part, [34], also belongs to it. (As far as the city is concerned, this axiom states merely that wherever two units overlap, the area of overlap is itself a recognizable entity and hence a unit also. In the case of the drug store example, one unit consists of the newsrack, sidewalk, and traffic light. Another unit consists of the drug store itself, with its entry and the newsrack. The two units overlap in the newsrack. Clearly this area of overlap is itself a recognizable unit, and so satisfies the axiom above which defines the characteristics of a semi-lattice.)

The tree axiom states:

A collection of sets forms a tree if and only if, for any two sets that belong to the collection, either one is wholly contained in the other, or else they are wholly disjoint.

The structure illustrated in diagrams C and D is a tree. Since this axiom excludes the possibility of overlapping sets, there is no way in which the semi-lattice axiom can be violated, so that every tree is a trivially simple semi-lattice.

However, in this paper we are not so much concerned with the fact that a tree happens to be a semi-lattice, but with the difference between trees and those more general semi-lattices which are *not* trees because they *do* contain overlapping units. We are concerned with the difference be-

C

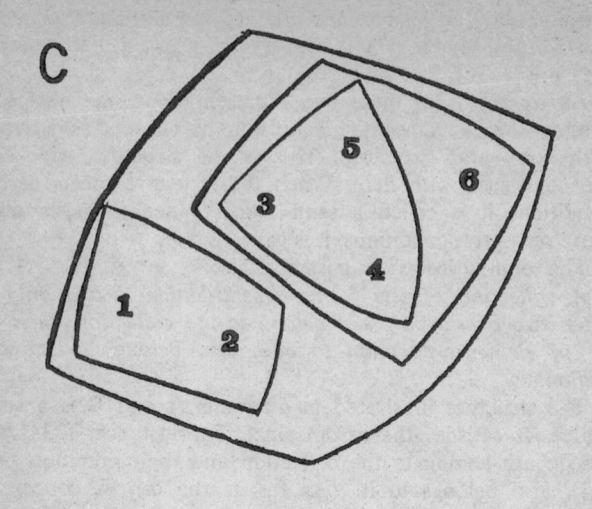

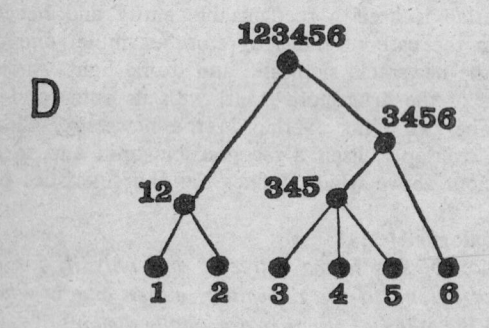

D

tween structures in which no overlap occurs, and those structures in which overlap does occur.

It is not merely the overlap which makes the distinction between the two important. Still more important is the fact that the semi-lattice is potentially a much more complex and subtle structure than a tree. We may see just how much more complex a semi-lattice can be than a tree in the following fact: a tree based on 20 elements can contain at most 19 further subsets of the 20, while a semi-lattice based on the same 20 elements can contain more than 1,000,000 different subsets.

This enormously greater variety is an index of the great structural complexity a semi-lattice can have when compared with the structural simplicity of a tree. It is this lack of structural complexity, characteristic of trees, which is crippling our conceptions of the city.

To demonstrate, let us discuss some modern conceptions of the city, each of which I shall show to be essentially a tree. It will perhaps be useful, while we talk about these plans, to have a little ditty in our minds:

> Big fleas have little fleas
> Upon their back to bite 'em,
> Little fleas have lesser fleas,
> And so ad infinitum.

This rhyme expresses perfectly and succinctly the structural principle of the tree.

1. Columbia, Maryland, Community Research and Development Inc.: Neighborhoods, in clusters of five, form "villages." Transportation joins the villages into a new town. The organization is a tree.

2. Greenbelt, Maryland, Clarence Stein: This "garden city" has been broken down into superblocks. Each superblock contains schools, parks, and a number of subsidiary groups of houses built around parking lots. The organization is a tree.

3. Greater London plan (1943), Abercrombie and Forshaw: It is made of a large number of communities, each sharply separated from all adjacent communities. Abercrombie writes, "The proposal is to emphasize the identity of the existing communities, to increase their degree of segregation, and where necessary to reorganize them as separate and definite entities." And again, "The communities themselves consist of a series of sub-units, generally with their own shops and schools, corresponding to neighborhood units." The city is conceived as a tree with two principal levels. The communities are the larger units of the structure; the smaller sub-units are neighborhoods. There are no overlapping units. The structure is a tree.

4. Tokyo plan, Kenzo Tange: This is a beautiful

example. The plan consists of a series of loops stretched across the Tokyo Bay. There are four major loops, each of which contains three medium loops. In the second major loop, one medium loop is the railway station and another is the port. Otherwise, each medium loop contains three minor loops which are residential neighborhoods, except in the third major loop where one contains government offices and another industrial offices.

5. Mesa City, Paolo Soleri: The organic shapes of Mesa City lead us, at first, to believe that it is a richer structure than our more obviously rigid examples. But we find precisely the same principle of organization. Take, particularly, the university center. Here we find the center of the city divided into a university and a residential quarter, which is itself divided into a number of villages (actually apartment towers) for 4,000 inhabitants, each again subdivided further and surrounded by groups of still smaller dwelling units.

6. Chandigarh (1951) by Le Corbusier: The whole city is served by a commercial center in the middle, linked to the administrative center at the head. Two subsidiary elongated, commercial cores are strung out along the major arterial roads, running north-south. Subsidiary to these are further administrative, community and commercial centers, one for each of the city's 20 sectors.

7. Brazilia, Lúcio Costa: The entire form pivots about the central axis, and each of the two halves is served by a single main artery. This main artery is in turn fed by subsidiary arteries parallel to it. Finally, these are fed by the roads which surround the superblocks themselves. The structure is a tree.

8. Communitas, Percival and Paul Goodman: Communitas is explicitly organized as a tree: it is first divided into four concentric major zones, the innermost being a commercial center, the next a university, the third residential and medical, and fourth open country. Each of these is further subdivided: the commercial center is represented as a great cylindrical skyscraper, containing five layers: airport, administration, light manufacture, shopping and amusement; and, at the bottom, railroads, buses and mechanical services. The university is divided into eight sectors comprising natural history, zoos and aquariums, planetarium, science, laboratories,

plastic arts, music and drama. The third concentric ring is divided into neighborhoods of 4,000 people each, not consisting of individual houses, but of apartment blocks, each of these containing further individual dwelling units. Finally, the open country is divided into three segments: forest preserves, agriculture, and vacation-lands. The over-all organization is a tree.

9. The most beautiful example of all I have kept until last, because it symbolizes the problem perfectly. It appears in Hilberseimer's book called *The Nature of Cities*. He describes the fact that certain Roman towns had their origin as military camps, and then shows a picture of a modern military encampment as a kind of archetypal form for the city. It is not possible to have a structure which is a clearer tree.

The symbol is apt, for, of course, the organization of the army was created precisely in order to create discipline and rigidity. When a city is endowed with a tree structure, this is what happens to the city and its people. Hilberseimer's own scheme for the commercial area of a city is based on the army camp archetype.

Each of these structures, then, is a tree. Each unit in each tree that I have described, moreover, is the fixed, unchanging residue of some system in the living city (just as a house is the residue of the interactions between the members of a family, their emotions, and their belongings; and a freeway is the residue of movement and commercial exchange).

However, in every city there are thousands, even millions, of times as many more systems at work whose physical residue does not appear as a unit in these tree structures. In the worst cases, the units which do appear fail to correspond to any living reality; and the real systems, whose existence actually makes the city live, have been provided with no physical receptacle.

Neither the Columbia plan nor the Stein plan, for example, corresponds to social realities. The physical layout of the plans, and the way they function, suggests a hierarchy of stronger and stronger closed social groups, ranging from the whole city down to the family, each formed by associational ties of different strength.

In a traditional society, if we ask a man to name his best friends and then ask each of these in turn to name their best friends, they will all name each other so that they form a closed group. A village is made of a number of separate closed groups of this kind.

But today's social structure is utterly different. If we ask a man to name his friends and then ask them in turn to name their friends, they will all name different people, very likely unknown to the first person; these people would again name others, and so on outwards. There are virtually no closed groups of people in modern society. The reality of today's social structure is thick with overlap—the systems of friends and acquaintances form a semi-lattice, not a tree (Fig. 1).

In the natural city, even the house on a long street (not in some little cluster) is a more accurate acknowledgment of the fact that your friends live not next door, but far away, and can only be reached by bus or automobile. In this respect Manhattan has more overlap in it than Greenbelt. And though one can argue that in Greenbelt too, friends are only minutes away by car, one must then ask: Since certain groups *have* been emphasized by the physical units of the physical structure, why are just these the most irrelevant ones?

I shall further demonstrate why the living city cannot be properly contained in a receptacle which is a tree—that indeed, its very life stems from the fact that it is not a tree.

Finally, I shall try to show that it is the process of thought itself which works in a treelike way, so that whenever a city is "thought out" instead of "grown," it is bound to get a treelike structure.

So far, we have seen that the units of which an artificial city is made up are organized to form a tree. So that we get a really clear understanding of what this means, and shall better see its implications, let us define a tree once again:

Whenever we have a tree structure, it means that within this structure no piece of any unit is ever connected to other units, except through the medium of that unit as a whole.

The enormity of this restriction is difficult to grasp. It is a little as though the members of a family were not free to make friends outside the family, except when the family as a whole made a friendship.

A City Is Not a Tree

FIG. 1

Traditional Society

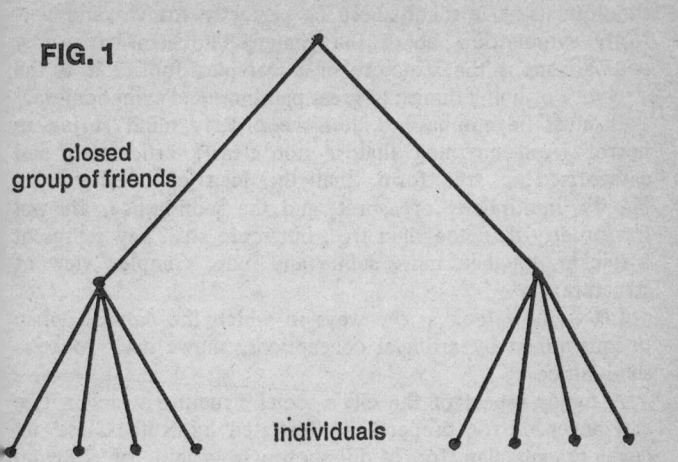

closed group of friends

individuals

Open Society

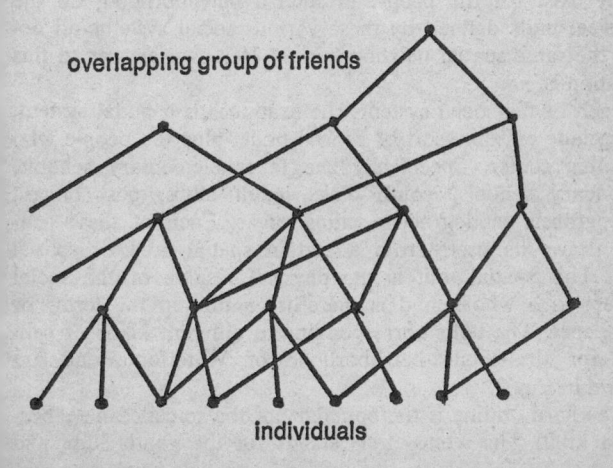

overlapping group of friends

individuals

In simplicity of structure the tree is comparable to the compulsive desire for neatness and order that insists the candlesticks on a mantlepiece be perfectly straight and perfectly symmetrical about the center. The semi-lattice, by comparison, is the structure of a complex fabric; it is the structure of living things; of great paintings and symphonies.

It must be emphasized, lest the orderly mind shrink in horror from anything that is not clearly articulated and categorized in tree form, that the idea of overlap, ambiguity, multiplicity of aspect, and the semi-lattice, are not less orderly than the rigid tree, but more so. They represent a thicker, tougher, more subtle and more complex view of structure.

Let us now look at the ways in which the natural, when unconstrained by artificial conceptions, shows itself to be a semi-lattice.

A major aspect of the city's social structure which a tree can never mirror properly is illustrated by Ruth Glass' redevelopment plan for Middlesborough, a city of 200,000 which she recommends be broken down into 29 separate neighborhoods. After picking her 29 neighborhoods by determining where the sharpest discontinuities of building type, income, and job type occur, she asks herself the question: "If we examine some of the social systems which actually exist for the people in such a neighborhood, do the physical units defined by these various social systems all define the same spatial neighborhood?" Her own answer to this question is, *no*.

Each of the social systems she examines is a nodal system. It is made of some sort of central node, plus the people who use this center. Specifically she takes elementary schools, secondary schools, youth clubs, adult clubs, post offices, greengrocers, and grocers selling sugar. Each of these centers draws its users from a certain spatial area or spatial unit. This spatial unit is the physical residue of the social system as a whole, and is therefore a unit in the terms of this paper. The units corresponding to different kinds of centers for the single neighborhood of Waterloo Road are shown in Fig. 2.

The hard outline is the boundary of the so-called neighborhood itself. The white circle stands for the youth club, and

FIG. 2

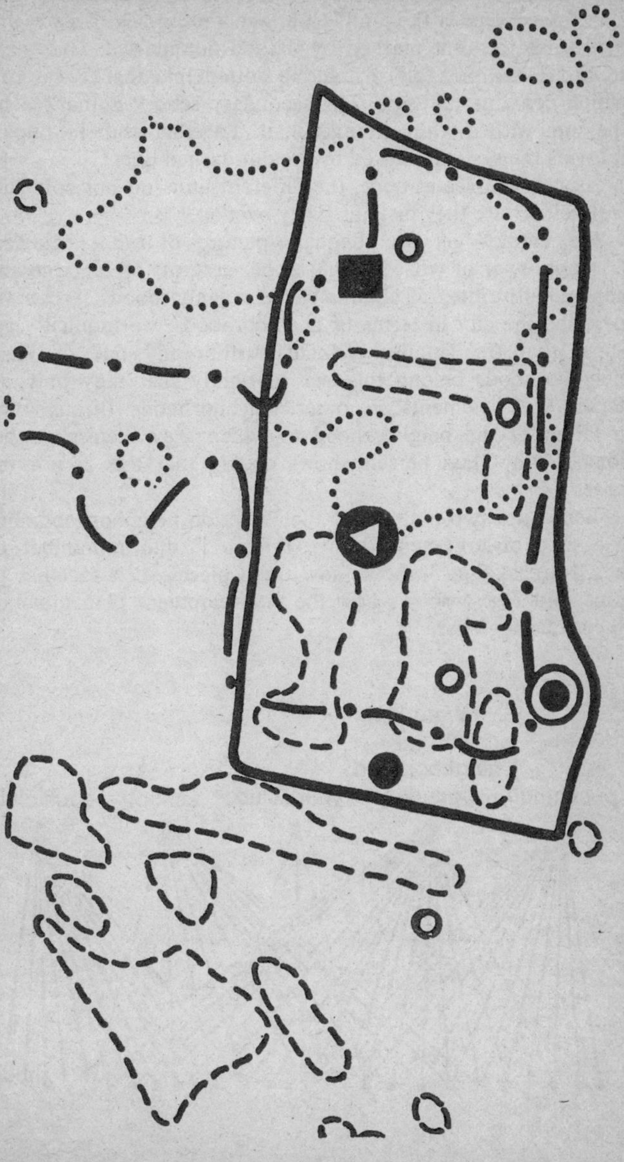

120   Surviving the City

the small solid rings stand for areas where its members live. The ringed spot is the adult club, and the homes of its members form the unit marked by dashed boundaries. The white square is the post office and the dotted line marks the unit which contains its users. The secondary school is marked by the spot with a white triangle in it. Together with its pupils, it forms the system marked by the dot-dashed line.

As you can see at once, the different units do not coincide. Yet neither are they disjoint. They overlap.

We cannot get an adequate picture of what Middlesborough is, or of what it ought to be, in terms of 29 large and conveniently integral chunks called neighborhoods. When we describe the city in terms of neighborhoods, we implicitly assume that the smaller elements within any one of these neighborhoods belong together so tightly that they only interact with elements in other neighborhoods through the medium of the neighborhood to which they themselves belong. Ruth Glass herself shows clearly that this is not the case.

Below are two pictures of the Waterloo neighborhood. For the sake of argument I have broken it into a number of small areas. Fig. 3 shows how these pieces stick together in fact, and Fig. 4 shows how the redevelopment plan pretends they stick together.

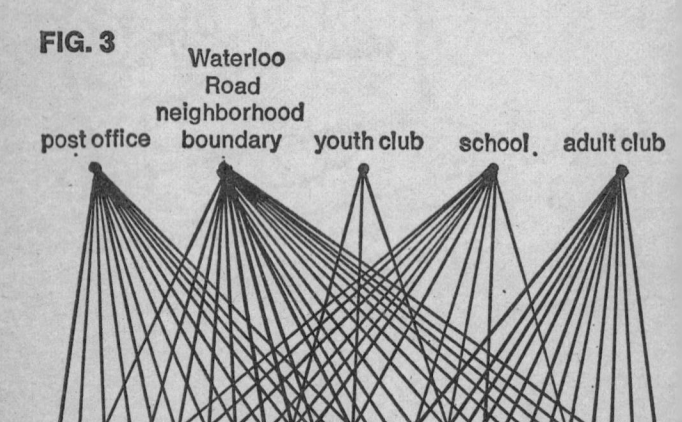

FIG. 3

Waterloo Road neighborhood

post office   boundary   youth club   school   adult club

FIG. 4

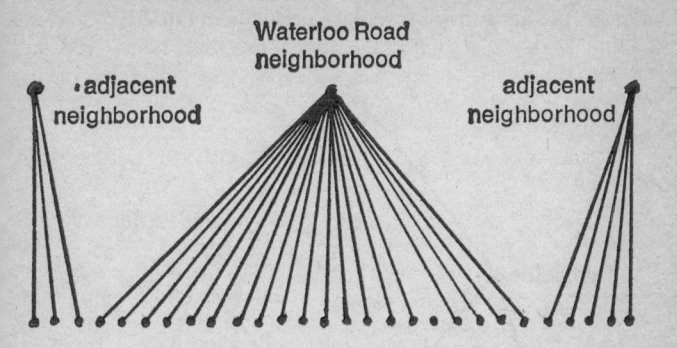

Figure: Waterloo Road neighborhood with adjacent neighborhoods on either side.

There is nothing in the nature of the various centers which says that their catchment areas should be the same. Their natures are different. Therefore the units they define are different. The natural city of Middlesborough was faithful to the semi-lattice structure they have. Only in the artificial tree conception of the city are their natural, proper, and necessary overlaps destroyed.

Take the separation of pedestrians from moving vehicles, a tree concept proposed by Le Corbusier, Louis Kahn, and many others. At a very crude level of thought this is obviously a good idea. It is dangerous to have 60-mile-an-hour cars in contact with little children toddling. But it is not *always* a good idea. There are times when the ecology of a situation actually demands the opposite. Imagine yourself coming out of a Fifth Avenue store; you have been shopping all afternoon; your arms are full of parcels; you need a drink; your wife is limping. Thank God for taxis.

Yet the urban taxi can function only because pedestrians and vehicles are not strictly separated. The prowling taxi needs a fast stream of traffic so that it can cover a large area to be sure of finding a passenger. The pedestrian needs to be able to hail the taxi from any point in the pedestrian world, and to be able to get out to any part of the pedestrian world to which he wants to go. The system which contains the taxicabs needs to overlap both the fast vehicular traffic system and the system of pedestrian circulation. In Manhattan pedestrians and vehicles do share certain parts of the city, and the necessary overlap is guaranteed (Fig. 5).

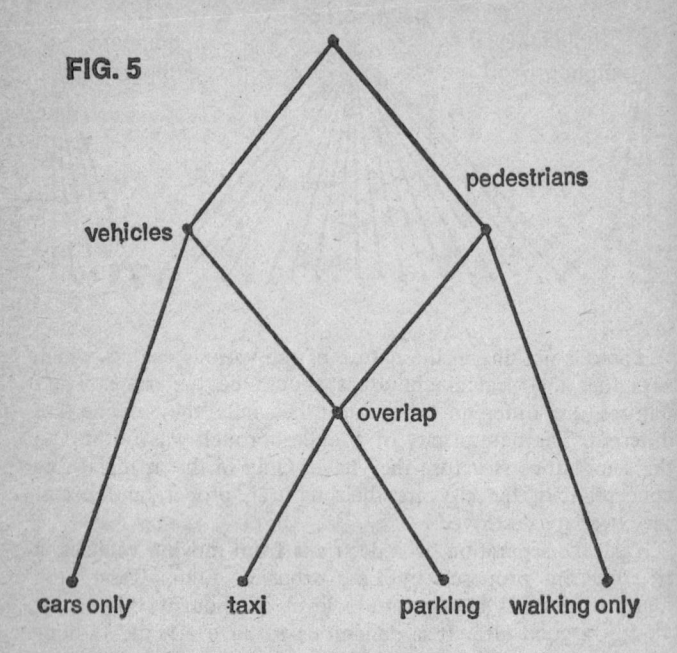

FIG. 5

```
              •
             / \
            /   \
           /     \
          /       • pedestrians
  vehicles•       /\
         /\     /  \
        /  \   /    \
       /    \ /      \
      /      •overlap \
     /      / \        \
    /      /   \        \
   •      •     •        •
cars only taxi parking walking only
```

Another favorite concept of the CIAM theorists and others is the separation of recreation from everything else. This has crystalized in our real cities in the form of playgrounds. The playground, asphalted and fenced in, is nothing but a pictorial acknowledgment of the fact that "play" exists as an isolated concept in our minds. It has nothing to do with the life of play itself. Few self-respecting children will even play in a playground.

Play itself, the play that children practice, goes on somewhere different everyday. One day it may be indoors, another day in a friendly gas station, another day down by the river, another day in a derelict building, another day on a construction site which has been abandoned for the weekend. Each of these play activities, and the objects it requires, forms a system. It is not true that these systems exist in isolation, cut off from the other systems in the city. The different systems overlap one another, and they overlap many other systems besides. The units, the physical places recognized as play places, must do the same.

In a natural city this is what happens. Play takes place in a thousand places—it fills the interstices of adult life. As they play, children become full of their surroundings. How can a child become filled with his surroundings in a fenced enclosure? He cannot.

The Isolated Campus

A similar kind of mistake occurs in trees like that of Goodman's Communitas, or Soleri's Mesa City, which separate the university from the rest of the city. Again, this has actually been realized in common American form of the isolated campus.

What is the reason for drawing a line in the city so that everything within the boundary is university, and everything outside is non-university? It is conceptually clear. But does it correspond to the realities of university life. Certainly it is not the structure which occurs in non-artificial university cities.

Take Cambridge University, for instance. At certain points Trinity street is physically almost indistinguishable from Trinity college. One pedestrian crossover in the street is literally part of the college. The buildings on the street, though they contain stores and coffee shops and banks at ground level, contain undergraduates' rooms in the upper stories. In many cases the actual fabric of the street buildings melts into the fabric of the old college buildings so that one cannot be altered without the other.

There will always be many systems of activity where university life and city life overlap: pub-crawling, coffee-drinking, the movies, walking from place to place. In some cases whole departments may be actively involved in the life of the city's inhabitants (the hospital-cum-medical school is an example). In Cambridge, a natural city where university and city have grown together gradually, the physical

FIG. 6

Cambridge

University *City*

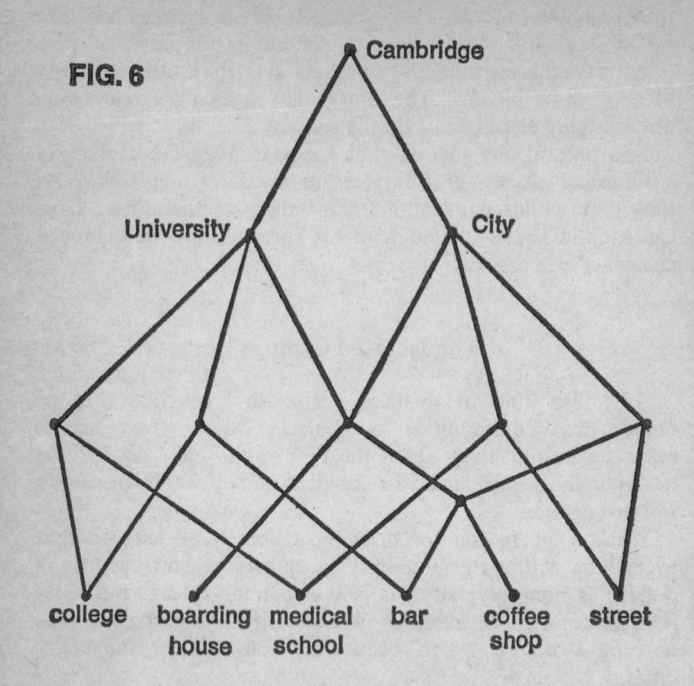

college boarding house medical school bar coffee shop street

units overlap because they are the physical residues of city systems and university systems which overlap (Fig. 6).

Let us look next at the hierarchy of urban cores, realized in Brazilia, Chandigarh, the MARS plan for London, and, most recently, in the Manhattan Lincoln Center, where various performing arts serving the population of greater New York have been gathered together to form just one core.

Does a concert hall ask to be next to an Opera House? Can the two feed on one another? Will anybody ever visit them both, gluttonously, in a single evening, or even buy tickets from one after going to a concert in the other? In Vienna, London, Paris, each of the performing arts has found its own place, because all are not mixed randomly. Each has created its own familiar section of the city. In Manhattan itself, Carnegie Hall and the Metropolitan Opera House were not built side by side. Each found its own place, and now creates its own atmosphere. The influence of each overlaps the parts of the city which have been made unique to it.

The only reason that these functions have all been brought together in the Lincoln Center is that the concept of performing art links them to one another.

But this tree, and the idea of a single hierarchy of urban cores which is its parent, do not illuminate the relations between art and city life. They are merely born of the mania every simple-minded person has for putting things with the same name into the same basket.

The total separation of work from housing, started by Tony Garnier in his industrial city, then incorporated in the 1929 Athens Charter, is now found in every artificial city and accepted everywhere where zoning is enforced. Is this a sound principle? It is easy to see how bad conditions at the beginning of the century prompted planners to try to get the dirty factories out of residential areas. But the separation misses a variety of systems which require, for their sustenance, little parts of both.

Jane Jacobs describes the growth of backyard industries in Brooklyn. A man who wants to start a small business needs space, which he is very likely to have in his own backyard. He

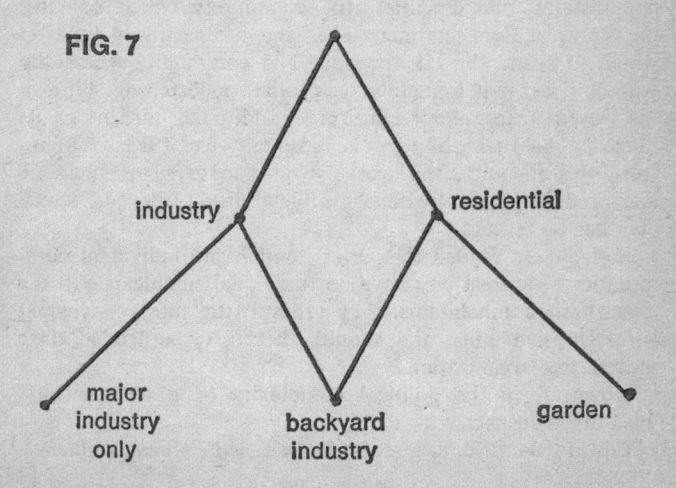

FIG. 7

also needs to establish connections with larger going enterprises and with their customers. This means that the system of backyard industry needs to belong both to the residential zone, and to the industrial zone—these zones need to overlap. In Brooklyn they do (Fig. 7). In a city which is a tree, they can't.

Finally, let us examine the subdivision of the city into isolated communities. As we have seen in the Abercrombie plan for London, this is itself a tree structure. The individual community in a greater city has no reality as a functioning unit. In London, as in any great city, almost no one manages to find work which suits him near his home. People in one community work in a factory which is very likely to be in another community.

There are, therefore, many hundreds of thousands of worker-workplace systems, each consisting of a man plus the factory he works in, which cut across the boundaries defined by Abercrombie's tree. The existence of these units, and their overlapping nature, indicates that the living systems of London form a semi-lattice. Only in the planner's mind has it become a tree.

The fact that we have so far failed to give this any physical expression has a vital consequence. As things are, whenever the worker and his workplace belong to separately administered municipalities, the community which contains the workplace collects huge taxes and has relatively little on which to spend the tax revenue. The community where the worker lives, if it is mainly residential, collects only little in the way of taxes, and yet has great additional burdens on its purse in the shape of schools, hospitals, etc. Clearly, to resolve this inequity, the worker-workplace systems must be anchored in physically recognizable units of the city which can then be taxed.

It might be argued that, even though the individual communities of a great city have no functional significance in the lives of their inhabitants, they are still the most convenient administrative units, and should, therefore, be left in their present tree organization.

However, in the political complexity of a modern city, even this is suspect.

Edward Banfield, in a recent book called *Political Influence*, gives a detailed account of the patterns of influence and control that have actually led to decisions in Chicago. He shows that although the lines of administrative and executive control have a formal structure which is a tree, these formal chains of influence and authority are entirely overshadowed by the ad hoc lines of control which arise naturally as each new city problem presents itself. These ad hoc lines depend on who is interested in the matter, who has what at stake, who has what favors to trade with whom.

This second structure, which is informal, working within the framework of the first, is what really controls public action. It varies from week to week, even from hour to hour, as one problem replaces another. Nobody's sphere of influence is entirely under the control of any one superior; each person is under different influences as the problems change. Although the organization chart in the mayor's office is a tree, the actual control and exercise of authority is semi-lattice-like.

Trapped in a Tree

Now, why is it that so many designers have conceived cities as trees when the natural structure is in every case a semi-lattice? Have they done so deliberately, in the belief that a tree structure will serve the people of the city better? Or have they done it because they cannot help it, because they are trapped by a mental habit, perhaps even trapped by the way the mind works; because they cannot encompass the complexity of a semi-lattice in any convenient mental form; because the mind has an overwhelming predisposition to see trees wherever it looks and cannot escape the tree conception?

I shall try to convince you that it is for this second reason that trees are being proposed and built as cities—that it is because designers, limited as they must be by the capacity of the mind to form intuitively accessible structures, cannot achieve the complexity of the semi-lattice in a single mental act.

Let me begin with an example.

Suppose I ask you to remember the following four objects: an orange, a watermelon, a football, and a tennis ball. How will you keep them in your mind, in your mind's eyes? However you do it, you will do it by grouping them. Some of you will take the two fruits together, the orange and the watermelon, and the two sports balls together, the football and the tennis ball. Those of you who tend to think in terms of physical shape may group them differently, taking the two small spheres together—the orange and the tennis ball and the two larger and more egg-shaped objects—the watermelon and the football. Some of you will be aware of both.

Let us make a diagram of these groupings (Fig. 8).

Either grouping taken by itself is a tree structure. The two together are a semi-lattice. Now let us try and visualize these groupings in the mind's eye. I think you will find that you cannot visualize all four sets simultaneously—because

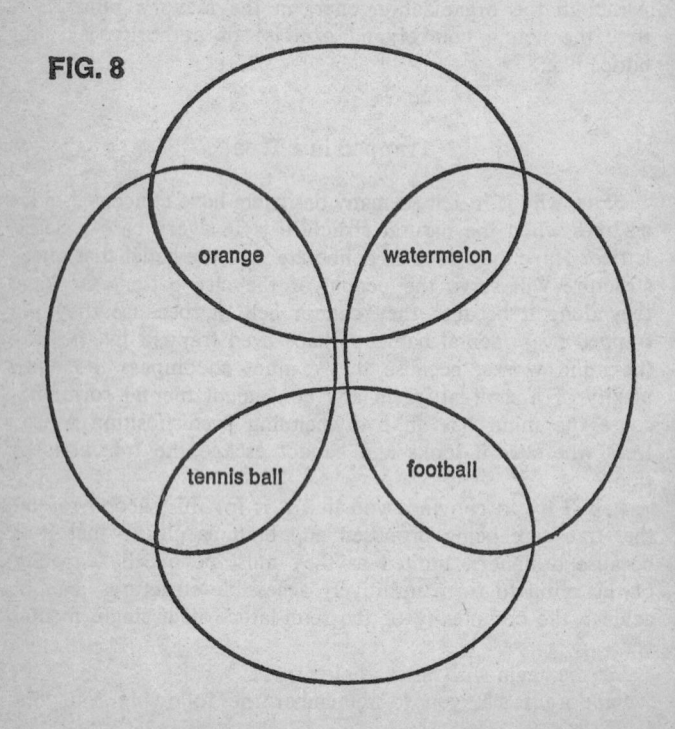

FIG. 8

orange watermelon tennis ball football

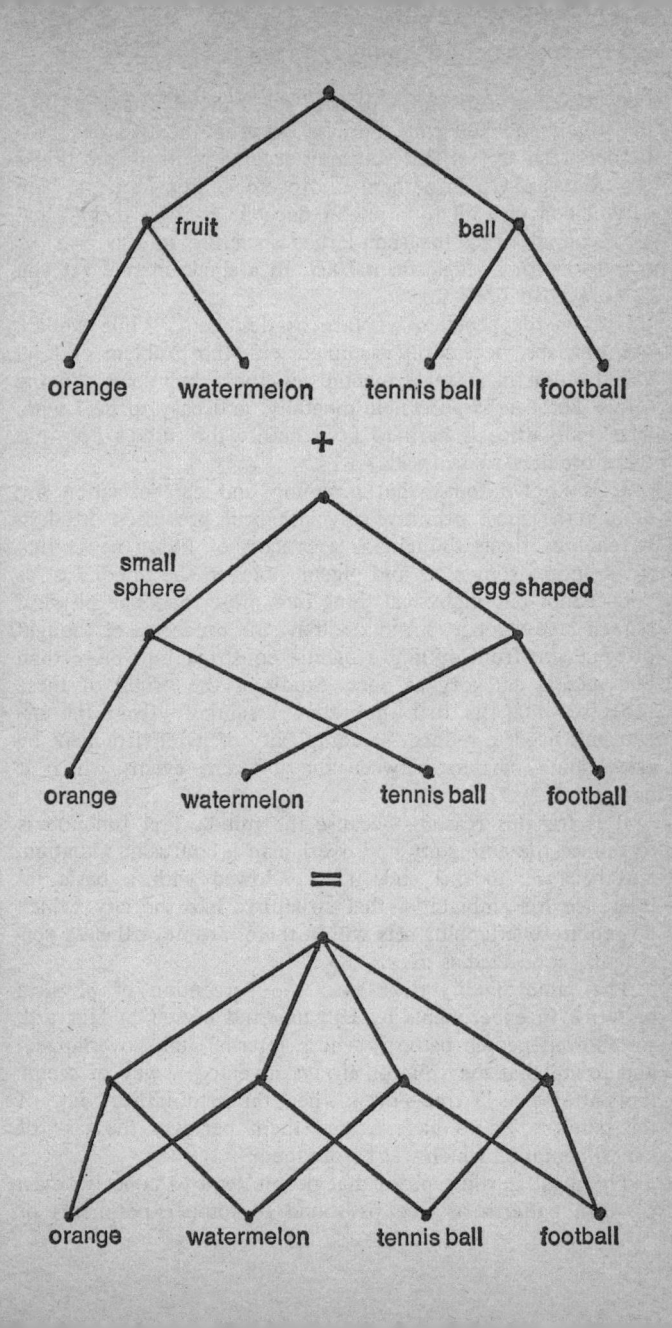

fruit ball

small sphere egg shaped

+

=

they overlap. You can visualize one pair of sets and then the other, and you can alternate between the two pairs extremely fast, so fast that you may deceive yourself into thinking you can visualize them all together. But in truth, you cannot conceive all four sets at once in a single mental act. You cannot bring the semi-lattice structure into a visualizable form for a single mental act. In a single mental act you can only visualize a tree.

This is the problem we face as designers. While we are not, perhaps, necessarily occupied with the problem of total visualization in a single mental act, the principle is still the same. The tree is accessible mentally, and easy to deal with. The semi-lattice is hard to keep before the mind's eye, and therefore hard to deal with.

It is known today that grouping and categorization are among the most primitive psychological processes. Modern psychology treats thought as a process of fitting new situations into existing slots and pigeon holes in the mind. Just as you cannot put a physical thing into more than one physical pigeon hole at once, so, by analogy, the processes of thought prevent you from putting a mental construct into more than one mental category at once. Study of the origin of these processes suggests that they stem essentially from the organism's need to reduce the complexity of its environment by establishing barriers between the different events which it encounters.

It is for this reason—because the mind's first function is to reduce the ambiguity and overlap in a confusing situation, and because, to this end, it is endowed with a basic intolerance for ambiguity—that structures like the city, which do require overlapping sets within them, are nevertheless persistently conceived as trees.

The same rigidity dogs even the perception of physical patterns. In experiments by Huggins and myself at Harvard, we showed people patterns whose internal units overlapped, and found that they almost always invented a way of seeing the patterns as a tree—even when the semi-lattice view of the patterns would have helped them perform the task of experimentation which was before them.

The most startling proof that people tend to conceive even physical patterns as trees is found in some experiments of

FIG. 9

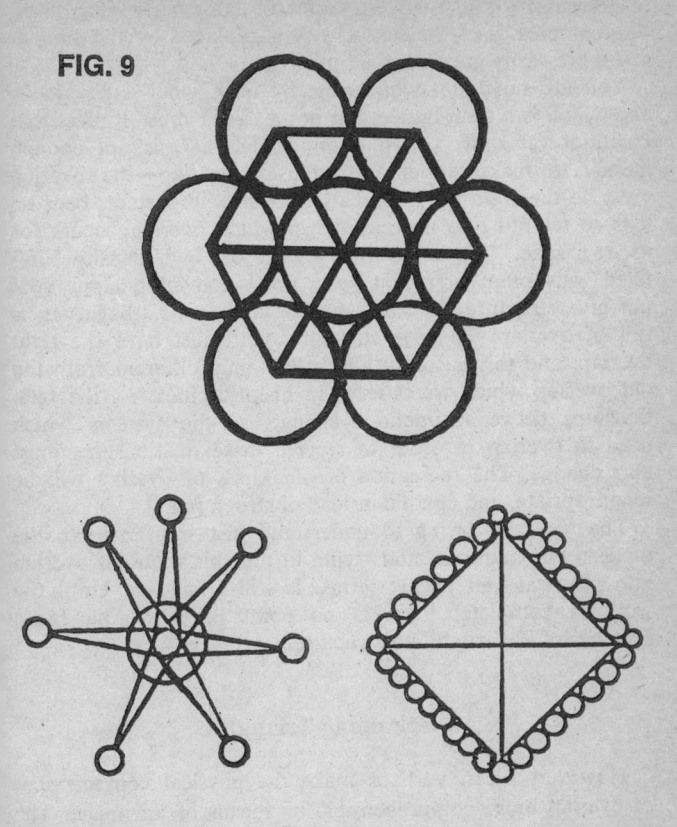

Sir Frederick Bartlett. He showed people a pattern for about one quarter of a second and then asked them to draw what they had seen. Many people, unable to grasp the full complexity of the pattern they had seen, simplified the patterns by cutting out the overlap. In Fig. 9, the original is shown at the top, with two fairly typical redrawn versions below it. In the redrawn versions the circles are separated from the rest; the overlap between triangles and circles disappear.

These experiments suggest strongly that people have an underlying tendency, when faced by a complex organization, to reorganize it mentally in terms of non-overlapping units. The complexity of the semi-lattice is replaced by the simpler and more easily grasped tree form.

You are no doubt wondering, by now, what a city looks like which is a semi-lattice, but not a tree. I must confess that I cannot yet show you plans or sketches. It is not enough merely to make a demonstration of overlap—the overlap must be the right overlap. This is doubly important, because it is so tempting to make plans in which overlap occurs for its own sake. This is essentially what the high density "life-filled" city plans of recent years do. But overlap alone does not give structure. It can also give chaos. A garbage can is full of overlap. To have structure, you must have the right overlap, and this is for us almost certainly different from the old overlap which we observe in historic cities. As the relationships between functions change, so the systems which need to overlap in order to receive these relationships must also change. The recreation of old kinds of overlap will be inappropriate, and chaotic instead of structured.

The work of trying to understand just what overlap the modern city requires, and trying to put this required overlap into physical and plastic terms, is still going on. Until the work is complete, there is no point in presenting facile sketches of ill thought out structure.

Overlapping Triangles

However, I can perhaps make the physical consequences of overlap more comprehensible by means of an image. The diagram represents a recent painting by Simon Nicholson (Fig. 10). The fascination of this painting lies in the fact that although constructed of rather few simple triangular elements, these elements unite in many different ways to form the larger units of the painting—in such a way indeed, that if we make a complete inventory of the perceived units in the painting, we find that each triangle enters into four or five completely different kinds of unit, none contained in the others, yet all overlapping in that triangle.

Thus, if we number the triangles and pick out the sets of

FIG. 10

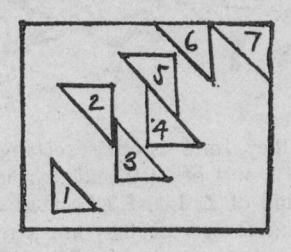

triangles which appear as strong visual units, we get the semi-lattice shown in Fig. 11.

Three and 5 form a unit because they work together as a rectangle; 2 and 4 because they form a parallelogram; 5 and 6 because they are both dark and pointing the same way; 6 and 7 because one is the ghost of the other shifted sideways; 4 and 7 because they are symmetrical with one another; 4

FIG. 11

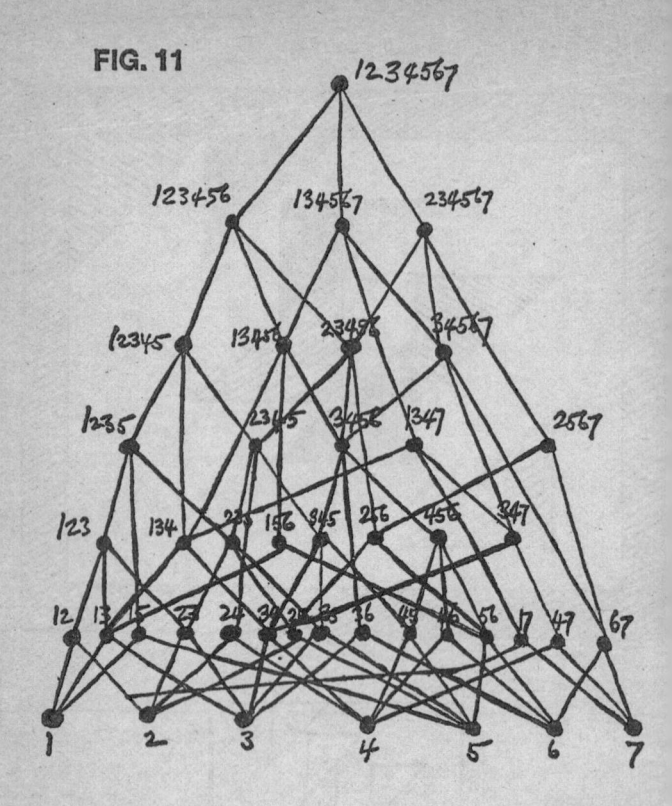

and 6 because they form another rectangle; 4 and 5 because they form a sort of Z; 2 and 3 because they form a rather thinner kind of Z; 1 and 7 because they are at opposite corners; 1 and 2 because they are a rectangle; 3 and 4 because they point the same way as 5 and 6, and form a sort of off-center reflection; 3 and 6 because they enclose 4 and 5; 1 and 5 because they enclose 2, 3, and 4. I have only listed the units of two triangles. The larger units are even more complex. The white is more complex still, and is not even included in the diagram because it is harder to be sure of its elementary pieces.

The painting is significant, not so much because it has

overlap in it (many paintings have overlap in them), but rather because this painting has nothing else in it except overlap. It is only the fact of the overlap, and the resulting multiplicity of aspects which the forms present, that makes the painting fascinating. It seems almost as though the painter had made an explicit attempt, as I have done, to single out overlap as a vital generator of structure.

All the artificial cities I have described have the structure of a tree rather than the semi-lattice structure of the Nicholson painting. Yet it is the painting, and other images like it, which must be our vehicles for thought. And when we wish to be precise, the semi-lattice, being part of a large branch of modern mathematics, is a powerful way of exploring the structure of these images. It is the semi-lattice we must look for, not the tree.

When we think in terms of trees we are trading the humanity and richness of the living city for a conceptual simplicity which benefits only designers, planners, administrators and developers. Every time a piece of a city is torn out, and a tree made to replace the semi-lattice that was there before, the city takes a further step toward dissociation.

In any organized object, extreme compartmentalization and the dissociation of internal elements are the first signs of coming destruction. In a society, dissociation is anarchy. In a person, dissociation is the mark of schizophrenia and impending suicide. An ominous example of city-wide dissociation is the separation of retired people from the rest of urban life, caused by the growth of desert cities for the old like Sun City, Arizona. This separation is only possible under the influence of tree-like thought.

It not only takes from the young the company of those who have lived long, but worse, it causes the same rift inside each individual life. As you will pass into Sun City, and into old age, your ties with your own past will be unacknowledged, lost, and therefore, broken. Your youth will no longer be alive in your old age—the two will be dissociated, your own life will be cut in two.

For the human mind, the tree is the easiest vehicle for complex thoughts. But the city is not, cannot, and must not be a tree. The city is a receptacle for life. If the receptacle severs the overlap of the strands of life within it, because it is a tree, it will be like a bowl full of razor blades on edge, ready to cut up whatever is entrusted to it. In such a receptacle life will be cut to pieces. If we make cities which are trees, they will cut our life within to pieces.

The Social Effects of the Physical Environment

Irving Rosow

Much of the force behind the movement for housing reform is epitomized by one of its most articulate exponents: "The tenants' entire social life may hang on the smallest whim of the greenest draftsman or rent collector."[3]* Although it is an extreme statement—and one which, if taken too literally, imposes a severe responsibility—it sums up a basic operational assumption of idealistic housing practitioners. As a movement and ideology, housing and planning rest on the premise that by the manipulation of the physical environment, we can control social patterns. If housing exerts an independent influence on how people live, then the creation of certain housing conditions can change social relationships. We can affect the choice of friends, family adjustments, and generally how people spend their time. All this is subject, of course, to given cost limitations. But apparently, within these restrictions, different housing decisions may have different social consequences. The problem of the housers is to learn more about how and in what way factors of design do indeed affect patterns of social life.

In this paper, we should like to assess this premise against the findings of a growing body of housing research. This is by no means a systematic, exhaustive coverage of the literature or of housers' working "hypotheses." It is more of an interim clarification, now that "some of the early research returns are in," of those assumptions which tend to be more

Reprinted by permission from *Journal of Marriage and the Family*, August, 1957, copyright by the National Council on Family Relations.

*Numbers refer to references listed at the end of this article.

effective than others in realizing social policies which are at once the housers' goals and guides.

The assumptions may be classified into several general categories to which they refer: 1) social pathology and social efficiency; 2) "livability" of the dwelling unit; 3) neighborhood structure and integration; and 4) esthetics. Our concern here is mainly, though not exclusively, with low- and middle-income public housing or similar planned neighborhoods.

Social Pathology

The housers have effectively won their point that slum clearance pays dividends in terms of social welfare and hard cash. The correlation between poor housing and the incidence of crime, disease, juvenile delinquency, mortality, et cetera, have been established beyond doubt. Planners no longer have to deal seriously with the objection that correlations do not prove causal relationships. Enough work has already shown re-housing to be a sufficient condition to produce a sharp, significant decline in these morbidities.[5,6,10] Slum clearance and the elimination of obviously substandard housing have reduced some virulent social problems and contributed to health and welfare among underprivileged groups.

Furthermore, Rumney, among others, has demonstrated impressively that the dividends of re-housing are not only to be reaped in social values like health, but also in dollars and cents.[38,39] Slums have been highly profitable rental and speculative properties to their owners, but largely at public expense. Municipalities have subsidized slums indirectly. For thirteen major cities, the public expenditures on blighted areas have exceeded revenues from them by ratios of 2.2 to 9.9.[39] In other words, the direct costs of public services (relief, police and fire, welfare, et cetera) were between two and ten times as high as the taxes which these areas contributed to the public coffers. These ratios are reversed for high-rental residential districts which tend to yield considerably more revenue than expense, thereby providing the funds for slum services. Despite certain difficulties with such indices,[14] the over-all outline is clear. Depressed housing areas represent social and financial liabilities which are greatly eased by clearance and re-housing.

Livability

The factor of livability is the most instrumental aspect of design and is most commonly related to the individual dwelling unit.[33,34,35] It refers to the utilitarian organization of space and facilities which best accommodates the needs of the occupants and minimizes frictions and frustrations from factors of layout and design.[17] According to one sociologist of housing:

> Modern architecture does its best to accommodate in the most utilitarian manner the informal aspects of private family living . . . . Room arrangements [are favored] that serve the everyday life of the family and reduce household chores to a minimum . . . . Relaxation and informality in the relations between different family members are promoted.[32]

Livability thus becomes an expression of the "functional" goals of modern architecture and design, and its norms are efficiency. It implies a careful adaptation of design to use, and frequently specific features or space are designed for specific purposes.

But there is evidence of "nonconforming" usage. Many features are neglected, used for purposes other than those intended, the activity takes place elsewhere, or does not take place at all in the confines of the plan. This applies both to the dwelling unit and to the neighborhood.

In the private dwellings, for example, study space is commonly provided in the "children's bedroom" where, at desks or built-in desk shelves, the younger generation can do its lessons in privacy. This nominally removes them from the distractions of family intercourse without imposing undue restraint on the rest of the family. Yet the picture of the teenager with homework scattered over the living room floor and the radio or TV set blaring in his ear has become almost a stereotype, although to the writer's knowledge it has not been examined in research.

Other features have had a varying fate in non-conforming usage. The short-lived experiment with the tiny "Pullman" kitchen is a case in point. Another, in private houses, is the basement recreation room which matures into a conventional storage space. Or in residential suburbs, the façade of house after house may have enormous "picture windows" which are covered by venetian blinds or drapes (often made-to-measure) to give some privacy to the occupants.

Similar nonconforming usage is found in community facilities, with the community center a conspicuously neglected amenity.[16] In one interracial development, for example, a professionally-staffed community center was created to promote interracial activities and contact. But only 15 percent of the women reported meeting women of the other race in the center compared with almost 60 percent who named the community laundry.[25]

These few illustrations are typical. They can be multiplied, although these suffice to make the point here. Nonconforming usage is important because it almost invariably represents fixed installations which become an economic liability. The space and cost might have been otherwise invested. The occupants are thereby penalized in some sense for incorrect predictions about use or the plasticity of habits.

In mass housing, livability of the domicile necessarily takes on a more restricted meaning than the ideals represented by modern architecture. Cost limitations and family patterns which vary in time, in stage of the family cycle, and from one group to another forbid detailed attention to individual preferences and force standardization of design. In effect, this reduces livability largely to considerations of housekeeping and mechanics—choices of kitchen layout; easy-to-clean wall, floor, and window surfaces; convenient storage; et cetera. Not only are these decisions sharply restricted by cost factors (viz. consolidating fixtures about plumbing cores), but they frequently involve choices between space and appliances. In this respect, public housing may represent rather few differences from *any* new housing. This is especially true to the extent that, aside from *gross blunders* of design, housekeeping ease may be increased more by appliances than by design decisions. The availability, for example, of a clothes dryer may save more time and exasperation than a brilliant, subtle detail of planning.

Beyond housekeeping mechanics, livability problems can essentially be reduced to factors of space which afford the room for group activities *and* for privacy. In the arrangement of space the designer can make ingenious decisions which minimize frictions. But this is most true in relatively expensive residential housing. In middle- and low-income dwellings, the cost limitations severely restrict the amount of space available. And only so many alternatives exist as realistic choices. The different livability consequences between them may be even more limited.

The effect of the space variable on livability is not simply in crowding (whether persons per room or use-crowding) or space for social activities. Usually there is enough room for those activities in which the family engages together, although larger social affairs such as parties, et cetera, may suffer in small dwellings. The basic problem boils down to privacy. To some extent it is possible to isolate part of the dwelling by clever design: careful solutions of circulation, sound insulation from closet placement, et cetera. But real privacy requires room for comfortable retirement; and unless this space is "manufactured," the lack of privacy may become a source of friction and frustration. The difficulty of creating space without sacrificing other indispensables is a problem of which designers are only too well aware.

The problem of livability may be viewed in a somewhat different perspective. We may properly ask under what conditions livability factors are positive causes of frustration, friction, and tension, and the extent to which they are significant in the social adjustment of the family. In Westgate, a prefabricated housing project for married students, there were extremely serious livability difficulties.[20] Notwithstanding, Festinger reported:

> This general satisfaction [with living in the community] existed in spite of, and seemed to compensate for, many physical inadequacies of the houses. At the time of our study there were many physical nuisances in the houses. Some were incompletely equipped, the grounds were muddy and had not yet been landscaped, they were difficult to heat in the winter, and the like. One example of the reaction to such

physical inadequacies will suffice, however, to illustrate the point. At the time of the investigation many of the houses had trouble with the roofs. The houses were prefabricated, and many of the roofs had not been assembled properly . . . in the interviews about one-third of the residents reported that the roofs leaked. Any rain accompanied by a moderately strong wind would apparently raise the roof slightly, and water would pour down the walls. One family reported that in a particular strong rain the roof had started to blow off; the husband had to go outside and hold the roof down until the wind subsided.

It is remarkable, however, that even such *serious physical inconveniences did not create a strong impression on the residents.* Typically the reaction was, "Oh yes, there are many things wrong with these houses, but we love it here and wouldn't want to move."

The adequate and satisfying social life was sufficient to override many inconveniences. The result was a rather happy social and psychological existence.[19] (Italics inserted.)

This is not to recommend such Spartan trials as built-in housing features. But housing attitudes are far too complex to ascribe them specifically to livability frustrations which may be much less relevant than housers suppose. The adjustment of family members to one another is a function of social and personal factors to which the dwelling may contribute relatively little. In another study, for example, of thirty-three families who built homes, five had absolutely no dissatisfaction with their previous dwelling and the complaints of the others centered about highly discrete details which were annoying.[36]

The almost standard response of housers to such evidence is, "Aha, but these people don't know what it can be like to live in a well-designed dwelling." This is largely true. But on the other hand, there is little evidence that satisfaction with new housing is directly related to livability resulting *from design per se* except when there is a significant improvement in housing, especially where people came from substandard housing, or occupants are particularly conscious of housing in highly literate, sophisticated terms.

This brings us to a second point regarding space and privacy. There is evidence of important class differences in the meaning and valuation of privacy. In a study of fifty families in New York state, Cutler found that exactly one half of the people in lower class families complained about the lack of privacy in comparison with only 10 percent of the middle class and none of the upper class.[9] Furthermore, in defining the elements of privacy, lower class respondents mentioned having a room of one's own twice as frequently as upper class people (70 percent versus 34 percent). Conversely, 44 percent of the upper class compared with 8 percent of the lower class mentioned such factors as outdoor privacy, rooms that could be closed off, extra baths, extra guest rooms, and the maid living away from the family. In other words, higher social groups take for granted amenities which the lower classes would like. The lower class groups basically want more space than they have available. Although satisfaction with housing is clearly related to size of dwelling[8,9,13]—which is in turn related to many other features as well—crowding, privacy, and space limitations may not be so important to working-class groups as to other segments of the population. Dean found in a Steubenville sample that although 21 percent of the semi-skilled and unskilled workers were doubled-up with relatives, only 6 percent specifically complained about this in terms of overcrowding, whereas in the white collar group 6 percent were living with relatives, but 29 percent complained of overcrowding.[13] This is consistent with other findings in which space was subordinate to other features in housing complaints of working-class groups.

Thus, conceptions of privacy and adequate space have different class meanings; and there is little evidence that these assume drastic importance in family adjustment *provided* that some adequate space standards are met and that the class culture does not demand private space for highly individual personal activities. Chapin, for example, observes:

> Thus privacy becomes a value. One may question the validity of imputing to others the desires, needs, and wants that are characteristic in this respect of nervously high-strung, sophisticated, and responsive intellectual persons. Perhaps the common run of home occupants is not as sensitive to deprivation of privacy as some, but it is safer to assume that some individuals born to the common run of humanity will be sensitive . . . . Privacy is needed for thinking, reflection, reading and study, and for esthetic enjoyment and contemplation. Intrusions on the fulfillment of personal desires need to be shut off . . . .[7]

This is a statement of highly personal goals pursued in the home. As Chapin indicates, it tends to be highly class-selective in its relevance—or indeed, to characterize particular social types within classes, particularly middle and upper class intellectuals and esthetes. Their needs can ultimately only be satisfied with space, which again involves cost more than design factors.

In general there tends to be an incompatability between highly individuated housing goals and standardization imposed by mass housing. Virtually the only manipulable variable in large-scale projects is the diversification of dwelling-unit sizes within the over-all budget. This is perhaps the most opportune way to juggle space to satisfy the needs of specialized groups—whether by providing larger units for larger families and those with high privacy activities or by smaller units for smaller families (young and old couples, et cetera).

The provision of space poses additional problems, since large increments of floor space may have to be provided to realize small increments of actual free space. In studies of the Pierce Foundation, for example, middle-class families tended to fill free space with furnishings so that from one family to another, similar amounts of open space were found despite different sizes of comparable rooms. Some of these furnishings were for storage and others for decoration. It is important to note, however, when the designer assumes that he is squeezing out several more cubic feet of open space in reality he may be creating a "vacuum" which the occupant will "abhor" and fill at the earliest possible opportunity.

Further, although surveys and the like may reveal considerable agreement about the *categories* of housing complaints or desired housing features, the research on livability has not "weighted" these factors, especially by class and social typology variables, to reveal how important housing values actually are to different groups. Who is willing to sacrifice how much of what (including money) to get the kind of housing he wants? For example, a New York realtor not long ago expressed amazement at his middle-class tenants who preferred to give up a bedroom and sleep on a studio couch in the living room in order to own a car. Or as one houser put it:

We are inclined to look down our noses at the family who lives in a shack so they can own an automobile, or the six persons who live in one room and yet pool their resources to buy a television set; but are we sure we are right?[18]

Nowhere does the problem of relative class values become so acute as the question of livability. The planners, designers, architects, and housers must operate with assumptions about how people do live, how they want to live, how they would live if given a chance.[37] Most of them conventionally assume that the people for whom they are designing must be "educated" to appreciate and exploit the housing advantages being placed at their disposal. When the tenants fail to respond, this is often written off as "no fair test" because the housing itself was too restricted and not enough design influence was brought to bear. On the contrary, there is ample reason to believe that design factors generally represent only conditions of the physical environment which do not significantly alter human outlooks apart from the significant social experience which housing may not provide. And it remains to be seen how the average new project or even the better ones which have been built with strong cost restrictions can affect the relations of family members to one another— for those people who did not come from substandard housing. Or more precisely, it is an open question whether livability factors can be significantly separated from the sheer fact of re-housing lower-class groups or custom-building for upper-class families. The intermediate range may be slightly but not substantially affected by livability provisions.

In summary, the factors of livability which can be influenced by design tend to apply selectively to class groups and to those with highly specialized housing needs. It is mainly the lower-class group, moving into new housing from conspicuously poor dwellings, who benefit most from factors of livability. The more specialized needs of people with strong privacy desires can scarcely be met in new dwellings except at high cost.

Community Integration

Intimately bound up with the planning movement is a reaction to the fragmentation and segmentalization of urban life. There is an effort to recapture an "organic" environment in which people will be integrated into communities on a residential basis. This is epitomized in the controversy over the neighborhood plan in its various names and guises.[1,10,11,15,24,31,42]

A series of studies has amply demonstrated the effect of residential placement on group formation and the selection of friends.[4,16,20,21,23,28,29,30 et al] The evidence is well known and so clear that it warrants little elaboration. In planned communities friendship groups are determined by two variables: proximity of neighbors and orientation of dwellings. People select their friends primarily from those who live nearby and those whom their home faces.

The full significance of these patterns, however, is less clear. Housers interpret this to mean that people are indeed being integrated into community or neighborhood structures. But these patterns are adumbrated by several factors: deviant cases in which planned communities did *not* result in this spontaneous cohesiveness[12,19]; that they characterized the earliest period in the life of the community, but then became instable and gave way to the extension of friendships farther afield outside the neighborhood[16,22]; that the neighborhood community developed a system of social stratification which was not solidary in its effects;[12,16,21,23,26,29] that community integration was most directly related to homogeneous social composition and inversely related to length of residence.[22] In other words, when people of a similar type (*viz.* students, war plant workers, et cetera) are brought together into a new community for a relatively impermanent period, considerable social solidarity springs up. But the longer people stay and the more diversified the group, the more is solidarity affected by status differentiation and the establishment of friendships elsewhere.

The deeper issues presented here center about the significance of homogeneous social composition. Some critics of

The Social Effects of the Physical Environment 147

the neighborhood concept have contended that homogeneous communities tend to formalize social segregation and defeat the very democratic objectives which neighborhood planners seek.[24] According to others, the contrary desire to establish socially heterogeneous communities will not necessarily achieve democratic aims. Some argue that there is no reason to assume that people will spontaneously or willingly enter heterogeneous planned neighborhoods any more than similar unplanned neighborhoods.[22] If they do, there is no assurance that they will interact harmoniously, but may, on the contrary, perpetuate existing differences.[12,26,43]

Some changes are perceptible. For example, in interracial housing, attitudes toward Negroes became more favorable on closer contact.[25] In two projects with internal segregation of Negroes, between two thirds and three fourths of the white occupants favored segregation while in two others with no internal segregation, about 40 percent of the whites favored segregation. These attitudes were accompanied by extremely sharp differences in association between the races. In the segregated projects, less than 5 percent of the white women knew any Negro woman by first name or engaged in such cooperative activity as baby-sitting, shopping together, helping in illness, et cetera. In contrast to this, the proportion of white women in the non-segregated projects varied from one fourth to three fourths who had such associations with Negroes. The occupancy patterns evidently served to reinforce negative attitudes in the segregated projects.

Jahoda and West indicate the strong influence exerted by previous interracial experience on attitudes.[25] Of those whites who had previously lived in racially mixed neighborhoods, 19 percent expected trouble and 17 percent found relations better than they had expected; but of those who had no prior biracial experience, 56 percent expected trouble and 43 percent were pleasantly surprised by the absence of conflict. But under the best conditions, among the whites who had *both* previous residential experience *and* worked with Negroes, only 45 percent favored interracial housing. Although whites' desire to move from an interracial project was directly related with their expectations of a Negro invasion, among those who expected no change in the proportion of Negro residents, 50 percent nonetheless planned to move—not necessarily, of course, as a reflection of their racial attitudes. In this project, the management's policy of a "quota" system maintained a stable proportion of the races through time. But in the same town, a comparable project without a "quota" showed the proportion of Negroes gradually reaching between 80-90 percent.

Unquestionably, the influence of greater contact on racial images had an impact on stereotypes, but the over-all picture is one of accommodation rather than community integration. Changes in attitude ultimately depended on more than sheer contact. Jahoda and West indicate, "But in part, also, the more favorable expectations [of whites] are the result of that kind of *sustained* interracial contact which displaces racial stereotypes."[25] (Italics inserted.)

The factor of residential mobility has bearing both on the necessary condition of sustained contact in changing racial stereotypes and on the friendship patterns of homogeneous communities. Apparently about three fourths of the American people changed their residence during the 1940-50 decade.[2] Furthermore, among the working classes most eligible for planned projects, there is the highest residential mobility and the lowest integration into the local neighborhood. Higher class groups who are less mobile and have longer residential tenure have more friends within their immediate neighborhood. Nonetheless, in terms of *sources* of friendships, the lower-class groups draw upon immediate neighbors more than twice as frequently as middle and upper class groups (33 percent versus 14 percent).[41] The reasons for the mobility may vary—economic opportunity, desire to own a home, middle-class aspirations, changing stages in the family cycle, et cetera.[14,36] The motives are less important than the implications for the integration of the community. High mobility is not a condition favoring *sustained* contacts necessary to change racial attitudes. Nor is either high mobility or long tenure in planned neighborhoods conducive to the sustained solidarity and friendship patterns observed in the newly formed communities.

One may properly inquire what the alternative friendship patterns may have been in homogeneous *unplanned* neighborhoods. Apparently they were of a similar character to those of the planned neighborhood. Lower-class groups draw heavily upon the local area for their friendships, but because they move frequently, their friends are spread about; upper class people have more diverse sources of friendships, but with more stable residence they gradually extend their local contacts and become integrated into the community.[41] Planned communities of a given density and layout provide X-number of conveniently located neighbors with whom friendships are established. It remains to be shown that unplanned neighborhoods of equal density and equally homogeneous composition do not provide the identical patterns of friendship formation and group structure.

We may here be the innocent victims of a research bias. Housing research has concentrated heavily on the planned community and findings have been interpreted as changed social patterns, although no base point for change was established. In fact, we may have inadvertently discovered basic patterns which have been operating in urban environments but which were not intensively investigated prior to the modern housing developments.

Under these circumstances, one is forced to ask anew, "What are the *social patterns* which housing and design have changed?" If anything, one is impressed perhaps less by the changes than by the continuities and the persistence of previous social patterns—with the exception of the easing of social pathology by the movement from substandard housing areas. There is little conclusive evidence of more than ephemeral changes in social patterns through the medium of planned communities. Particularly, the integration of the community does not seem to be significantly greater than is found in homogeneous, unplanned neighborhoods. Stratification and racial divisions remain effective forces.

Thus, to all intents and purposes, it remains to be established how planning does significantly more than shift or regroup active—not latent—social relations into new settings.

Esthetics

The final factor which concerns us is the commitment of planners and housers to an esthetic way of life. In this, their assumptions of psychological effects of esthetic atmospheres may be on firmer ground. Light, air, greenery, variety of color, materials, forms—within the dwelling unit and the neighborhood—may create interest which affects people's moods. In extreme cases this is clear. One need only allude to women's customary responses to blue fluorescent light.

There is reason to suspect class differentials on the importance of the variable of esthetics. But planners have here a more intangible factor which, despite its subjectivity, may have subtle effects on mood and thereby potentially affect tolerance thresholds and the texture of social interaction. Very little research has been done on the psychological impact of different esthetic environment (beyond some preliminary research into effects of colors), so there is little ground on which to evaluate the importance of design from this standpoint. Certainly we know its importance in merchandising—although housers may not be identified with the esthetics in some proven packaging. In housing, however, we would expect the esthetic element to involve much more of a Gestalt perception process rather than segmental responses. Esthetic judgments will have to await further research.

References

1. American Public Health Association, Committee on the Hygiene of Housing, *Planning the Neighborhood*, Chicago: Public Administration Service, 1948.

2. Bauer, Catherine, "Social Questions in Housing and Community Planning," *Journal of Social Issues*, 7, Nos. 1 & 2 (1951), pp. 1-34. Special Housing Issue.

3. Bauer, Catherine, "Good Neighborhoods," *Annals*, 242 (1945), pp. 104-15.

4. Caplow, Theodore, and R. Forman, "Neighborhood Interaction in a Homogeneous Community," *American Sociological Review*, 15 (June, 1950) pp. 357-66.

5. Chapin, F. Stuart, "The Effects of Slum Clearance and Rehousing on Family and Community Relationships in Minneapolis," *American Journal of Sociology*, 43 (1938), pp. 744-63.

6. Chapin, F. Stuart, "An Experiment on the Social Effects of Good Housing," *American Sociological Review*, 5 (Dec., 1940), pp. 868-79.

7. Chapin, F. Stuart, "Some Factors Related to Mental Hygiene," *Journal of Social Issues*, 7, Nos. 1 & 2 (1951), Special Housing Issue.

8. Cottam, Howard, *Housing and Attitudes Toward Housing in Rural Pennsylvania*, State College, Pa.: Pennsylvania State College School of Agriculture, 1942.

9. Cutler, Virginia, *Personal and Family Values in the Choice of a Home*, Ithaca, N.Y.: Cornell University Agricultural Experpmental Station, 1947.

10. Dahir, James, *Communities for Better Living*. New York: Harper & Bros., 1950.

11. Dahir, James, *The Neighborhood Unit Plan*, New York; Russell Sage Foundation, 1947.

12. Danhof, R., "The Accommodation and Integration of Conflicting Cultures in a Newly Established Community," *American Journal of Sociology*, 48 (1943), pp. 14-43.

13. Dean, John, "The Ghosts of Home Ownership," *Journal of Social Issues*, 7, Nos. 1 & 2 (1951), Special Housing Issue.

14. Dean, John, "The Myths of Housing Reform," *American Journal of Sociology*, 54 (1949), pp. 271-88.

15. Dewey, Richard, "The Neighborhood, Urban Ecology and City Planners," *American Sociological Review*, 15 (Aug., 1950), pp. 502-07.

16. Durant, Ruth, *Watling*, London: P. S. King & Son, 1939.

17. Federal Public Housing Authority, *The Livability Problems of 1000 Families*, Washington: National Housing Agency, 1945.

18. Ferrier, Clarence, "Frontiers of Housing Research," *Land Economics* 25 (1949), supplement.

19. Festinger, Leon, "Architecture and Group Membership," *Journal of Social Issues*, 7, Nos. 1 & 2 (1951), Special Housing Issue.

20. Festinger, Leon, Stanley Schachter, and Kurt Back, *Social Pressures in Informal Groups*, New York: Harper & Bros., 1950.

21. Form, William, "Status Stratification in a Planned Community," *American Sociological Review*, 10 (Oct., 1945), pp. 605-13.

22. Form, William, "Stratification in Low and Middle Income Housing Areas," *Journal of Social Issues*, 7, Nos. 1 & 2 (1951), pp. 109-31, Special Housing Issue.

23. Infield, H., "A Veterans' Cooperative Land Settlement and its Sociometric Structure," *Sociometry*, 6 (1947), pp. 50-70.

24. Isaacs, Reginald, "The Neighborhood Theory," *Journal of the American Institute of Planners*, 14 (1948), pp. 15-23.

25. Jahoda, Marie, and Patricia Salter West, "Race Relations in Public Housing," *Journal of Social Issues*, 7, Nos. 1 & 2 (1951), Special Housing Issue.

26. Jevons, R., and J. Madge, *Housing Estates*, Bristol, Eng.: University of Bristol, 1946.

27. Kilbourn, Charlotte, and Margaret Lantis, "Elements of Tenant Instability in a War Housing Project," *American Sociological Review*, 11 (Feb., 1946), pp. 57-64.

28. Kuper, Leo, *Living in Towns*, London: Cresset Press, 1953.

29. Merton, Robert, "Patterns of Interpersonal Influence and Communications Behavior in a Local Community," in Paul Lazarsfeld and Frank Stanton (eds.), *Communications Research, 1948-49*, New York: Harper & Bros., 1949.

30. Merton, Robert, "The Social Psychology of Housing," in Wayne Dennis (ed.), *Current Trends in Social Psychology*, Pittsburgh: University of Pittsburgh Press, 1948, pp. 163-217.

31. Perry, Clarence, *Housing for the Machine Age*, New York: Russell Sage Foundation, 1939.

32. Riemer, Svend, "Architecture for Family Living," *Journal of Social Issues*, 7, Nos. 1 & 2 (1951), Special Housing Issue.

33. Riemer, Svend, "Designing the Family Home," in H. Becker and R. Hill (eds.), *Family, Marriage and Parenthood*, Boston: D. C.. Health, 1948.

34. Riemer, Svend, "Maladjustment to the Family Home," *American Sociological Review*, 10 (Oct., 1945), pp. 442-48.

35. Riemer, Svend, "Sociological Perspective in Home Planning," *American Sociological Review*, 12 (April, 1947), pp. 155-59.

36. Rosow, Irving, "Home Ownership Motives," *American Sociological Review*, 13 (1948), pp. 751-55.

37. Rosow, Irving, "Housing Resarch and Administrative Decisions," *Journal of Housing*, 8 (1951), pp. 285-87.

38. Rumney, Jay, and S. Shuman, *The Cost of Slums in Newark*, Newark: 1946.

39. Rumney, Jay, "The Social Costs of Slums," *Journal of Social Issues*, 7, Nos. 1 & 2 (1951), Special Housing Issue.

40. Rumney, Jay, and S. Shuman, *The Social Effects of Public Housing*, Newark: Newark Housing Authority, 1944.

41. Smith, Joel, William Form, and Gregory Stone, "Local Intimacy in a Middle-Sized City," *American Journal of Sociology*, 60 (Nov., 1954), pp. 276-85.

42. Sweetser, Jr., Frank, "A New Emphasis for Neighborhood Research," *American Sociological Review*, 7 (Aug., 1942), pp. 525-33.

43. Wright, H., *Rehousing Urban America*, New York: Columbia University Press, 1935.

The Human Implications of Current Redevelopment and Relocation Planning

Herbert J. Gans

I

A number of large American cities are currently initiating or carrying out renewal projects which involve the clearance of a neighborhood and the relocation of a large number of families. This paper attempts to analyze and evaluate some of the social and planning problems in this process, as they were observed in the redevelopment of Boston's West End. It is submitted as a case study, because many of the conditions described exist also in other American cities.

The 48-acre West End project area[1] is part of a 72-acre working-class residential district in downtown Boston.[2] The project area is covered almost solidly with five-story apartment buildings, which replaced older three-story single- and multifamily structures around the turn of the century. The

Reprinted by permission from *Journal of the American Institute of Planners*, Vol. XXV, No. 1, February, 1959, copyright by the American Institute of Planners.

[1] The terms West End and project area will hereafter be used interchangeably.

[2] The eastern boundary of the project area fronts on Massachusetts General Hospital and the back of Beacon Hill; the northern, on the Charles River; the southern, on a number of blocks much like the West End, although in poorer condition, and on Scollay Square. This is one of Boston's major skid-row areas, soon to be redeveloped as a government center. The western boundary faces a major railroad station and a wholesaling-industrial area which separates the West End from the North End.

land coverage is very high, as is the ground density.[3] However, the apartments were built at a time when families were much larger, so that for many households the floor density is low. In the last twenty-five years, the West End has been mainly an area of first and second settlement for Italian and Polish families. In 1950, the area was estimated to have 12,000 residents. At the time of the city's "taking" the land under eminent domain in May, 1958 about 2,800 households and 7,500 residents remained.[4]

The redevelopment plan proposes total clearance, except for a half dozen community-wide institutions and buildings of architectural interest. The area is to be redeveloped with up to 2,400 apartments, most of them in elevator buildings, at rents currently estimated to be $45 per room, and with parks, shops, and parking areas for the new tenants. Massachusetts General Hospital is also expanding its plant and parking areas on an adjacent site.

II The Redevelopment Plan

A planning analysis of this redevelopment project must begin with the question of whether or not the area is a slum. The term slum is an evaluative not an empirical one, and any definition must be related, implicitly or explicitly, to the renewal policy in which it is used. Popular definitions of the slum include two criteria, the social image of the area and its physical condition. Federal standards for determining eligibility for renewal funds focus almost exclusively on the latter. However, it is the local agency which selects the area to be proposed for clearance; and, in most communities, the area's physical condition is a necessary but not suffi-

[3]"Buildings now cover 72% of the net land area in the West End, excluding streets and vacant lots. Of the total of 48 blocks 11 have building coverages of over 90%. . . . ," Boston Housing Authority, "West End Project Report," Boston, 1953, p. 5. This refers to the 72-acre study area. An unpublished Housing Authority report indicated that according to the 1950 census, the ground density was in excess of 152 dwelling units per net residential acre, "Supporting Documentation to the Redevelopment Plan," Boston, September 1955, p. 7.

[4]This paper is based largely on conditions at the time of the taking; the figures are from a survey made by the Boston Redevelopment Authority just prior to the taking.

The Human Implications of Current Redevelopment 155

cient criterion. What seems to happen is that neighborhoods come to be described as slums if they are inhabited by residents who, for a variety of economic, cultural, and psychological reasons, indulge in overt and visible behavior considered undesirable by the majority of the community.[5] The community image of the area gives rise to feelings that something should be done, and subsequently the area is proposed for redevelopment.[6] Usually, the physical condition of the area is such that it is eligible for redevelopment; however, there are areas, such as Boston's North End, which meet physical criteria, but which are socially and politically strong enough to discourage any official or politician from suggesting them for clearance.[7]

The federal and local housing standards which are applied to slum areas reflect the value pattern of middle-class professionals. These professionals, like the rest of the middle class, allot a higher value to housing (as measured by percentage of income to be spent for shelter) and place greater emphasis on the status functions of housing than does the working class. Their evaluation of the behavior of slum residents is also based on class-defined standards, and these often confuse behavior which is only culturally different with pathological or antisocial acts.[8]

Generally speaking, these standards are desirable bases for public policy, despite their class bias; and many of them should be applied to the poorer areas of the city, *if they were followed by a program which provided the residents of*

---

[5] For an analysis of the kinds of people who live in the slums and the ways in which they deviate from the rest of the urban population, see John Seeley "The Slum: Its Nature, Use, and Users," pp. 7-14 herein.

[6] Consequently, the planning reports which are written to justify redevelopment dwell as much on social as on physical criteria and are filled with data intended to show the prevalence of antisocial or pathological behavior in the area. The implication is that the area itself causes such behavior, and should therefore be redeveloped (see, for example, "West End Project Report" cited above).

[7] Actually, a considerable number of West End families had moved into the area from the North End during the 1930's and 1940's since West End apartments were more spacious and modern and had their own, rather than shared, bathrooms.

[8] The latter point is developed further in the author's unpublished paper, "Some Notes on the Definition of Mental Health: An Attempt from the Perspective of the Community Planner," 1957.

these areas with better housing. Presently, however, these standards are used to tear down poor neighborhoods; but the better housing for the residents is not provided. This assertion will be supported by the analysis that follows.

Slum and Low-Rent Districts: A Redefinition

Consequently, unless urban renewal policy is drastically altered, other definitions of the slum should be developed. Existing physical standards fail to make a distinction between *low-rent* and *slum* districts, or low-rent and slum housing, community facilities, street patterns, etc. This distinction is an important one. *Slum dwellings, etc., may be defined as those which are proven to be physically, socially, or emotionally harmful to their residents or to the community at large. On the other hand, low rent dwellings, etc., provide housing and the necessary facilities which are not harmful to people who want, or for economic reasons must maintain, low rental payments and are willing to accept lack of modernity, high density, lack of privacy, stair climbing, and other inconveniences as alternative costs.*[9]

A set of equitable social standards is more difficult to define, because of the problem of causality. In most cases people move into what are known as slum areas because they have problems or unacceptable behavior patterns; economic, social, and psychological conditions, rather than the slum, cause these. The social environment may "infect" a few people previously without problems, but this is much rarer than commonly thought. However, for purposes of definition in connection with renewal policy, it is possible to distinguish between undesirable patterns which are related causally to the neighborhood and those which are not. *Thus, for renewal purposes, a slum may also be defined as an area which, because of the nature of its social environment can be proved to create problems and pathologies, either for the residents or for the community at large.*

---

[9] Planners like to describe such housing as "obsolescent." However, it is obsolescent only in relation to their own middle-class standards and, more important, their incomes. The term is never used when alley dwellings of technologically similar vintage are rehabilitated for high rentals, e.g., in Georgetown, Washington, D.C.

For example, if children are drawn into illegal activities and it can be *proved* that the neighborhood, rather than conditions of lower-class life, was responsible, that neighborhood might be called a slum.[10] The same would apply if residential overcrowding inhibited privacy and led to intra- or inter-familial conflict. However, overcrowding is probably caused by socioeconomic deprivations that force people to live under such conditions, rather than by the neighborhood itself; and clearance does not solve this problem.

The West End as a Low-Rent District

In my opinion, and given existing renewal policies, most of the West End cannot be described as a slum. I would estimate that at the time of the land taking, probably from 25 to 35 percent of the buildings in the project area were structurally unsound, uninhabitable because they had been vacant for some time, or located on alleys too narrow for proper sanitation and fire prevention.[11] Some of the deterioration was due to the fact that in 1950, when the plans for redevelopment were first announced, landlords were advised not to make extensive repairs on their properties. Many residents claim—with some justification—that parts of the area deteriorated rapidly as a result, especially where apartments

---

[10] A number of West End mothers want to isloate their children from the culture of "the street." Since peers are a strong influence on older children and teenagers, the conflict between the norms of home and street within the child may be resolved in favor of the latter. Only systematic research can determine whether or not such neighborhood characteristics as high density and the mixture of "respectable" and "rough" working-class residents are responsible for any subsequent delinquency. I suspect that relations within the family, and the external socio-economic and cultural factors creating them, are probably more important.

[11] Because of the high land coverage, the first- and second-floor apartments of many buildings receive less air and sunlight than desirable, although there is no evidence that this had deleterious effects. This may be owing in part to the fact that many West Enders spend much time outside, since the street is a major location for neighborhood sociability. I would not defend such apartments as desirable, but I can understand the preferences of low-income West End residents for these dwellings at rentals of $30 a month over those with more air and sunlight at $75.

or entire buildings became and remained vacant in the years that followed.[12] However, reduction of maintenance during the period of rent control and the housing shortage, especially by absentee landlords with big holdings, also contributed to the decay.[13]

Nevertheless, the majority of the structures provide low-rent rather than slum dwellings. Rents are extremely low—often below those charged in public housing; and during the postwar prosperity, most West Enders were able to modernize the interiors of their apartments.[14] The low rents enable the many people in the area who have never escaped the threat of work layoffs to keep their fixed housing costs low enough to survive such a layoff, and the location of the area is within walking distance of the central business district where most of the residents are employed. Also, the minimal rents and the familiar neighbors enable the many old people in the area who retired on social security and some income from a building to maintain independent households.

The exteriors of the buildings have not been well maintained. This is in part because West Enders pay little attention to the status symbols connected with housing. The proximity of family and ethnic group and the availability of local institutions catering to their needs are valued by residents more highly than the status image of the neighbor-

---

[12]The eight-year interim period was taken up by the usual technical and political problems that make up the "natural history" of a redevelopment project. However, owing to poor newspaper coverage and the West Enders' inability as well as unwillingness to understand the complex administrative process, many of the residents were convinced until the last minute that what they called "the steal" of their neighborhood would never go through. The less sanguine suffered greatly from the uncertainty as to whether the project would or would not go through, as did the landlords and the businessmen, who lost tenants and customers during this period. This is one of the hidden costs of redevelopment paid by the West Enders.

[13]The stereotype of the "greedy" slum landlords who fail to maintain their buildings applied mainly to the absentee owners. The resident owners with one or two buildings generally kept up their buildings until the land taking. Most of the vacancies in the area were in absentee-owned buildings; the resident owners had been able to hold their tenants, partly because many of them were friends or relatives.

[14]Visitors were often surprised that West End apartments differed little from those in lower middle-class neighborhoods and could not easily reconcile this with the stereotype of slum housing.

The Human Implications of Current Redevelopment 159

hood.[15] Nor do they regard the high density as a problem, except for parking. Privacy is not evaluated here as highly as it is in middle-class culture, and West Enders consider it more important to have large numbers of relatives, friends, and neighbors at hand. Cultural differences between middle- and working-class families thus affect the applicability and validity of some of the planner's housing standards.

Nor does the West End satisfy the social criteria which would make it a slum. There are "problem residents" in the area, because of the spill-over from the adjacent skid-row and because the low rents have attracted transients, broken families, and new immigrants. For some years now, the West End has been the main first area of settlement for newcomers to Boston; and it has thus served an important, though unrecognized, function in the city.[16] Problems and pathologies associated with ethnic and economic status are also present.[17] But these problems are not created by the

---

[15] Because most of the residents are of Italian or Polish descent, some aspects of life in the West End resemble that of the European villages from which they or their parents came. The extended family plays an important role, since relatives often reside in adjacent apartments. People here live within an intricate social network and a multitude of informal groups which are crucial to the functioning of people in a culture in which the individualism of the middle-class professional is unknown. Despite published statistics, antisocial behavior among permanent West End residents was low, in part because of the strict (though decreasing) parental control over children and of the persuasive sanctions against any kind of nonconformity.

[16] Some of the people who left the West End after 1950 were young people who participated in the suburban boom. They were replaced by people of lower incomes and more transitional living habits, single transients, gypsies, and families with obvious pathological characteristics. Such people found a home in the West End because landlords with vacant units could no longer afford to reject what they defined as "undesirable tenants." The arrival of the new kinds of tenants also helped to convince the community at large that the West End was a slum. Despite this self-fulfilled prophecy, the majority of the West Enders who lived there before 1950 remained until the time of the land taking. Many had lived in the area for from twenty to forty years.

[17] The Redevelopment Authority claimed that delinquency statistics in the area were among the highest in the city, but these figures were questioned by local sources, including the police. The disparity is due in part to the fact that youngsters from other neighborhoods perpetrated their antisocial acts in the West End, just as some West End teenagers, true to the code of protecting the in-group and hurting only the stranger, were delinquents in other neighborhoods.

neighborhood. In fact, for the newcomers the West End has provided an opportunity to avoid the problems that they would have faced in the other major location for first settlement, the South End. Moreover, the highly developed system of informal social control in the West End makes it possible for people with different standards of living and ethnic backgrounds to live together peaceably, tolerant of those with problems.

Some Other Reasons for the Redevelopment Decision

The certification of the West End for redevelopment was not due solely to its physical and social characteristics. Because of its central location adjacent to Beacon Hill and near the downtown retail area, real estate men had long felt the West End was "ripe for higher uses." The Charles River frontage was considered desirable for high-rent apartments. Moreover, the desire of the hospital and other powerful Boston institutions that the low-income population be moved out of the area, the city's desperate need for a higher tax base and its equally urgent search for some signs of economic revival,[18] and the belief that the shrinkage of the central retail area could and should be halted by settling "quality shoppers" nearby, all contributed to justify clearance of the area. The fact that a developer was available made the plan a potential reality. Meanwhile, other Boston neighborhoods in which the housing is more deteriorated and even dangerous receive a much lower priority for renewal, because they are not suitable for high-income housing or because there is less interest among the community's major decision-makers.*

---

[18] For the past few years, politicians and other community leaders have used West End redevelopment as a major symbol of Boston's emergence from its economic doldrums. This may be a false hope, since the apartments to be built in the area will probably draw tenants primarily from other parts of Boston and there is little indication that the project represents any significant amount of new growth.

*As this article went to press, a group of private investors proposed a multimillion dollar project of low and middle-income "ideal apartment efficiency units" in a substandard area of Boston (see the *Boston Herald*, December, 30, 1958).

Costs and Benefits of Redevelopment

The proposed redevelopment will be profitable for the builders and will add to Boston's tax base; and it should provide a psychological lift to the city. Several questions can be raised however, about its over-all benefit to the community, especially when some generally unrecognized and perhaps unintended consequences are taken into consideration. An examination of some of these probable consequences follows:

1) The project has been planned on the assumption that high- and middle-income residents are of benefit to the city, whereas low-income residents are only a burden and a source of public expense. This assumption ignores the vital economic and social functions played in the city economy by low-income people—and by the availability of low-rent housing. The reduction of the city's low-rent housing supply by close to 3000 units makes it more difficult for the present and future industrial force of a low-wage city to find centrally located, economic housing. The need to relocate 2,800 households in the reduced supply will thus overcrowd the remainder, or increase further the outmigration from the city.

2) The economic benefits from the redevelopment may be counteracted by the loss of property values and tax yields in the areas from which tenants will be drawn. Moreover, the central business district which is intended to benefit by the redevelopment may actually lose because a) the redevelopment plan calls for a sizeable shopping center; b) the people likely to rent the new apartments probably already do much of their shopping downtown; and c) the West Enders who will leave the city will probably shop in outlying centers, whereas previously they did all but their food buying in the downtown stores.

3) West Enders with social, economic, and other problems are faced by yet further problems brought on by the need to move from a familiar, permissive, and inexpensive neighborhood. Although some will undoubtedly find better housing, others will be forced to the real slums of the city or will overcrowd other low-rent districts to the point where

they become slums. The need to move and to pay higher rents will increase the burdens of these West Enders and of the community agencies helping them now.

More detailed analyses of the project would have to be made to determine whether or not the benefits outweigh the costs for the community as a whole and for the sectors of the population affected by the project.

The Hidden Costs

However, such analyses would not take into consideration the hidden social, economic, and other costs paid by the West Enders in being forced out of their neighborhood with nothing more than the $100 moving allowance.

1) West Enders must bear the financial burdens that result from having to pay higher rentals for new apartments that are unlikely to be better in quality than the old ones. For many West Enders, this will require drastic budgetary changes with consequent deprivations in other spheres of life.[19] Because of the shortage of rental housing, some people will be encouraged to buy houses in the suburbs at prices beyond their ability to pay. Moreover, because of the negative publicity leveled at the West End by the press, apartment-hunting tenants from there are likely to be faced with rent gouging by landlords who know that West Enders are at the mercy of the market, as well as with discrimination or refusals because they are "slum dwellers."[20]

2) Landlords who were able to live modestly from the rentals of one or more West End buildings will lose their incomes; the amount of money they will receive for these buildings is not likely to be large enough to allow them to purchase others.

3) Many small businessmen in the area will lose their incomes and livelihood. Although federal relocation regulations allot them $2,500 for moving expenses if they re-

---

[19] Many of these people were being subsidized by low rentals. However, the proportion of their total income paid for rent was not lower than that of the average high-income Bostonian.

[20] Evidence of both types of discrimination came to my attention even before relocation had formally begun.

establish their business, many will be unable to find a new location, since Boston is already oversupplied with small stores.[21] Many of these businessmen are too old to be hired by employers, so both economically and psychologically their future is grim.

4) There are social and psychological losses that result from the breakup of the neighborhood. Clearance destroys not only housing, but also a functioning social system, the existence of which is not even recognized by current relocation procedures. The scattering of family units and friends is likely to be especially harmful to the many older people. The younger West Enders feel that they can adjust to a new neighborhood, but they expect that many of the older ones will not be able to do so and will die during the process.[22]

The variety of costs which West Enders will pay as a result of clearance and relocation (to be discussed below) represent hidden subsidies to the redevelopment program. In effect, the present low-income population will subsidize the clearance of their neighborhood and the apartments of their high-income successors, both by their own losses and by their share of the federal and local tax monies used to clear the site. To balance these costs, the only benefit to be received by most residents is the moving allowance.

Some West Enders, especially the most poorly housed, will undoubtedly benefit from the development by being able to find better apartments. Others will gain by being given a push toward a move to the suburbs they had wanted to make anyway but which they had delayed because of

[21] Thus the businessmen who are economically strong enough to relocate will receive funds for the move, but those who are most in need of aid will receive nothing. Redevelopment officials justify this by the argument that the small stores are already marginal and are being driven out by economic processes, not by redevelopment policies. However, these stores are less marginal in their present neighborhoods; and in addition, they serve a variety of social and communication functions. There are also a number of small businessmen and semiprofessionals in the area who were able to escape from factory jobs by being able to rely on low residential rentals. These will also be forced out of business when their rent bills go up.

[22] Several deaths among older residents at the time that West Enders realized the area would be cleared were attributed by informants to the shock of this recognition.

inertia; however, many of the families in this position had already left the West End between 1950 and 1958.[23]

III The Relocation Plan

While considerable attention has been devoted to the planning of the physical redevelopment phase of the project, less planning has been done for the relocation of the present West End residents. The local relocation plan, approved by federal officials, is based on the assumption that the 60 percent of the population eligible for public housing will accept such units and that private housing is available for the remainder. Neither of these assumptions has yet been tested, and both were open to serious question in May, 1958.

Many eligible West Enders are unwilling to go into public housing. This is so in part because they have been affected by the negative image given public housing by the Boston newspapers, because they will be unable to live with relatives, friends, and neighbors from their own ethnic group, because they consider public-housing tenants to be below them in status, and because they do not wish to be subjected to administrative regulation of their activities.[24] Nor is it entirely clear whether there are sufficient vacant public-housing units for even those West Enders who will accept them.[25]

As a result, considerably more than the 40 percent estimated by the relocation planners will be competing for low-

---

[23] The other beneficiaries will be the absentee landlords, who were losing money on partly or totally vacant buildings and will now be able to sell their buildings to the city. Since they have the funds for legal fees and the political know-how to choose the right lawyers, they can go to court and may be able to get higher prices for their buildings than can the small resident owners.

[24] This is owing in part to the animus against authority and middle-class bureaucracy in Italian-American working-class culture. West Enders are particularly opposed to the review of income and to the raising of rents with increases in earnings.

[25] The West Enders I talked with were willing to accept units in the small projects in or near middle-class districts, but were violently opposed to the large institutional projects built in recent years. Since the former already have long waiting lists, the Housing Authority plan was to move West End people into vacancies in the latter.

rent and low-cost *private* housing. Moreover, no adequate study has been made of the private-housing market,[26] so at the time of the land acquisition, no one knew how much of such housing was available.[27] In addition, since most West End people are used to living amidst their own ethnic group, those of Italian descent (approximately 60 percent of the present population) would like to move to a handful of Italian communities in the Boston area. However, these probably cannot house more than a small percentage of the relocatees.

As a result, many people inside and outside the West End believe that there is not sufficient relocation housing to meet either the needs of the 2,800 West End households or the federal regulations calling for their rehousing in decent, safe, and sanitary dwellings.[28]

Consequences of Relocation

The relocation procedures that have been developed from the nation-wide experience of the past few years also present some problems in relation to the culture and the needs of the West End residents. These problems are discussed below and are in addition to the four types of problems described earlier.

1) Relocation procedures were developed by middle-class professionals and thus assume the self-sufficiency of the nuclear family-household. In the West End, however, many of these physically individual households are tied to those of other families by strong bonds, either of kinship or peer-group membership. If households are relocated individually,

[26] The Authority based its estimate on newspaper rentals, without knowing whether or not these were eligible to be used for relocation. Federal provisions require that relocatees must be moved into decent, safe, and sanitary (i.e., standard) housing.

[27] The more West Enders go into public housing, the more competition there will be among those leaving public housing and the remaining West Enders for the limited supply of private low-rent or low-cost housing.

[28] Since the relocation will take several years, the trickling-down process may throw some low-cost units on the regional housing market, and thus reduce somewhat the discrepancy between supply and demand for relocation housing.

so they are not accessible to these other households with whom they live, negative social and emotional consequences may result. For many of the old people, accessibility means pedestrian accessibility, and thus they will suffer most from being separated from West End relatives and neighbors. Younger people can come together again by car or public transportation, but only if they are relocated in relatively accessible neighborhoods.[29]

2) Differences exist between relocation officials and West End residents in the evaluation of physical and social "standardness" of housing. Thus, what the former define as physically standard may be located in areas which the latter will consider socially undesirable. Since social criteria are more important to many West Enders than physical criteria, they may reject on this basis the units offered to them by relocation officials. Conversely, they may relocate themselves in dwelling units that are substandard by federal provisions, but not by the West Enders' priority of social over physical values.

3) As presently indicated, the scheduling of relocation is based on the requirements of the clearance program. If relocation takes longer than expected, this may force officials to interpret the federal relocation provisions as written, and limit the apartment choices of the relocatees to the number required by law.[30] Given the differences in housing standards between officials and residents, some people may be forced to move into dwelling units and neighborhoods they do not want. Others may be hurried into panicky voluntary relocation with much the same results.

4) Since relocation procedures do not allow for the transfer of the social system, the shock of the relocation process itself is likely to affect negatively a number of people who have never lived anywhere except in the West End, and whose social and emotional ties are entirely within the neighborhood.

[29] One of the reasons families like to live in the West End is its central location with respect to other Italian neighborhoods in the Boston area, so that family members scattered over them can be visited easily.

[30] At the start of relocation, officials indicated that they would be more liberal than the law requires in allowing West Enders to reject apartments offered to them.

Cultural and Political Obstacles to Communication

A fifth problem involves communication difficulties between the redevelopment agency and the West End residents that threaten to make the prospective relocation even more painful. This problem deserves more elaborate discussion than accorded others because these difficulties are an expression of more fundamental problems.

During the eight years in which the Housing Authority and its successor, the Redevelopment Authority, endeavored to implement the redevelopment plan, considerable hostility developed among the residents toward the city agencies. This hostility was based primarily on opposition to the destruction of the West End. However, there were other causes. Working class people are frequently hostile toward governmental authority in general, and feel that the politicians as well as the city officials seek to deprive them of things they value, or are trying to cheat them out of their belongings.[31] This attitude was strengthened in the West End by the fact that in a city inhabited by people of Italian and Irish descent in about equal numbers, the latter retain control over its government and political life. Moreover, as a result of the transformation of the Boston City Council from a ward to an at-large system in 1950, the West End was for all practical purposes disenfranchised.[32]

The Housing and Redevelopment Authorities acted as strict administrators of the law, and failed to take residents' attitudes into consideration. For example, their communica-

---

[31] Thus, many West Enders were convinced that the redevelopment was just another instance of government action to benefit those with greater economic resources and political influence. Since a member of the redeveloper firm had managed the mayor's election in 1950 and had subsequently served in his office, they believed that the redevelopment project was set up to pay off a political debt and also to fatten the mayor's purse before he left office. Such beliefs can arise in Boston more easily than in other cities, since the city government has been unusually inefficient, and in recent years more attentive to the demands of the business interests than to those of the rest of the population.

[32] Although one of the city's nine councilors came from the West End, and another from the North End, there were not enough voters in the West End to make it politically possible for these representatives to support the West End at the expense of other districts.

tion with the West End followed local and federal regulations, and they were extremely careful not to give out any information about which they were not absolutely certain, or which was not required by the rule books. The informational vacuum thus created in the West End was filled with rumors. Moreover, the officials assumed that West End residents were as expert as they in understanding the complex administrative processes of redevelopment, and could thus interpret properly the cryptic news releases which the agency issued periodically.[33]

However, since West Enders have little contact with bureaucratic procedure, they tend to interpret such procedure in personal terms. Because of their generally suspicious view of city governmental activities, they reinterpreted the agency's communications accordingly. For example, the long years of delay between the announcement of redevelopment and the final taking were generally assumed to be due to the city's desire to confuse the residents, scare them out of the West End, and thus reduce the acquisition costs of property and the relocation problem.

The redevelopment officials did not seem to consider the effects of their announcements, especially since vocal opposition to the redevelopment was minimal. This was interpreted by the agency as a general acquiescence on the part of West Enders toward the fate of their neighborhood.

Actually, since 1950, the residents who read so many news stories announcing an early start of the redevelopment that many were convinced it would never take place. Although a small group of determined West Enders had begun to fight the city's plan in 1954, they received little support from residents for this reason.[34]

[33] The Boston press was of little aid to the West Enders, since it was very much in favor of the redevelopment and also seemed to assume that West Enders do not read the papers.

[34] There were other reasons. First, many working-class people rarely think in community-wide terms, since they believe that the community is exploiting them. Second, they are not inclined to, or skilled in, the middle-class pattern of community participation; and they expect their political representatives to take care of this function. Finally, the protest organization was led by a Beacon Hill resident and a small group of West Enders of middle-class background, who were not "natural leaders" by the standards of most of the residents of Italian and Polish descent.

The pattern of poor communication on the part of the redevelopment officials and the negative interpretation of any communication by the residents continued after the Authority had set up a project area relocation office and had announced the taking of the properties by eminent domain. The agency continued to be vague on those topics of most importance to the residents, for example, on the relocation and clearance schedules. This was particularly frustrating to those people who, finally relieved of eight years of uncertainty, now want to plan ahead.[35] Other West Enders took admonitions to move as soon as possible to mean that the relocation office was set up to scare people out of the area. Suggestions about the availability of vacant housing in areas of lower socio-economic status than the West End were reinterpreted to mean that the city wanted to push West Enders into the worst slums of Boston. The redevelopment agency's official notification to landlords that their structures had been purchased for $1 under eminent domain procedures, plus its failure to include this token payment or to explain why it was not included, convinced many people that the city was not keeping its promises to treat them fairly and was going to cheat them out of their payments. Likewise, the way in which the redevelopment agency took the land caused considerable hurt among the older immigrants. They could not understand how the buildings they had worked so hard to own could suddenly be taken away from them, with no assurance as to when they would be paid or how much. Moreover, at the same time they were told to pay rents for their own apartments in these buildings or face eviction. Thus, many of the landlords who earned their livelihoods from the rents they collected were at the same time deprived of both a source of income and the funds with which to pay the rent demanded from them.[36]

---

[35] However, many residents were not planning ahead. Since they have traditionally suffered from economic uncertainty, they have adjusted to this by a flexible and fatalistic day-to-day philosophy of living. The kind of planning familiar to middle-class households would have raised too many false hopes and left them psychologically unprepared to accept sudden job losses and the like.

[36] Kindly relocation officials attempted to soften the hurt by allowing owners to postpone their rent payments until they had been reimbursed for their buildings.

Although the residents and redevelopment officials attributed the communication failure to each other's negative motivations, the difficulties were based on cultural factors. The redevelopment agency was concerned mainly with following local and federal regulations governing relocation. These regulations said nothing about understanding the consequences to the residents of its official acts. Thus, the agency had no real opportunity for learning how the West End received its letters and announcements or interpreted its actions. However, it is questionable whether such an opportunity would have been exploited. The officials concerned were not policy-makers; they were hired to carry out their prescribed duties. They felt sorry for some of the West Enders, especially those with serious problems; and they tried to help them in various ways not required by their job. But, since they believed that relocation would improve the living conditions for most of the residents and that the redevelopment was for the good of the city, they could not really understand why the West Enders were hostile and often unwilling to cooperate.

These beliefs about the virtues of relocation and the unilateral desirability of redevelopment are written into existing local and federal renewal policy. *As a result, when redevelopment officials take action affecting project area residents, they are not required to take into account the attitudes and the situation of the residents.* There is no opportunity for the correction of such actions by feedback from the residents. As a result, the relocation procedures developed so far in most American cities include no techniques that would ease the burden of the people who are to be moved.

Relocation, the Residents' Subsidy of Redevelopment

American redevelopment planning so far has proceeded on the assumption that relocation is secondary to redevelopment. Thus, great pains are taken with planning for clearance and the reuse of the site, but plans for the present occupants of the site are treated as by-products of the redevelopment proposal. For example, the local and federal redevelopment agencies had detailed maps of the West End's street and utility system, but they did not seem to know the simple fact that a number of owners living in the area depended on the rents they collected for their income.

Perhaps the clearest indication of the relatively low priority of relocation in the redevelopment process is the fact that the funds allocated to relocation are less than five percent of the total cost of taking and clearing the land, and this represents only about one percent of the cost of clearance and redevelopment. The real cost of relocation is very much higher, but is paid in various ways by the people being moved out. Under present conditions, the redevelopment of American cities is economically possible only because of the hidden subsidies provided by the residents of the areas to be cleared.

IV Some Recommendations

This critique is not directed either at renewal or relocation per se, but at the present policies which use public funds to subsidize—if only indirectly—the erection of high-rent housing and which penalize the low-income population, without clear proof that these policies are in the public interest.

Moreover, the specific criticisms made of Boston procedures are not intended as "blame" of any individuals within the local or federal agencies. It is important to emphasize that what has happened cannot be attributed to evil motives. No laws have been broken, and many officials have acted with only the best intentions toward the West Enders.[37] However, good intentions can lead to harmful consequences if the basic procedures are at fault. Thus, the responsibility for what has happened rests to a considerable extent on the system of procedures that has emerged from years of legislative and administrative decision-making since the passage of the 1949 Housing Act, and on the unintended

---

[37]Needless to say, more farsighted and analytically oriented officials might have ameliorated the process to some extent. Moreover, if there had been some criticism of the program on the part of planners (commissioners as well as professionals), some changes might now be under way. However, some planners seem to feel that relocation is not their responsibility, even though it is a direct consequence of their plans.

or unrecognized consequences of these procedures when they are actually implemented. However, this system is tied to the economic and political structure, which must therefore also be implicated. For example, since redevelopment agencies must provide sufficient incentives to attract a redeveloper, some of their policies, such as site selection, must be shaped by the demands, or the anticipated demands, of these redevelopers.

Proposals for Redevelopment

Urban renewal and the rehousing of slum dwellers are necessary and desirable objectives. However, the means of achieving them ought to be chosen in relation to these objectives, rather than to extraneous ones.[88] Thus, redevelopment should be pursued primarily for the benefit of the community as a whole and of the people who live in the slum area, and not for that of the redeveloper or his eventual tenants.[89] The recommendations that follow are based largely on this principle. Although they stem from the Boston observations, many of them are undoubtedly applicable to renewal and relocation procedures in other large cities.

1) Renewal projects should be located first in those areas which are slums as defined above, i.e., in which it can be proven that the housing and facilities present social and physical dangers to the residents and to the larger community. The availability of a redeveloper ought to be a consideration, but one of lesser priority.

2) Before areas for renewal are finally determined, independent studies should be made which provide proof of the area's character but take into account the values and

[88] For example, objectives such as attracting middle and upper-income citizens back from the suburbs, contributing potential shoppers to a declining central retail area, creating symbols of "community revival," or providing more statusful surroundings (and parking lots) for powerful community institutions.

[89] This statement is based on a comment made by Ruth Glass, the British planner, after her observations of American renewal. She described it as primarily for the benefit of the redeveloper and his tenants, where as British renewal tries to aid mainly the present residents of the slum area.

The Human Implications of Current Redevelopment

living patterns of the residents.[40] These studies should be made by persons who have no connection either with the project area or the redevelopment agency.

3) Renewal proposals which call for the clearance of an entire neighborhood should be studied closely to determine whether the existing social system satisfies more positive than negative functions for the residents. If this is the case, planners must decide whether the destruction of this social system is justified by the benefits to be derived from clearance.

4) Projects which require large-scale relocation[41] should be studied in a similar manner. Such projects should not be initiated until the community has built sufficient relocation units to assure the proper[42] rehousing of the residents. If private enterprise is unable to provide them, city, state, and federal funds will have to be used. Moreover, if relocation housing is built prior to the renewal project, and in sufficient quantity, and if it is attractive, it is likely to draw enough people out of the slum areas to reduce the market value of slum structures. Consequently, some of the costs of providing such relocation housing will be returned by reduced acquisition costs at the time of renewal.

5) If a community is unwilling or unable to provide the required relocation housing, it should not be permitted to engage in renewal operations.

6) City planners ought to recognize the functions performed in the city by the low-income population. They

---

[40] Studies made by redevelopment agencies rarely concern themselves with the characteristics and needs of the project area residents, or the ways in which they live. Instead, they try to prove, on the one hand, how undesirable the area is in order to persuade the federal and local agencies to provide funds for renewal, and, on the other, how desirable the area is for potential redevelopers. Thus, they judge the area from the narrowly class-determined values of their clients, and ignore the neighborhoods' positive functions. The previously cited West End Project Report is a particularly blatant example. The fault here lies not so much with the local agency that writes such a report as with the federal procedures which permit no real alternative.

[41] This is defined as any relocation proposal that requires the rehousing of more people than is possible, given the existing low-rent housing supply of the community.

[42] "Proper" should be defined by the standards of the residents who are to live in the relocation units as well as by those of the housing and planning officials.

should make sure that sufficient housing is available for them and in the proper locations (including some near the central business district) for their and the city's needs. The federal government should encourage the renewal of such housing by increasing its subsidies when the renewal plan calls for the rehabilitation or construction of low-income dwellings.

7) Greater emphasis should be placed on the rehabilitation of low-rent housing, and less on its clearance. Such rehabilitation should be based on standards that provide decent, safe, and sanitary—but economically priced—dwelling units. In order to make this possible, existing standards should be restudied, to distinguish requirements which bring housing up to a standard but low-rent level, from those which are "fringe benefits" that price rehabilitated units out of the low-rent market.[43]

8) In the future, when renewal becomes an accepted urban governmental activity, experiments should be made with:

   a) Flexible subsidies, so that federal contributions are increased if the reuse is low- or middle-income housing; and reduced if it is luxury housing.
   b) Requirements that the redeveloper construct or finance some relocation housing, especially if he proposes to redevelop the site with housing out of the price range of the present site residents.

Proposals for Relocation

If the purpose of urban renewal is to improve the living conditions of the present slum dwellers, relocation becomes one of the most important, if not the most important, phases of the renewal process. This principle suggests a number of proposals for procedural change:

1) The relocation plan should take priority over the renewal phases of the total plan, and no renewal plan should be approved by federal or local agencies until a proper relocation plan has been developed.

---

[43] Current rehabilitation frequently takes low-rent apartments and transforms them into dwelling units that fit the demands, tastes, and pocketbooks of middle- and upper-class people, but not those of their present residents.

2) This relocation plan should be based on a thorough knowledge of the project area residents, so that the plan fits their demands and needs and so that officials have some understanding of the consequences of their actions before they put the plan into effect. The federal agency ought to re-evaluate its relation to the local agencies, raising its requirements for approval of the local relocation plan and relaxing its requirements for such phases as rent collection. The latter would make it possible for the local agency to be more sensitive to certain needs of the project area residents.

3) Any renewal plan which requires the clearance of an area and large-scale relocation should contain provisions for the rehabilitation of site structures if changes in market conditions suddenly reduce the amount of land required by the redeveloper.[44]

4) Local and federal agencies should provide interest-free or low-interest loans to relocatees who wish to buy new homes.

5) These agencies should provide similar loans to project area landlords whose present buildings provide decent, safe, and sanitary housing, to allow them to purchase new buildings in other areas or to rehabilitate such buildings and to make them available to project area residents.

6) Landlords with units eligible for relocation housing anywhere in the community should be encouraged to rent to relocatees, through such incentives as rehabilitation loans, subsidies for redecorating, and the like.

7) When project area rents have been low, so that residents' housing costs are raised sharply as a result of relocation, the federal and local agencies should set up a rent moratorium to allow relocatees to save some money for future rentals. The length of this moratorium should be based on the gap between project area and relocation area rentals.

8) Liquidation funds in lieu of moving allowances

---

[44] For example, where the reuse is luxury housing, clearance of existing housing should be scheduled so that if the market for high-rent units suddenly shrinks, the remaining stock of existing housing can be rehabilitated for low- or middle-income tenants, or redeveloped for them if necessary.

should be provided to small store owners and other businessmen who will not be able to reopen their firms elsewhere. Other federal and local programs should be made available to provide occupational retraining and other vocational aids to those who want them.

9) Communication between the redevelopment agency and the residents should be set up so that:
- a) The amount of information given to site residents is maximized, and the development of rumors due to information vacuums is prevented.
- b) Officials are trained to understand the inevitably deprivatory nature of relocation for the residents, so that they have more insight into what relocation means to the residents, and can develop a more tolerant attitude towards their reactions of shock and protest.

10) The relocation staff should be strengthened by the addition of:
- a) Social workers who can provide aid to residents faced with additional problems resulting from relocation, and can make referrals to other city agencies that deal with such problems.[45]
- b) Real estate technicians who can develop a thorough inventory of the city's housing supply, and can also weed out unscrupulous landlords who are likely to exploit the relocatees.

11) In relocation projects that involve the destruction of a positive social system, experiments should be conducted to:
- a) Find ways of relocating together extended families living together in separate but adjacent households—provided they want to be moved en masse.
- b) Make it possible for important project area institutions and organizations to re-establish themselves in those neighborhoods which have received the majority of relocatees, or in central locations

---

[45] The relocation office in the West End has done some pioneering work in this respect. The relocation staff should also call on resource persons in those areas to which site residents are moving, and employ them to facilitate the adjustment of the relocatees in their new neighborhoods.

where they are accessible to scattered relocatees.
c) Develop group relocation methods to allow members of an ethnic group who want to stay together to move into an area as a group. This is especially important if there are neighborhoods with available relocation housing in which there are presently no members of that ethnic group.

12) Previous relocation projects suggest that most people relocate themselves, and only a small proportion are relocated by the agency. In the future, procedures should be revised on this basis. Then, the major functions of the relocation agency should be:
  a) To make sure that the supply of relocation housing is sufficient to give relocatees a maximal choice of decent, safe, and sanitary dwelling units at rents they are willing to pay and in neighborhoods in which they want to live.
  b) To provide information and other aids that will enable relocatees to evaluate these dwelling units, and to make the best housing choice in relation to their needs and wants.
  c) To offer relocation service to those who want to be moved by the agency.

Implications for the Future of Urban Renewal

Many of these proposals will increase the cost of relocation, which will in turn raise the cost of renewal. This is equitable, since project area residents should not be required to subsidize the process as they do presently. In time, the higher cost of renewal will become the accepted rate. Moreover, since redevelopers often stand to make considerable profit from their renewal operation, they should eventually be asked to bear part of this increased cost.[46]

[46]Thus, the redeveloper could be asked to include some proportion of relocation expenses in his costs, and pass them on to his tenants as their share of the renewal charges. Alternatively, the city could bear relocation costs initially, and require the redeveloper to repay part of them if his project shows more than an agreed upon reasonable profit. In either case, the lower the rentals of the redevelopment housing, the lower should be the share of relocation costs to be paid by the redeveloper.

Current renewal and relocation procedures have been discussed mainly in terms of the inequities being borne by the project area residents. However, these procedures can be shown to have undesirable consequences for renewal itself. For example, projects based on inadequate relocation plans simply push site residents into the next adjacent low-income area, and create overcrowding that leads to the formation of new slums. Thus, the city is saddled with additional problems, and new costs, which eventually overwhelm the apparent short-run benefits of the renewal project. Moreover, poorly handled relocation frequently results in political repercussions which can endanger the community's long-range renewal plans. Consequently, the critique and proposals suggested here have implications not only for the site residents, but for the future of urban renewal itself.[47]

Author's Note

This paper is based on the conclusions of an eight-month sociological community study which I made in the West End of Boston. During this period, I lived in the neighborhood as a participant-observer, and conducted formal and informal interviews with many West Enders, as well as with redevelopment officials. The study was conducted under the auspices of the Center for Community Studies, affiliated with the Department of Psychiatry, Harvard Medical School, and Massachusetts General Hospital. The Center is conducting a five-year research project, "Relocation and Mental Health: Adaptation Under Stress," under a grant from the National Institute of Mental Health. Drs. Erich Lindemann and Gerald Caplan are coprincipal investigators; Dr. March Fried is coordinator of research.

The field work for this article was carried out independently of the longer study, and the conclusions discussed here are therefore strictly the author's, and not necessarily those of the rest of the research staff. From a scientific standpoint,

---

[47] Many of the conclusions and recommendations described here were reached also by a thorough Philadelphia study, "Relocation in Philadelphia," Philadelphia Housing Association, November, 1958, which was published after this article had been written.

these conclusions are hypotheses and preliminary findings based on observational and interview evidence. Although the author talked with many West Enders, he probably had less contact with the poorest, least educated residents, who lived in the worst buildings in the area, than would be desirable from a research point of view. However, they are the least likely to talk to a middle-class researcher.

The five-year research project is measuring the effects of clearance and relocation on the people of the West End in a systematic manner, and should provide scientifically tested data on many of the observations presented here. It will also show to what extent these effects are beneficial or detrimental.

Mass Housing:
Social Research and Design

Brent C. Brolin and John Zeisel

Technically adequate mass housing is often socially inadequate. An important reason for many failures in large-scale modern design is that it does not fit the way people live. The designer, unable to intuit the needs of a group with which he is unfamiliar, often imposes his own values and needs on those for whom he builds. To prevent this, he must be able to identify social patterns necessary to the group and incorporate them into his plans. This paper, with its design solutions based on observations of behavior, will attempt to show one way in which social research can be used to help the architect.

Since the beginning of the Industrial Revolution, mass housing has been designed *for* the worker, not *by* the worker, and has had a dehumanizing and degrading effect in imposing new ways of life on its tenants. This is in sharp contrast to unplanned housing—built by the inhabitants themselves, changing over a period of time, and serving social functions not apparent to architects who are not of that culture. Urban redevelopment and new town programs are often based on what the designer considers adequate for himself. Often when he consciously tries to build for those different from himself, he unconsciously imposes his own values.

Modern architecture asserted the principle of functional design, but the architect's concept of function has usually been limited to *manifest* functions: kitchens for cooking,

Reprinted by permission from *Architectural Forum*, July-August, 1968, copyright by Whitney Publications.

stores for buying, streets for driving. He does not usually take into account the *latent* functions of behavior required for social and psychological stability in cultures or subcultures other than his own: for example, driving a car as a means of demonstrating a certain status as well as a means of transportation.

In building for different cultures or subcultures, architects have introduced—along with modern sanitary standards—middle-class assumptions of privacy, comfort, forms of sociability and community living. Western middle-class norms, as we can see, have often proved inappropriate.

The Brazilian government built apartment buildings in Pedregulhos for the inhabitants of the shantytown around Rio de Janiero and then destroyed their primitive shacks. Several months later, the tenants of the project rebuilt their shacks and moved back.

A modern low-income community was built by the Hungarian government in Budapest for families from a physically deteriorated district in the city. Many of these people sold their new apartments to middle-class families from the old district and, exchanging apartments, moved back to their old but familiar physical slum.

Riots in Kingston, Jamaica in the summer of 1966 reportedly "were partly prompted by resistance to public housing proposed to replace familiar 'slums.' "

Although the cause of these violent reactions is complex and demands investigation, the situation is partly encouraged by socially inadequate, though technically adequate, mass housing.

Unfamiliar Cultures

When a person moves from the country or from a small urban neighborhood into urban mass housing, one way of life is cut off for him and another begins. His new environment is often incompatible or hostile to his way of life. When traditional living patterns are denied him it is always with the implication that they are wrong or inappropriate, and that he must now imitate the new way of life around him.

But if left to his own choice, the urban migrant often seeks to retain his cultural identity.

It is easy to document the many socially exclusive towns which grew up across the country in the 19th century; it is more difficult to find examples of the successful integration of different cultures within a single city. The assimilation of ethnic groups was a challenge that the American city met with neither grace nor efficiency. In addition, cultural integration may not be felt possible, or desirable, by all minority groups. Instead of asking if America has lost its power of integration, we should ask whether America ever had that power.

For moral as well as for practical reasons, it is vitally important to respect the different customs of groups within our own society, and within urbanizing societies throughout the world. The social parameters of housing are as important as the legal, economic, and physical. The architect and planner need detailed information about the living patterns of people who are of different cultures or subcultures. This information about the functional requirements of urban subcultures, or rural cultures in transition to urban life, can be provided by analyzing the *latent social structure* and living patterns as they relate to the architectural environment. The architect must then be able to translate this information into a form useful in three-dimensional planning.

Observations

To determine what information about social behavior is useful to the designer we have drawn freely from Herbert Gans' *The Urban Villagers*,* an insightful description of working-class Italian life in the West End of Boston. This group was chosen for our study because of the availability of substantial information. Our method could be applied to any group—ethnic, class, age, institutional. Although it was not originally intended to be used by planners, we have put part of Gans' material into guidelines for the designer. From these guidelines we have designed housing which might have

*Included as the previous article in this collection.—J.G.

replaced the physically substandard housing in the neighborhood Gans studied without destroying the healthy, low-income community.

The West End has since been torn down by urban renewal. Thus, although we had considerable information about people's behavior, we had little knowledge of their surroundings. To demonstrate the method of using specific research for design, and to place our study in a relevant physical context, we chose an existing site in the North End of Boston. This area is physically, ethnically, and demographically similar to the old West End.

From Gans' report, which followed his living in the West End and studying it over a period of months, we chose statements about the social behavior of the inhabitants. Since these observations were not intended to indicate how the architect should adapt his designs, we translated them into specific requirements for the architect to meet. Some samples of the original observations, and their translation into architectural requirements, follow:

Observation: "Food preparation serves as an example of the woman's skill as a housewife and mother. When company is present, it enables her to display her skills to relatives and peers." *Requirement:* Area for cooking visible to where women visitors gather.

Observation: ". . . the normal tendency is for men and women to split up, the men in one room and the women in another." *Requirement:* Privacy between men's and women's social gathering areas.

Observation: "While the teenage groups were sexually segregated, girls' groups in the West End met near the corners where the boys hung out." *Requirement:* Adolescent girls' areas visible to boys' areas.

We then grouped together the requirements that referred to behavior taking place in the same physical area: apartments, groups of apartments, areas of informal social activity, and commercial areas. The architectural design followed from this. Therefore, on each of the drawings, there is a set of observations as well as the requirements met by the drawing.

Relevance of Observations

Since Gans did not aim at a specifically architectural orientation, this pilot study and the resulting drawings are not able to cover all aspects of design related living patterns. Furthermore, it is not quite clear what an "architectural orientation" is. At first we picked those comments we felt could help the architect to meet the social needs of that community. We began with over 200 observations of behavior, most of which described an activity taking place in a physical setting. Many of these, although telling us how the West Enders behaved, were not necessarily helpful to the architect: "Girls from about age ten are expected to help with the household tasks . . . . Adolescents and young adults are frequent movie-goers."

Whether or not young girls help around the house does not tell us about the preferred apartment layout or the size of rooms. Nor does the second observation, as it stands, guide the architect's work; he knows no better whether the movie theater should be in the center of the area or its outskirts, or whether the movies downtown are just as good. He must know who else is involved in movie-going. If he knew, for instance, that when going to the movies, teenagers were seen by other young people from the neighborhood—and avoided adults—he would know that the social significance of this activity is related to its physical location in the area. The theater should be visible to teenagers doing other things and not be easily visible from areas of adult activity.

Another type of observation tells us more about physical location: "The peer group meets regularly in the kitchens and living rooms of innumerable West End apartments." But here, too, we do not know what factors, physical or otherwise, make these rooms more desirable than others. Further, we do not know which peer groups meet regularly in the kitchens and living rooms.

In sum, the observations we found to be useful to the architect possessed the following attributes: 1) *a primary actor and his activity;* 2) *the significant others in the situation;*

Mass Housing: Social Research and Design

and 3) *the relationship between the primary actor and the significant others.* This relationship is the means of including or excluding the significant others from the realm of the primary actor.

In the example above, the movie-going teenagers are the actors, the significant others are nonmovie-going teenagers and adults. The relationship in the teenagers' case is visual and auditory connection, and in the adults' case, visual and auditory separation. The field observer, by asking: *"Who is doing what, including or excluding whom?"* will most likely encompass all of the necessary sociological components in his observations.

Furthermore, in spelling out the relationship—the means of inclusion or exclusion—we get the "requirement" to be fulfilled by the new physical form. This is the link between social behavior and physical form, by which we can specify how an area in which a given activity takes place should be connected to or separated from another area. From the sample list of observations and requirements:

Area for cooking *visible* to where women visitors gather.

Privacy between men's and women's social gathering areas.

Adolescent girls' areas *visible* to boys' areas.

These requirements indicate the social connection that the designer can either break or allow to exist. If we see the design process in large part as putting up or leaving out different kinds of barriers, by defining where these walls are socially desirable, we can help the designer meet people's needs.

The Existing Environment

The requirements are the design implications of social behavior. We must also see the social implications of the existing physical environment that is to be replaced. Although a simple description is necessary—apartment layouts, relationship among spaces, size of rooms, where the stores are, where the playground is—this is not sufficient. Two things must be established: 1) Is the existing physical form compatible with the prevalent social patterns? and 2) What patterns does the physical form make difficult or easy?

Some indicators of *incompatibility* between the existing physical form and social needs are: changes made in the original form—windows painted black, doors nailed shut, ramps built over stairs: aspects of the environment totally unused—playgrounds, balconies, park benches; and aspects falsely used—children playing in the street instead of a nearby park, dinner cooked on the fire escape, the car parked in the living room.

Indicators of *compatibility*, on the other hand, will be the absence of these changes in form or use, as well as little destruction, much use, relatively low turnover, and conscious efforts at beautification by the inhabitants.

Avoiding Mistakes

To find out what patterns the physical form allows, we translate an observation of the existing physical environment into the requirement it seems to fulfill. If that aspect is compatible, the requirement is one to be fulfilled by new designs, while the requirements reflected in incompatible form are clearly to be avoided. By taking into account both the social implications of the environment and the indicators of conflict, we can avoid present mistakes.

The field observer could apply the method we have described in the following ways: 1) *Looking at behavior*. He notices repeatedly that boys play ball in the street. Looking for the significant others in the situation, he finds that girls of the same age often sit around watching the boys, while adults stop to look and comment. The primary actors—the boys—are related visually to two groups of significant others —the girls and the adults. This complete observation is translated into the requirement: boys' play areas should be visibly connected to where the girls hang out and to where adults are. If other observations indicate a similar requirement, the designer might build a playground near the shopping area or subway station, as well as near the stoops where young girls get together. 2) *Looking at the environment*. A playground with basketball courts is far from both the busy life of the street and from the door stoops and shops where the teenage girls hang out. By asking, "Who can play in the playground, including or excluding whom?" we translate this simple observation into the social pattern it allows: teenagers, mostly male, can play basketball there. While other boys, both younger and older, may be included, both adults and girls of the same age are excluded. Since this playground is rarely used by anyone, it is evident that we should avoid the separation of the boys' play area from that of the girls' and from "where the [adult] action is." More simply, we come up with the previous requirement: The boys' play area should be visibly connected to these other places.

This observation alone would, of course, not be enough to make a final judgment. Both repeated observations and the use of other techniques—surveying attitudes, informal interviewing, counting how often people do things—are necessary to validate findings.

Appropriateness of the Method

Although it should be augmented with survey techniques, this observational method is very different in content. Most people will answer questions about a proposed plan in terms of what they have experienced or what they want. When the respondent is a potential buyer in a housing market, it is important to know his preferences. But this often has little to do with the latent functions of behavior that are integral to the social stability of a group. We therefore distinguish these conscious wants from unconscious needs.

This approach and method is appropriate for both new and redeveloped urban areas. It may be applied to people already living in cities and to rural in-migrants. Its value in the last case should be clear. When people move from the country to the city or from primitive to more modern housing, their patterns of living undergo strain. Taking these patterns into account when planning new housing will not limit behavior, but, by accommodating familiar life styles and providing alternatives, it will make the transition easier for them.

In urban redevelopment it has been argued that, when

the architect tries to reinforce the social structure, he reinforces the pathology of the slum. The distinction between a physical and a social slum must be clarified. A physical slum refers to an area with a large percentage of substandard housing. A social slum, on the other hand, might be characterized by a loosely connected social structure, anomic inhabitants and a social pathology reflected in violent crime, suicide, drug addiction, and other deviant behavior. Often these two go together, but often they do not. City planners, as they did in the West End, often tear down a physical slum and at the same time tear apart a healthy social climate in which social pathologies are relatively low and people take an active part and interest in the community. Applying the approach of this paper may not enable the architect to revive this healthy social atmosphere, but it may help him to avoid contributing to its decline and to the eventual development of social as well as physical slums.

We must be aware that the designer has only limited control over the social lives of the people in his buildings. He can neither limit people's social behavior nor force them to change by building a socially inhibiting environment. Their living patterns will stay the same or change regardless of the physical environment in which they live. If the designer does try to limit behavior when change is imminent, or to force change when the inhabitants neither want it or are ready for it, he can cause potentially harmful conflicts. This conflict can have several consequences: the physical environment may be altered, misused, or not used at all, and the people may suffer social and psychological stress. To stop this we would have the designer understand the social behavior of those who opt to live in his buildings, and try to avoid putting up barriers to their way of life in the physical environment.

Design Freedom

The results of this type of research define a minimum set of social behavior patterns which the physical structure should not prohibit. The means that one designer uses to achieve this end as well as the number of nonconflicting alternative he offers is in no way limited. For example, to separate the cooking area from the social area we use a folding partition. This allows the alternative of connecting these areas. Many different walls, both more stationary and more adaptable, could meet the same requirement.

The social parameters specified by these requirements are ideals; it is difficult to meet them all equally well. One essential next step is to determine the hierarchy of requirements, so that there is a basis for making choices where conflict occurs among the requirements. We must, therefore, determine the relative importance of the behavior's latent function to the social stability of the group. We might also define the architectural means for separating or connecting the activities related in the requirements.

In applying this research-design method we must consider that the living patterns of those for whom we design will eventually change. But any change will have its starting point in existing social patterns. If the Italian community of Gans' research becomes more middle-class, it will still retain many of its present social customs. In any case, to design now in a way that we know will not fit existing life styles is to make the hypothetical misfit of the future a reality of the present.

Neighborhood Concepts in Sociological Perspective

Dr. Suzanne Keller

Introduction

Both in physical planning and in sociology the term neighborhood has been widely, variously, and often inconsistently, used. At times it seems to refer to an area having certain physical properties, at times to a set of human activities or relationships, and then again to an area in which such activities or relationships may, but need not, occur. C. H. Cooley, the American social theorist, considered the neighborhood, along with the family and playmates, to be a primary group, and many physical planners similarly confound the spatial and the social dimensions of neighboring. Before one can properly assess the current state of knowledge of neighborhoods in modern urban settings, therefore, one must first clarify the various conceptions and assumptions contained within that ambiguous term.

The existing confusion is the result of at least three factors:
1) conceptual ambiguity, particularly the failure to distinguish between three essential, yet separate, elements: that of the neighbor as a special role and relationship, of neighboring, as a set of socially defined activities, and of neighborhood, as a delimited area in which neighboring and other activities involving neighbors may occur;
2) contradictory evidence based on research whose ambiguous assumptions have been incorporated into

Reprinted by permission from *Ekistics*, Vol. 22, July, 1966, copyright by The Athens Center of Ekistics.

ambiguous research tools. So we are told, for example, that there is little sense of neighborhood in community X because few poeple indicated that they were friends with their neighbors. But even the most impeccable research findings regarding friendly ties among neighbors cannot supply the needed information on *neighborly* ties among neighbors if these two are, as appears to be the case, distinct relationships. If most neighborly relations are in fact not relations of friendship, then to ask only about those that are makes us miss the large majority that are not. In addition, without having clearly defined the phenomenon, it is next to impossible to distinguish its essential from its accidental aspects and so to discover genuine rather than spurious empirical variations in neighboring activities and relationships. Moreover, ignoring the conceptual distinction between friend and neighbor has led to unwarranted inferences about the alienation of modern urban man and to unwarranted idealization of the friendly neighbors in small towns and peasant villages. The failure of planners to recreate such "friendly" neighborhoods may thus be due less to any professional shortcomings than to their being ill-advised as to the conditions making for friendship and for neighborliness in village and city;

3) the problem of rapid social change which upset the traditional balance between neighbors, neighboring, and neighborhoods, and leaves in its wake a residue of incoherent fragments of such neighborhoods. When relatively compact and easily identified sub-areas of small towns and stable cities disintegrated under the impact of the industrial-urban tidal wave, often only the broken bits of such neighborhoods remained. Studies of these partial neighborhoods then showed them to be not only areas of variable and vague boundaries but also areas of incoherent sets of activities and relationships. Instead of more or less unified social and spatial entities there emerged sprawling, seemingly formless, rapidly changing aggregates, within which the mobile ur-

ban multitude was forging the personal and social relations of its period. This posed great difficulties to a study of the problem. Even in the most distinctive natural areas of cities (with homogeneous populations, a historic identity, strong social traditions, and considerable stability), a continual back and forth movement of people and goods, responding to the ceaseless play of diverse social and cultural forces, transforms these neighborhoods into hybrid creatures between past and future. In the absence of clearly defined concepts it is not even possible to form correct impressions of these events, not to speak of recording and measuring them precisely. . . .

Methods for the Study of Neighboring and Neighborhoods

Our understanding of any phenomenon depends on the nature and the interpretation of available evidence. Interpretation consists of logically connected inferences drawn from observed data whose quality and utility is in turn dependent on the sources of information and the techniques used to obtain it. Two of the chief sources of information on neighboring and neighborhoods are knowledgeable or representative samples of informants and collected (tabulated or mapped) statistics. The techniques used to tap these sources of information have been observation and informal recording of neighborhood life as in participant observation of local communities, the direct asking of questions in formal interview settings as in sample surveys, and the inferring of neighboring activities and relationships from specially computed rates of collective characteristics and behavior. Most investigators have been interested in the following two problems: 1) how much neighboring exists in a given area or among a given group, and 2) do neighborhoods exist and function as distinct spatial entities within larger communities?

The Extent of Neighboring

In general, studies of this aspect are based on interview and questionnaire data. People are asked to indicate whom they see, know, talk to, visit, or help within a given area, at which times, and for what reasons. They may be asked a series of simple, unstructured questions to which they may give their "free" associations, or the questions may be precisely structured and demand fairly categorical answers, which may be scaled. Thus Fava used Wallin's neighboring scale in studying the propensity for neighboring in socially similar, ecologically dissimilar, samples of residents, and Caplow and his coworkers applied a scale of Neighboring Intensity in their San Juan study; (Fava, in Dobriner, 1958, pp. 123-131; Caplow et al., 1964, p. 69; Bott, 1957, p. 49, proposes tracing through networks of social relationships in urban areas rather than merely sampling proportions).

Because of inadequate conceptualization of the phenomenon, many existing studies, while interesting and suggestive, fail to add up to a balanced, comprehensive account in the aggregate. The absence of a systematic framework leads this investigator to ask only about visiting, that one mainly about exchange of help, and a third about friendly sentiments among neighbors, and thus yields uneven, piecemeal information. Not surprisingly, the results of these divergent and diversified inquiries are often not easy to interpret.

Investigations of the Existence of Neighborhoods

To locate distinct neighborhoods, our investigators used two main methods based on objective and on subjective indicators. In the first the investigator identifies and locates physically distinct neighborhoods on the basis of statistical and census data, physical reconnaissance of the area, and information supplied by selected informants especially knowledgeable about the area. For example, Glass, in her pioneering efforts, plotted the distributions of selected indicators of such area characteristics as net population densities, ages and conditions of dwellings, ethnic and religious composition of the populations, occupational distributions, and figures on school attendance, and then noted where these overlapped. By tracing boundaries around these areas of concentrated and overlapping distributions, 26 potential neighborhoods were identified (Glass, 1948). More recently, a study in West Philadelphia, seeking to locate sub-areas for more intensive analysis, asked 21 well-informed local persons to "name the areas which they thought of as neighborhoods"; newspapers, historical accounts, and organizational records provided supplementary information, and eventually yielded 16 identifiable areas ranging in population from 10,000 to over 40,000 persons (Herman, 1964).

Another method draws on information about where people in a given area shop, work, and play, and the spatial distribution of these phenomena then provide the basis for the tracing of boundaries around them. For example, in early investigations of village neighborhoods, areas were marked off according to the uses of village centers; usually this left some marginal areas unaccounted for and therefore unclassifiable. Instead of asking adults where they shop or work, one may ask school children attending particular schools where their parents go for particular services and then plot their answers in relation to their individual residences. A variant of this technique is to obtain the addresses of clients, members, or customers, from village stores, schools, weekly newspapers, and churches, and then plot these service areas to see whether and where they overlap (Warren, 1963, p. 24).

A second method is to ask respondents themselves to indicate the boundaries and extent of their neighborhoods (Riemer, 1951). Often this method is used in conjunction with the first and serves as a check on its utility (Herman, 1964; McGough, 1964).

Assessments of the Functioning of Neighborhoods

Even the most ardent partisans of the neighborhood as a purely spatial phenomenon would agree that the location of geographically demarcated areas is as yet no proof of the existence of actual neighborhoods. Some additional information is usually considered necessary to ascertain whether the residents in such physically distinct areas perceive these areas as distinct social and symbolic units. Thus, Glass, having identified 26 distinct territorial groupings, then went on to consider whether these also exhibited a given concentration of social activities. This involved a comparison of the geographic units with the "catchment areas" of the following facilities and services for degree of boundary coincidences: the catchment area (i.e., the spatial distribution of members) of all elementary and secondary schools, of Youth and Adult Clubs, of Post Offices, and of greengrocers and shops for sugar registration (Glass, 1948).

In an intensive study of three West Philadelphia sub-areas previously identified as possessing some neighborhood potential, the following dimensions were studied further to see whether this potential was being realized: identifiability of the area, identification with the area, presence of friends and relatives within the area, use of local stores, churches, and recreational facilities, attitudes toward the area, and presence of organized local groups for the handling of local problems (Herman, 1964). Another investigator participating in this board inquiry into local neighborhood life selected 12 sub-areas by means of social area analysis, a technique used to locate distinctive sub-areas of larger census tracts, and asked 100 randomly selected respondents in each of these to identify the sub-area by name and boundaries and to evaluate the area as a place to live (McGough, 1964). This study, in not pre-selecting its neighborhoods, has an advantage over those that do, in not inadvertently concentrating on areas of known neighborhood potential. As a result, however, this as well as the study by Glass which it resembles in some respects, found very little overlap between potential neighborhoods and actual neighborhood identity, use, and participation. (See also Bell, in Sussman, 1959, pp. 61-92).

A knowledge of the predominant social character of an area, as tapped by various indices of living conditions, residential stability, and population characteristics, may be used as clues to its neighborhood potential. If we know, for example, that a given area has a high concentration of home owners of particular income and educational levels in skilled manual occupations, we might estimate their neighboring activities to be low on the basis of what we generally know about neighboring in such groups. Or, the presence of certain facilities may reveal the sort of population we are dealing with. Pawnshops or second-hand stores may signal the presence of low income groups; selected churches and schools, that of high income ones. In fact, Baltzell suggests the presence of certain schools and churches as a convenient way to trace the neighborhood migrations of fashionable society and thereby the rise and decline of fashionable upper-class neighborhoods (Baltzell, 1958, pp. 182, 194).

Information about boundaries, use of facilities, or relations among neighbors do not tell us how adequate, suitable, or desirable such local areas are. For this, objective standards or yardsticks are required. Since such standards are lacking, relative comparisons and subjective judgments are most frequently used, though this whole matter has been least systematically studied so far. Neither relative comparisons, such as ranking areas according to the presence of certain facilities or activities in relation to one another, nor unstandardized subjective judgments permit us to make valid generalizations (Glass, 1948, pp. 41 ff.). The two questions most frequently used to assess subjective neighborhood satisfaction are: 1) Do you consider this neighborhood of yours a good place to live? and 2) Do you intend to remain in this neighborhood permanently? (Caplow et al., 1964, p. 196; Dennis, 1963, p. 8). The answers to these questions, whose precise meaning is often vague, are then correlated with other characteristics of the respondents, the area, or both. Sometimes, instead of a single question, several questions are used and an index is then constructed (note the Improvement Index, Caplow et al., 1964, p. 161). Or, a more refined attitude scale with several ratings for each item may be used (Wilson in Chapin and Weiss, pp. 359-399). Individuals may also be asked to describe their ideal neighborhood or to choose among several photographs of neighborhoods the one they prefer, and so on (*Ibid.*). A series of "games" has been devised to probe people's wishes and attitudes regarding neighborhood facilities and services, as when respondents are given fixed sums of money and asked to imagine what facilities and settings they would choose for a house they had won, or to select among a series of density figures and commuting patterns the ones that most suit them

(*Ibid.*, p. 387). In analyzing how they "spend" the money at their disposal, their values and preferences may thus be ascertained.

Some Problems in the Empirical Study of Neighborhoods and Neighboring

Boundaries: Trying to locate neighborhoods visa identification of boundaries founders on the fact that the most clearcut physical and symbolic boundaries go hand-in-hand with clear cut neighborhoods, of which the boundaries themselves are only indicators. Where neither tradition nor relative isolation help forge precise neighborhood boundaries, accurate boundaries apparently cannot be drawn. Thus Riemer points to the danger of studying a delimited and contiguous "patch of the urban fabric and recording activities sustained in such areas" since thereby, important social activities that do not take place in these areas remain hidden and are treated as nonexistent (Riemer, 1950, p. 197).

Sampling: Most studies of neighborhood activities and use of local facilities are based on interviews with housewives who supposedly engage in more neighboring and are more involved with local neighborhood activities. This is not, however, always kept in mind when generalizing from their answers to "families" or "the working class" or the "urban dweller". Even if these housewives are asked about their children's neighboring activities they may not be able to supply the correct information. Moreover, a certain bias is bound to be introduced when interviews concentrate on functioning households, thus excluding the more transient residents, the unmarried, the highly mobile, and others who may not be available for home interviews.

Questionnaire design: It is well known that the nature of the questions asked may determine the answers given. Frequently, a problem may have little saliency for individuals and yet elicit dutiful responses to direct questions. In the West Philadelphia study, for example, when people were asked what they considered to be the biggest problem in the area, one-third could think of none. These same respondents, however, when asked sepcific questions about particular problems involving housing, noise, crime, unemployment, and so on, were able to express their concern about these problems (Herman, 1964, pp. 24, 25; McGough, 1964, p. 64). Here as in the next question, some forcing of answers is probably unavoidable by the very structure of the questions. When urban residents in San Juan are asked to indicate their three best friends among their neighbors what do positive answers really mean here? Aside from not knowing what each respondent has in mind when he thinks of his "best" friend, the question somehow presupposes that there will be such friendships among neighbors. Similarly, if housewives are asked whether their husband's "three closest recreational friends" are the same as their own, will any of them say that they or their husbands have no close friends, or only one, or will they give the answers they feel are expected of them? (Caplow et al., 1964, Interview Schedule). The last two questions, drawn from one of the most sophisticated studies in this entire field, illustrates the difficulty of designing proper questions. The same holds true for other aspects of the study design such as sampling, interviewing, index formation, and scale construction—all useful if carefully designed, pretested, and applied but of dubious value if they are not.

Of the hundreds of studies consulted for this analysis not one is sufficiently comprehensive in scope, design, or locale, to serve as an absolutely reliable source of data or model of procedure. Most studies, confined to small areas of local communities or to limited samples, emphasize only a few of the relevant dimensions of this complex subject. As previously indicated, there is considerable ambiguity in the terms themselves and this conceptual confusion is often matched by confusing research evidence based on arbitrary definition of terms, inadequate samples, and unreliable instruments. Thus, by confounding the distinction between neighbor and friend, studies often report less neighboring in cities than would be shown to exist were other definitions of neighboring used. Nor is the meaning of replies always fully explored. If people are asked whether they like their neighborhood, they usually say yes, but without knowing where they draw the

Neighborhood Concepts in Sociological Perspective

boundary lines or which aspect of the neighborhood they may be thinking of—the people near them, the shops and cinemas, access to the center, or the reputation of the area as a smart place—it is virtually impossible to make sense of their answers and thereby to accumulate valid and reliable knowledge.

If we do not as yet have scientifically valid knowledge of the formation and functioning of neighborhoods it is probably due to the conceptual difficulties involved in designing studies to yield such knowledge. To help develop such designs it is necessary to collect and classify the existing evidence based on personal impressions and fragments of existing studies. By thus piecing together, as this report tries to do, the many varied bits of evidence gathered in as many varied ways, a fairly consistent set of relevant dimensions may be specified. This method, tedious, time-consuming, and cumbersome though it be, is useful as preliminary approach to the problem to help guide more systematic research efforts in the future.

And in truth it is astonishing that these hundreds of studies of respondents in different contexts answering, perhaps unreliably, lists of unsystematic questions, have managed to yield as consistent findings as they do regarding, for example, rural and urban differences in neighboring, the role of physical design in neighboring, and the like. Of course, their consistency and agreement is in part a function of the investigator's demands, since facts rarely tell their own story. However, armed with a few concepts, primitive and preliminary though they be, the exploration of existing data provides at least a reasonable beginning, a reasonable approximation of what we know and do not know about the role of neighboring and neighborhoods in the cities and towns of our era. . . .

Evidence on Neighborhoods

Where neighborhoods are clearly distinguishable by their geographic boundaries or by their distinctive ethnic or social characteristics, there their identification presents no problem. However, where, as is true in rapidly changing urban areas, neither geography nor culture presents a reliable guide, how can one know whether one is dealing with a neighborhood or not? Three separate alternative ways have been utilized:

1) to see how the people themselves identify an area,
2) to see how a given group uses the facilities in an area, and
3) to assess how people feel about an area.

These three dimensions—the cognitive, utilitarian, and affective—overlap primarily in the geographically or physically well-delimited areas that are clearly marked off from others by some physical barrier—be it distance, a highway, a ring road, an open space, or a railroad track—or in the closed milieus of certain ethnic, occupational, or social status enclaves. As these are rare in changing urban areas it is extremely difficult to locate coherent neighborhoods in them. And since there is little consistent overlap between these three dimensions the question arises as to which one or what combination of them to use as a yardstick.

The extent of neighboring in an area would seem to be of little help here, since not all people rely on neighbors and if they do they have contacts with very few of them. If neighborhoods were to be defined by people's attachments to neighbors, the areas delimited thereby would be too small and variable to provide either general standards or areas sufficiently large for systematic planning purposes. Moreover, person-to-person neighboring is at best only a partial datum. People may not engage in neighboring and yet make use of local areas in other ways. Most investigators and planners would therefore implicitly include a wider area in their conception of neighborhood. But how wide? And if it is possible to have neighborhoods in which little or no person-to-person neighboring occurs then how are these neighborhoods to be demarcated?

Neither subjectively identified boundaries, concentrated use of area facilities, neighborly relations, nor sentiments permit us to locate and classify distinctive urban neighborhoods. The most distinctive urban neighborhoods today are either poor and relatively isolated or extremely wealthy and exclusive so as to be equally isolated from the mainstream of urban life. The lack of overlap between neighboring, use of facilities, and social attachments means that these cannot be used as indices for consistently subdividing a larger urban area satisfactorily from both the physical and the social point of view.

On the basis of the admittedly sparse data on how people use given local areas, where they draw boundary lines, and whether they are attached to a local area, we can only conclude, while pleading for more and more systematic data, that the local area is no longer (or perhaps not as yet) of primary importance. With the exception of shopping—and the daily, grocery store variety at that—and perhaps of primary schools (but this varies according to income and other values), there are very few facilities that must be located close to home for everyone. And as regards neighborhood attachments, some urban residents are strongly involved, others only minimally. At best this is a subjective phenomenon greatly dependent on perceived and actual alternatives for friends, facilities, and dependency on a wider urban area. The economically better off are more mobile and less tied to their neighborhoods than the poorer urban residents but even here personality factors may make some men urban in orientation despite limited means. Expanded or narrow local horizons seem very much dependent on opportunities for mobility and on personal selectivity. Thus, though physical neighborhoods may be identified, social change in the family, work, and mass entertainments and amusements have displaced these from their leading positions as providers of information, identity, and social relations.

Concentration on the local area, no matter how imprecisely defined, seems to be most strongly correlated with a lack of alternatives, as when town centers are too distant, too costly or not appealing due to unfamiliarity or ignorance, and with isolation due either to local self-sufficiency or to strong ideological and social pressures. That is, where a solidary local network of close economic, cultural, social, and physical ties already exists, there local loyalties and activities will be strong. This does not, however, mean that the provision of local services will by themselves stimulate the desired local loyalties and sentiments in areas lacking the social and historic preconditions for such solidarity.

Today, it seems that local self-sufficiency and self-reliance are everywhere diminishing. Even remote villages are linked to the urban-industrial world via mass transport and mass media of communication, local branches of national associations, and personal use of urban centers for amusement or learning. The utility of the neighborhood conception has in consequence been re-examined by many planners who increasingly find it wanting. Before going on to discuss the implications of the sociological evidence here reviewed, a brief summary of the main conclusions is in order.

Conclusion

Two main questions have guided this inquiry:
1) According to existing evidence, how much and what kinds of neighboring occur in different types of settlements and what factors account for the patterns found? and
2) What is the evidence for the existence of neighborhoods in modern urban settings?

To answer the first question we had to consider the varying definitions of the role of neighbor, for it is this role that helps clarify the meaning of manifest neighboring activities. Despite wide variations in practice, in principle, this role assigns to neighbors a place intermediate between friends and relatives as regards their duties toward and feelings about one another. Neighbors are expected to assist each other during emergencies, to be sociable in a delimited way, and to do their part in maintaining common standards of conduct and physical upkeep in a given space.

Neighboring activities, more diffuse and difficult to grasp in their complex entirety, may be analyzed according to several different dimensions, each of them capable of independent variation. These are, the frequency of neighboring, its priority, intensity, extent, formality, locale, and the occasions for it. These were found to vary by setting, by group and class affiliations, and by personal inclinations. Neighboring activities and relationships are more fully integrated with social and economic life in small towns and villages or in special cultural and occupational enclaves in cities than in big urban centers, where friends tend to replace neighbors as sources of assistance and sociability. As individuals and groups become more self-sufficient and as the capacity of local institutions to meet current crises wanes, the need for neighborly assistance diminishes. Fewer crises, more alternatives for dealing with them, increasing individuality and selectivity, and more mobility and fluidity, all make neighboring less compulsory and also more variable.

Traditions of place and of social class seem to exert a general determinative influence on patterns of neighboring within which personal characteristics and physical design play their particular parts. The rise of new values and institutions, the shift from an extended to a conjugal, companionate family system, and the availability of alternative sources of amusement and employment, also change the content and meaning of neighboring. It is not so much a decline in interpersonal neighboring that we observe here as a change in the organization of life itself accompanied by new values, priorities, and preferences.

Neighboring, in dynamic urban areas, is no longer part of a tight network of interdependent activities and obligations concentrated within a small physical and social space, but simply one more segmentalized activity. Only the most isolated, poorest, most immobile segments of the population continue to rely on the local area and its inhabitants—though not even they do so exclusively, taking for granted a degree of choice and change that would have been inconceivable in a less dynamic era.

The consequences of spatial mobility on neighboring have often been observed though not always correctly assessed. The immediate rise in observed sociability following a move to certain suburbs or housing estates led to certain hasty and premature conclusions about the favorable effects of suburbs or better houses as such. But while such increased sociability among newcomers accompanies the early period of adjustment to a strange environment, it is by no means a permanent feature of their lives. Neighbors do turn to one another for assistance and fellowship during a period of stress and strangeness difficult for all, but once things get settled and familiar again, individuals become more selective in their neighboring and specialized in their interests. This is true both for working-class and middle-class groups, for individuals who came from solidary areas high in traditional neighboring as well as for those who have moved from areas where more segmentalized neighbor relations prevailed.

In all of this, the role of age, personal temperament, and individual taste must not be neglected, but neither are these among the primary determinants of neighboring. It is true that children and adolescents may neighbor more or closer to home, or that extroverts may do so more than introverts, but these cannot be considered apart from the broader context shaped by social traditions and the dynamics of social change. Similarly for the design of houses and dwellings. Under certain social conditions of like-mindedness, common footpaths, shared utilities, or shared spaces may help promote pleasant social encounters. But if these common facilities are to be shared by mutually antagonistic groups then the common footpaths may well turn into uncommon warpaths. The mixing of different social groups is a complex and delicate matter requiring a great deal of skill not yet contained in any existing formula.

As regards the existence of neighborhoods, we confront a number of unsolved problems. Using the existence of boundaries or the use of local facilities as indicators works very well where boundary and functioning neighborhood are in fact joined, each being an expression of the existence of the other. A problem arises when we try to use these indicators as independent measures, as "proofs" of the presence of neighborhoods; or worse, when we try to use them as promoters of neighborhood formation. There we usually and perhaps necessarily, fail. For it appears that such phenomena as clear cut boundaries, concentrated use of local facilities, and strong local loyalties are only the expressions of neighborhood cohesion, not their causes. By identifying physical boundaries, therefore, we have not yet taken more than a faltering first step in the location of neighborhoods, even though most functioning neighborhoods usually have either natural or man-made boundaries.

Moreover, the very same forces that have altered and in part eroded neighborhood activities and relations have also eroded neighborhoods. "Where one resides", Merton once wrote, "is not necessarily where one lives", (Merton, 1957,

Neighborhood Concepts in Sociological Perspective

p. 393). And this is by and large true not merely for the small town to which Merton referred but for urban aggregates in general. Generally, those neighborhoods that are in fact neighborhoods in the traditional sense, that is, clearly marked by physical and social boundaries, are also somehow atypical in being isolated or outside the mainstream of urban life—economically, as in extremely wealthy or extremely poor districts, socially, as in slums or suburbs, and culturally, as in racial or immigrant ghettos. To duplicate only their surface configurations without duplicating the conditions which gave rise to them is as unfeasible as it would be ineffectual.

The boundaries recognized or demarcated by individuals themselves may facilitate their subjective orientation to their environment but can hardly serve as more than that, since they are usually much smaller than those of political precincts, religious parishes, or planning units, as well as quite variable, hence unreliable, as an objective basis for demarcating neighborhoods. Moreover, there is as yet no evidence that these subjective boundaries coincide either with special attachments to or concentrated use of local areas.

Satisfaction with one's local area is no better criterion for identifying the existence of separate neighborhoods. First, because people are not quick to admit dissatisfactions or to find fault with the particular neighborhoods they live in, and it is only by means of careful and explicit probing that their tendencies toward a blanket endorsement of existing conditions may be pierced to uncover more meaningful discriminations. Second, because, paradoxically, it is not difficult to obtain complaints if one makes an effort to do so, for if people are prodded they will readily catalogue the negative features of their neighborhoods which may in no way however alter their overall favorable assessment of them. This whole problem of the relation between subjective judgments and objective inadequacies of neighborhoods has been all too little explored. Finally, many people may actually be greatly attached to their neighborhoods and yet leave them. The young and ambitious, the highly status-conscious, and certain personality types are generally more critical and more mobile irrespective of the objective characteristics of their environment. But even older, more stable settled residents may not hesitate to move from neighborhoods they like in order to take advantages of better opportunities elsewhere. Thus, liking an area—at least in urban places—is not necessarily indicative of establishing permanent roots there. Local attachments are, of course, greater among long-term residents of a neighborhood, among "block" rather than "city" dwellers as one classification would have it, and among those satisfied with or resigned to their current social status. But in a dynamic urban setting, these groups, no matter how empirically prevalent, do not typify the inherent tendencies of the urban-industrial age with its pressures for movement and variety. This does not of course imply that their particular needs and problems should be ignored or overlooked but it does urge that they be considered in the proper perspective. The dynamic forces of urban-industrial society are not concentrated in them or realized through them, since isolation and immobility are, perhaps unjustly, considered peculiar anachronisms or undesirable, and if possible temporary, marks of deprivation. More typical of the realities of this century are those individuals and families seeking to find more space, better jobs, higher status or greater amenities, for whom local areas or neighborhoods are but stepping-stones—not necessarily devoid of sentimental value—in the pursuit of happiness. Perhaps future research will tell us that 20th century urban man had a utilitarian rather than a sentimental attitude to the areas in which he resided. Perhaps, today, sentiment is itself a specialized emotion attaching itself to selected points in a wider area—to a particular street, perhaps, or a favorite dwelling, or an ancient monument—but not to the entire sub-area in which one happens to live. Like urban man himself, ever in pursuit of actual or imagined opportunities, his emotions and sentiments are not fixed but travel along with him, staying where he stays and moving as he moves, in the varied course of his dynamic life.

Bibliography

Aalto, Alvar, "Feinde der Architektur", *Schoner Wohnen*, September 1965, p. 37.

Allen, Walter, "Secret City", *New Statesman*, February 26, 1965.

Alston, John C., *Cost of a Slum Area* (Wilberforce, Ohio: Wilberforce State College, 1948).

Anderson, Nels, "Diverse Perspectives of Community", *International Review of Community Development*, No. 7, 1961, pp. 15-33.

Angus, Anne, "Middle Class Cheshire", *New Society*, April 8, 1965, pp. 5-7.

Baltzell, Digby E., *Philadelphia Gentlemen* (Glencoe, Ill.: The Free Press, 1958).

Ban, John, "New Towns as Anti-ghettoes?", *New Society*, April 1, 1965.

Baranov, N.V. (chairman) (USSR), "Planning and Construction of New Towns", United Nations Symposium, *Ekistics*, Vol. 18, No. 108, Nov. 1964, pp. 283-288.

Bauer, Catherine, *Social Questions in Housing and Town Planning* (London: University of London Press, 1952).

Bell, Wendell, "Social Areas: Typology of Urban Neighborhoods", Marvin B. Sussman (ed.), *Cummunity Structure and Analysis* (New York, 1959, pp. 61-92).

Bell, Wendell, "Social Choice, Life Styles, and Suburban Residence", Dobriner (ed.), *The Suburban Community* (New York, 1958, pp. 225-247).

Bernard, Jessie, "An Instrument for the Measurement of Neighborhood with Experimental Applications", *Southwest Social Science Quarterly*, Vol. XVIII, Sept. 1937, pp. 145-158.

Bashers, James M., *Urban Social Structure* (New York: The Free Press of Glencoe, 1962).

Beyer, Glenn H., "Home Selection and Home Management", *Marriage and Family Living*, Vol. XVIII, No. 2, May 1955, pp. 143-153.

Beyer, Glenn H., *Housing: A Factual Analysis* (New York: McMillan Co., 1958).

Bohlke, Robert H., "Social Mobility, Stratification, Inconsistency and Middle Class Delinquency", *Social Problems*, Spring 1961, 8, No. 4, pp. 350-363.

Bott, Elizabeth, *Family and Social Network* (London: Tavistock Publications, 1957).

Bracey, H.E., *Neighbors, Subdivision Life in England and the U.S.* (Baton Rouge: Louisiana State University Press, 1964).

Brafoss, Erik, "Place for the Year 2000—Growth and Structural Changes in the Norwegian Economy", (Frondheim, 1962).

Camus, Albert, "A Writer's Notebook", *Encounter*, March 1965, pp. 25-26.

Caplow, Theodore; Stryker, Sheldon; Wallace, Samuel E., *The Urban Ambience* (Totowa, N.J.: The Bedminister Press, 1964).

Chapin, F. Stuart, Jr., and Weiss, Shirley F. (eds.), *Urban Growth Dynamics in a Regional Cluster of Cities* (New York: John Wiley, 1962) Ch. X: Newcomer Enculturation. Ch. XI. Liveability of the City.

Chombart de Lauwe, P.: *The Sociology of Housing: Research Methods and Future Perspectives* (Rotterdam: Conseil International du Bâtiment, 1959), pp. 1-23.

Cohen, Henry, "Social Surveys as Planning Instruments for Housing", R.K. Merton (ed.), *Journal of Social Issues*, 1951, VII, No. 1 & 2, pp. 35-46.

Cohen, Lillian, "Los Angeles Rooming House Kaleidoscope", *American Sociological Review*, Vol. 16, No. 3, June 1951, pp. 316-326.

Colborn, Fern M., *The Neighborhood and Urban Renewal* (New York: National Federation of Settlements and Neighborhood Centers, 1963).

Conference on Space, Science and Urban Life (Washington, D.C.: National Aeronautics and Space Administration, 1963).

"DA Projects Revisited—Eastwick, Philadelphia", *DA Review*, Oct. 1, 1965, p. 11.

Dean, John P.: "The Ghosts of Home Ownership", R.K. Merton (ed.), *Journal of Social Issues*, 1951, pp. 59-68.

Dennis, Norman: "Who needs Neighbors?", *New Society*, No. 43, July 25, 1963.

Deschamps, Fanny: "Parisiennes Décentralisées", *Elle*, 1965.

Deutsh, Karl W., "On Social Communication and the Metropolis", Lloyd Rodwin (ed.), *The Future Metropolis*, pp. 129-143.

Dewey, Richard, "The Neighborhood, Urban Ecology and City Planners", Paul K. Hatt and Albert J. Reiss, Jr. (eds.), *Cities and Societies* (Glencoe, Ill.: The Free Press, 1957), pp. 783-790.

Dewey, Richard, "The Rural-Urban Continuum: Real But Relatively Unimportant", *American Journal of Sociology*, Vol. LXVI, No. 1, July 1960, pp. 60-66.

Dobriner, William M., "Local and Cosmopolitan as Contemporary Suburban Character Types", Dobriner (ed.), *The Suburban Community* (New York: G.P. Putnam's Sons, 1958), pp. 132-143.

Dore, R.P., *City Life in Japan* (Los Angeles: University of California Press, 1958).

Doxiadis, C.A., "The Ancient Geek City and the City of the Present", *Ekistics*, Vol. 18, No. 108, Nov. 1964 (reprint).

Doxiadis, C.A., "The Image of the City", *DA Review*, Sept. 1, 1965, pp. 12-16.

Duhl, Leonard J. (ed.), *The Urban Condition* (New York: Basic Books, 1963).

Dyckman, John, "The Changing Uses of the City", Lloyd Rodwin (ed.), *The Future Metropolis* (New York: George Braziller, 1961).

Feldman, Arnold S. and Tilly, Charles, "The Interaction of Social and Physical Space", *American Sociological Review*, Vol. 25, No. 6, Dec. 1960, pp. 877-884.

Fellin, Phillip, and Litwak, Eugene, "Neighborhood Cohesion Under Conditions of Mobility", *American Sociological Review*, Vol. 28, No. 3, June 1963, pp. 364-377.

Festinger, Leon; Schachter, Stanley; and Back, Kurt, *Social Pressures in Informal Groups: A Study of Human Factors in Housing* (London: Tavistock Publications, 1950).

Fleis Fava, Sylvia, "Contrasts in Neighboring: New York City and a Suburban Community", Dobriner (ed.), *The Suburban Community*, 1958, pp. 123-131.

Foley, Donald L., *Neighbors or Urbanites* (Rochester: University of Rochester, 1952).

Foley, Donald L., "The Use of Local Facilities in a Metropolis", Hatt and Reiss (eds.), *Cities and Societies*, 1957, pp. 607-616.

Foote, Nelson N.; Abu-Lughod, Janet; Foley, Mary Mix; and Winnick, Louis, *Housing Choices and Housing Constraints*. (New York: McGraw Hill, 1960).

Fried, Marc and Gleicher, Peggy, "Some Sources of Residential Satisfaction in an Urban Slum", *Journal of American Institute of Planners*, No. 27, 1961, pp. 305-315.

Galamison, Milton A., "Bedford-Stuyvesant—Land of Superlatives", *Freedomways*, Vol. 3, No. 3, Summer 1963.

Gans, Herbert J., "The Balanced Community", *Journal of American Institute of Planners*, Vol. XXVII, No. 3, Aug. 1961, pp. 176-184.

Gans, Herbert J., *Effects of the Move from City to Suburb*.

Gans, Herbert J., "Park Forest: Birth of a Jewish Community", *Commentary*, Vol. II, April 1951, pp. 330-339.

Gans, Herbert J., "Planning and Social Life", *Journal of American Institute of Planners*, Vol. XXVII, May 2, 1961, pp. 134-140.

Gans, Herbert J., "The Settlement House and the Attack on Urban Poverty". Prepared for presentation at the 1963 Northeastern Regional Conference, Philadelphia, May 2, 1963.

Gans, Herbert J., "The Suburban Community and Its Way of Life: Notes Toward a Description and an Evaluation". Paper read at the Eastern Canadian Sociological Association Conference, Toronto, Feb. 15, 1963.

Glass, Ruth (ed.), *The Social Background of a Plan: A Study of Middlesborough* (London: Routledge & Kegan Paul, Ltd., 1948).

Glazer, Nathan, "The Problem of Poverty and Race", *Ekistics*, Vol. 18, No. 104, July 1964, pp. 25-27.

Glazer, Nathan, and McEntire, Davis, *Studies in Housing and Minority Groups* (Los Angeles: University of California Press, 1960).

Glickson, Arthur, "Urban Design and New Towns and Neighborhoods", *Landscape Architecture*, April 1962, pp. 169-172.

Goss, Anthony, "Neighborhood Units in British New Towns", *The Town Planning Review*, Vol. XXXII, No. 1, April 1961, pp. 66-82.

Gross, Llewellyn, "The Use of Class Concepts in Sociological Research", *American Journal of Sociology*, Vol. LIV, No. 5, March 1949, pp. 409-421.

Gulick, John; Bowerman, Charles E.; and Back, Kurt W., "Newcomer Enculturation in the City: Attitudes and Participation", Chapin and Weiss (eds.), *Urban Growth Dynamics* (London: John Wiley & Sons, Inc.), pp. 315-358.

Gutkind, E.A., *Revolution of Environment* (London: Kegan Paul, 1946).

Henry, Jules, "White People's Time, Colored People's Time", *Transactions*, 2, No. 3, March/April 1965, pp. 31-34.

Herman, Mary W., *Comparative Studies of Identification Areas in Philadelphia*, City of Philadelphia Community Renewal Program, April 1964, Technical Report No. 9 (Mimeographed.)

Hodges, Harold M., Jr., *Social Stratification* (Cambridge, Mass.: Schenkman Publishers, 1964).

Hyman, Sidney, "Washington's Negro Elite", *Look Magazine*, April 6, 1965.

Jackson, J.B.: "Cumbernauld", *Landscape*, Vol. 12, No. 3, Spring 1963, pp. 17-19.

Jennings, Hilda, *Societies in the Making* (London: Routledge & Kegan Paul, 1962).

Kahn, J.H., "A Psychiatrist on New Towns", *Town and Country Planning*, Oct. 1961.

Keller, Suzanne, "The Role of Social Class in Physical Planning", *International Social Science Bulletin*, forthcoming.

Koppe, William A., "The Psychological Meanings of Housing and Furnishings", *Marriage and Family Living*, Vol. XVII, No. 2, May 1955, pp. 129-132.

Kuper, Leo, "Blueprint for Living Together", Kuper (ed.), 1953, pp. 1-203.

Kuper, Leo (ed.), *Living in Towns* (London: The Cresset Press, 1953).

Lee, Rose Hum, "The Decline of China Towns in the U.S.", *American Journal of Sociology*, Vol. LIV, No. 5, March 1949, pp. 422-432.

Litwak, Eugene, "Geographic Mobility and Extended Family Cohension", *American Sociological Review*, June 1960, pp. 385-394.

McGee, T.G., "The Cultural Role of Cities", A Case Study of Kuala Lumpur, *Ekistics* 18, 104, July 1964, pp. 19-22.

McGough, Donna M., *Social Factor Analysis*, Community Renewal Program, City of Philadelphia, Oct. 1964. Technical Report No. 11. (Mimeographed.)

McGovern, P.D., "New Towns as Regional Centers", *Town and Country Planning*, Vol. XXIX, No. 6.

Mackensen, Rainer; Papalekas, J.C.; Pfeid, E.; Schütte, W., and Burckhardt, L., *Daseinsformen der Grossstadt*, (Tübingen: J.C.B. Mohr, 1959).

Mackenzie, Norman, "Epitaph for a Borough", *New Statesman*, April 2, 1965.

McKinley, Donald Gilbert, *Social Class and Family Life* (Glencoe, Ill.: The Free Press, Dec. 1964).

Madge, Janet H., "Some Aspects of Social Mixing in Worcester", Kuper (ed.), *Living in Towns*, 1953, pp. 267-294.

Mann, Peter H., *An Approach to Urban Sociology* (London: Routledge & Kegan Paul, 1965).

Martin, Walter J., "The Structuring of Social Relationships engendered by Suburban Residence", Dobriner (ed.), *The Suburban Community*, 1958, pp. 95-108.

Mays, John B., "New Hope in New Town", *New Society*, No. 47, Aug. 22, 1963.
"Mental Health Aspects of Urbanization". Report of a Panel Discussion, World Federation for Mental Health, March 11, 1957.
Merton, Robert K., "Patterns of Influence: Local and Cosmopolitan Influentials", Merton (ed.), *Social Theory and Social Structure*, pp. 387–421 (Glencoe, Ill.: The Free Press, 1957).
Mestechkin, S., "Planning in the Kibbutz", *Landscape Architecture*, April 1962, pp. 173-175.
Meyerson, Martin, "Utopian Traditions and the Planning of Cities", Lloyd Rodwin (ed.), The Future Metropolis, New York: George Braziller, 1961.
Ministry of Housing and Local Government, *Grouped Flatlets for Old People: a Sociological Study* (London: Her Majesty's Stationery Office, 1962).
Mogey, J.M., "Changes in Family Life Experienced by English Workers Moving from Slums to Housing Estates", *Marriage and Family Living*, Vol. XVII, No. 2, May 1955, pp. 123-132.
Mogey, J.M., *Family and Neighborhood: Two studies in Oxford* (London: Oxford University Press, 1956).
Mowrer, Ernest R., "The Family in Suburbia", Dobriner (ed.), The Surburban Community, 1958, pp. 147-164.
Mowrer, Ernest R., "The Isometric Map as a Technique of Social Research", *American Journal of Sociology*, Vol. XLIV, No. 1, July 1938, pp. 86-97.
"Nachbarn sind laute Leute", *Stern*, 1964.
Neighborhoods and Community (Liverpool: University Press of Liverpool, 1954).
Nicholson, J.H., *New Communities in Britain* (London: N.C.S.S., 1961).
Norton, Perry L., "A Note on Community", Harvey Perloff (ed.), Planning and the Urban Community, 1961.
Osborn, Frederic J., and Whittick, Arnold, *The New Towns, the Answer to Megalopolis* (London: Leonard Hill, 1963).
Perry, Clarence Arthur, "The Neighborhood Unit", Regional Survey of New York and Its Environs, VII, pp. 22-140 (New York: Committee on Regional Plan of New York and Its Environs, 1929).
Pittman, David J., "Homeless Men", *Transactions*, Vol. 1, 2, Jan. 1964, pp. 15-16.
Porterfield, Austin L., "Traffic Facilities, Suicide, and Homicide", *American Sociological Review*, Vol. 25, No. 6, Dec. 1960, pp. 897-901.
Progressive Architecture (Editorial feature), "The Psychological Dimension of Architectural Space", April 1965, pp. 159-167.
Reiner, Thomas A., *The Place of the Ideal Community in Urban Planning* (Philadelphia: University of Pennsylvania Press, 1963).
Reiss, Albert J., Jr., and Rhodes, Albert Lewis, "The Distribution of Juvenile Delinquency in the Social Class Structure", *American Sociological Review*, Vol. 26, No. 5, Oct. 1961, pp. 720-732.
Remy, Jean, *Charleroi et son Agglomération* (Bruxelles: Centre de Recherches Socio-religieuses et SODEGEC, 1964).
Riemer, Svend, "Hidden Dimensions of Neighborhood Planning", *Land Economics* 26, May 1950, pp. 197-201.
Riemer, Svend, *The Modern City* (New York: Prentice Hall, Inc., 1952).
Riemer, Svend, "Villagers in Metropolis", *British Journal of Sociology*, Vol. II, No. 1, March 1951, pp. 31-43.
Riesman, David, "The Suburban Sadness", Dobriner (ed.), The Suburban Community, 1958, pp. 375-402.
Rodwin, Lloyd (ed.): *The Future Metropolis* (New York: George Braziller, 1961).
Rogler, Lloyed H., "A Better Life: Notes from Puerto Rico", *Transactions*, 2, No. 3, March/April 1965, pp. 34-36.
Rosenmayr, Leopold, "Wohnverhältnisse und Nachbarschaftsbeziehungen", Rosenmayr (ed.), *Wohnen in Wien* (Wien: Stadtbauamt der Stadt Wien, 1956), pp. 37-91.

Rosow, Irving, "The Social Effects of the Physical Environment", *Journal of American Institute of Planners*, XXVII, 2, May 1961, pp. 127-134.

Schnore, Leo F., "Some Correlates of Urban Size: A Replication", *American Journal of Sociology*, Vol. LXIX, No. 2, Sept. 1963, pp. 185-193.

Schorr, A., *Slums and Social Insecurity*, (U.S. Dept. of Health, Education and Welfare, Social Security Administration, 1963).

Schroeder, Clarence W., "Mental Disorders in Cities", *American Journal of Sociology*, Vol. XLVIII, No. 1, July 1942, pp. 40-47.

Slater, Philip E., "On Social Regression", *American Sociological Review*, Vol. 28, No. 3, June 1963, pp. 339-363.

Sorokin, Pitrim, *Social and Cultural Mobility* (Glencoe: The Free Press, 1959).

Spencer, John, *Stress and Release in an Urban Housing Estate* (London: Tavistock Publications, 1964).

Sprott, W.H., *Human Groups* (Baltimore: Penguin Books, 1958).

Stinchcombe, Arthur L., "Institutions of Privacy in the Determination of Police Administrative Practice", *American Journal of Sociology*, Vol. LXIX, No. 2, Sept. 1963, pp. 150-160.

Strotzka, Hans, "Spannungen und Lösungsversuche in Städtischer Umgebung", Rosenmayr (ed.), Wohnen in Wien, 1956, pp. 95-108.

Sussman, Marvin B. (ed.), *Community Structure and Analysis* (New York: Thomas Y. Crowell Co., 1959).

Tyrwhitt, Jaqueline, "The Size and Spacing of Urban Communities", *Journal of American Institute of Planners*, Summer 1949, pp. 10-13.

Tyrwhitt, Jaqueline, "Town Planning at the Local Levels", *The Municipal Journal*, Feb. 10, 1950.

Vagale, L.R., "Neighborhood Planning and Its Relation to Housing", Summary of Lecture at Bangalore, June 19, 1964, In Service Training Course organized by the National Buildings Organization, New Delhi.

Vereker, Charles, and Mays, J.B., *Urban Redevelopment and Social Change* (Liverpool: Liverpool University Press, 1961).

Vernoon, Raymond, *The Myth and Reality of Our Urban Problems* (Joint Center for Urban Studies of the M.I.T. and Harvard University, Cambridge, Mass., 1962).

Vogt, Evon Z., and O'Dea, Thomas F., "A Comparative Study of the Role of Values in Social Action in Two Southwestern Communities", *American Sociological Review*, 1953, pp. 645-654.

Warner, Lloyd W., and Lunt, Paul S., *The Social Life of a Modern Community* (New Haven: Yale, 1941).

Warner, Lloyd W., and Strole, Leo., *The Social Systems of American Ethnic Groups* (New Haven: Yale, 1945).

Warren, Roland L., *The Community in America* (Chicago: Rand McNally, 1963).

Wattel, Harold L., "Levittown: A Suburban Community", Dobriner (ed.), *The Suburban Community*, 1958, pp. 287-313.

Whyte, William H., Jr., *The Organization Man* (London: Jonathan Cape, 1957).

Willems, Emilio, "Racial Attitudes in Brazil", *American Journal of Sociology*, Vol. LIV, No. 5, March 1949, pp. 402-408.

Willmott, Peter, *The Evolution of a Community: A Study of Dagenham After Forty Years* (London: Routledge & Kegan Paul, 1963).

Willmott, Peter, "Housing Density and Town Design in a New Town", A Pilot Study at Stevenage. *The Town Planning Review* XXXIII, No. 2, July 1962, pp. 115-127.

Wilner, Daniel M., and Walkley, Rosabelle P., "The Effects of Housing on Health, Social Adjustment and School Performance", Paper presented at the 39th Annual Meeting of The American Orthopsychiatric Association, Los Angeles, Calif., March 23, 1962.

Wilner, Daniel M.; Walkley, Rosabelle Price; Pinckerton, Thomas C.; Tayback, Matthew, *The Housing Environment and Family Life* (Baltimore: Johns Hopkins Press, 1962).

Wilson, Robert L., "Liveability of the City: Attitudes and Urban Development", Chapin and Weiss (eds.), *Urban Growth Dynamics in a Regional Cluster of Cities* (New York: John Wiley, 1962), pp. 359-399.

Wilson, Roger, "Difficult Housing Estates", Tavistock Pamphlet No. 5, 1963.

Wurzbacher, Gerhard, *Das Dorf im Spannungsfeld industrieller Entwicklung* (Stuttgart: Ferdinand Encke, 1961), Ch. 5, pp. 112-151.

Young, Michael, and Wilmott, Peter, *Family and Kinship in East London* (Glencoe, Ill.: The Free Press, 1957).

Urban Design and Environmental Structuring

Frank L. Elmer and Duncan B. Sutherland, Jr.

For the urban designer, the "problem" of dealing with esthetic preference for different environments stems from the fact that individual values and standards cannot be objectively or specifically stated. Yet, clearly, individuals do develop relationships with their environments, varying from feelings of pleasure or distaste to active attempts to make changes in environmental elements.

The most basic relationship that may be assumed to exist between man and his physical environment, from an esthetic standpoint, is that situation in which the environment represents an extension of self. In this sense, environmental manipulations reflect both the value orientation (emotional life) and the perceptual experience of the individual.

Carrying this basic relationship one step further, it can be hypothesized that one of man's foremost impulses is to manipulate his environment, not only for survival purposes, but also to actively seek a balance between his perceptual experience of the world and his inner values or emotional life. This balanced state might be termed "environmental harmony."

Assuming that man is indeed constantly attempting to reduce any dissonance introduced by conflicts between his environmental state and emotional adaptation, what alternatives are available to restructure his situation so that environmental harmony is realized? Two alternative actions may be hypothesized: 1) change in emotional life (socio-cultural values) to conform to perceptual experience; or 2) change

Reprinted by permission from *Journal of the American Institute of Planners*, Vol. XXXVIII, No. 1, January, 1971, copyright by The American Institute of Planners.

in perceptual experience (environment) to conform to emotional life. The former might be defined as *passive structuralism* and the latter as *active structuralism*.

Passive Structuralism

The *passive structuralist* may react to dissonance by manipulating his emotional life (or by attempting to do so) to conform to his perceptual experience. He does so by adopting predetermined values induced by socio-cultural or peer group value constructs, pressure from the mass media, or more likely, a combination of the two. An environment becomes meaningful to the passive structuralist, not in and of itself, but in its social acceptability (Fromm, 1962). The passive structuralist is concerned about environments that are statements of "success" and fashionableness and resorts to trivial (and often conflicting) manipulations of the environment. He may express individualism by a narrow range of house color, rather than house form, or he may choose a residence that embodies accepted status symbols, such as the contemporary "New England Ranch," filled with early American antiques.

Active Structuralism

The active structuralist is constantly engaged in a series of environmental manipulations (of varying degrees and modes) that are intended to bring his perceptual experience into harmoney with his emotional life. He manipulates his environment with little or no regard for socio-cultural or peer group values. To the extent that an individual is effectively limited in his ability to manipulate his environment, either through restrictive rules or financial inability, environmental distaste may take extreme forms of expression. Some possible examples of active structuralism might be based on distaste, nostalgia, or artistic creativity.

Expressed distaste for environmental state may be expressed in a variety of ways, ranging from painting a slogan on a wall to joining a commune. *Graffiti,* as a universal form of self-expression, can be an effective pressure valve to relieve environmentally destructive impulses and to suggest "desired" social and environmental change.

Dilapidation and lack of maintenance can be viewed as more extreme, conscious expressions of lack of esteem for environmental state. Such reactions portray a definite "not caring for" attitude which has often been misconstrued as the inability to care.

Total environmental rejection is an extreme case, in which a whole form and value system is rejected in not only the most obvious associational elements such as housing, but also utensils, modes of transportation, and as many other elements as it is possible to do without. Today, one finds this reaction in the form of social communes, usually associated with hippies, but in reality reflecting a relatively complete cross section of Americana (Roberts, 1969). From the summer cottage to the commune, there is a continuum of environmental rejection, set in motion by the desire to escape from the competition, frustration, and "rat race" of urban life.

These suggested forms of expressed distaste may be perceived by passive structuralists as a threat to their own values. Thus, an environmental manipulation that tends to establish harmony for one may break it down for another (Huxtable, 1969). Depending on the severity of the threat, the passive structuralist may react by "erasing" it. Even the mild incidence of active structuralism involved in the creation of a "happy tree" was sufficiently threatening to passive structuralists so that the tree was cut down.

Nostalgic Structuralism Many individuals seek environments which they feel best express their emotional lives, regardless of rejection of these environments by their immediate peer groups. This tendency often manifests itself as environmental restoration. One might consider the nostalgic structuralist as returning to a satisfactory environment that has been passed over by contemporary socio-cultural values and standards.

Artistic Structuralism Some individuals manipulate forms to arrive at new solutions to the emotion-perception problem.

The artist or sculptor examines new materials and media in an attempt to find the ideal means of expression. Likewise, the artistic structuralist seeks new media and new forms that achieve harmony for him, regardless of socio-cultural acceptability. Supergraphics or super-mannerism serves as a good example of artistic structuralism (Huxtable, 1969). Another related example is "earth art," a new art form that employs the media of mountain tops, deserts, and wheat fields to create such constructions as a 520 mile long stretch of holes, dug in a desert floor (Bongartz, 1970). Earth art is an extreme example of the notion that the success or failure of a person as an individual depends on how well he manipulates his piece of environment as an expression of self.

Some Urban Design Implications

For summary purposes, it seems appropriate to hypothesize certain implications of active and passive structuralism that would be directly applicable to urban design concerns. Environmental destruction or an expressed distaste for environmental state is not confined to the poverty level resident. Destructive behavior is a predictable option in a conflict situation in which emotional life is not in harmony with perceptual experience.

Relative to *urban renewal*, it is suggested that while functional improvements to environments are important, opportunities for active environmental structuring are perhaps more important. Relocation of residents is an effective means of removing familiar environmental elements and often creates an emotion-perception conflict for those who are relocated. The ability to manipulate environmental elements is usually less than average for people affected by urban renewal. Therefore, redevelopment designs and schemes should provide more easily manipulable environments.

Relative to the *restoration of environmental districts*, it is suggested that success depends on the *location* of forces that influence the value structures of potential residents. Restoration will be successful if sold as fashionable to potential residents who tend toward passive structuralism to achieve environmental harmony. There will be a tendency for restoration to come about naturally if a restorable environment has meaning in and of itself for potential residents who tend toward active structuralism to achieve environmental harmony.

Relative to *urban design in general*, it is suggested that the significance of the designed environment should be judged in terms of the responses of its users. The more unfamiliar or contemporary a design, the less it will be understood emotionally and as designs become less understood emotionally, advertising and sales campaigns become more important.

Designs must provide the potential for people to become emotionally attached and should be flexible enough to be manipulated after completion. Urban design should be thought of as more than the art of providing "esthetically correct" and pleasing environments; it should provide an arena for the user's ongoing self-expression through environmental manipulation. This environmental manipulation (active structuralism) could be considered a form of continuing citizen participation.

Authors' Note

This project is supported by a grant from the National Endowment for the Arts in Washington, D.C., a federal agency created by Act of Congress in 1965.

References

Aldrich, Virgil C. (1968) "Beauty as Feeling," pp. 3-9 in Susanne K. Langer (ed.), *Reflections on Art* (New York: Oxford University Press).

Bongartz, Roy. (1970) "It's Called Earth Art—And Boulderdash," *The New York Times Magazine* (February 1), p. 16.

Fromm, Erich. (1962) "Alienation Under Capitalism," pp. 62-6 in Eric and Mary Josephson (eds.), *Man Alone* (New York: Dell Publishing Company).

Huxtable, Ada Louise. (1969) "Kicked a Building Lately?" *The New York Times* (January 12), p. 25D.

Josephson, Eric and Mary. (1962) "Introduction," pp. 9-53 in *Man Alone*.

Langer, Susanne K. (1966) "The Social Influence of Design," pp. 39-40 in Laurence B. Holland (ed.), *Who Designs America?* (Garden City, N.Y.: Doubleday & Company, Inc.).

Roberts, Steven V. (1969) "The Hippie Mystique," *The New York Times* December 15), p. 1.

Improving the Design Process in Urban Renewal

Roger Montgomery

Hundreds of urban renewal projects are under way all over the country, each built according to a plan. A look at the results shakes our faith in the efficacy of plans.

Can plans influence design? What kinds make good designs? Renewal planners examine their work, sense its frequent impotence, and look for new, foolproof types of plans. Recently this search has assumed new dimensions as experience with both renewal and design have led us to see these not as static objects but as processes.[1]

In the beginning, city planners recommended that renewal take place only in a well orchestrated relation to "the master plan of the whole urban territory."[2] Congress decided against such comprehensiveness in passing the Housing Act of 1949, which called for project plans only. The statutory requirement that each of these "indicate its relationship to definite local objectives"[3] operationally meant little in achieving comprehensive planning frameworks. Planners responded by making project plans into miniature city plans complete with land use and circulation maps, zoning ordinances, and the rest of the familiar apparatus of the comprehensive plan.

There are alternative approaches. Urban renewal plans need not be miniature city plans. Pittsburgh proved otherwise with the redevelopment plan for the Gateway project, written by a lawyer in 1950.[4] It contains no maps or zoning ordinances. It reads like a contract and declaration of principle, not a planning report or blueprint. Such plans are rare. Most efforts and most innovations aim to build in more

Reprinted by permission from *Journal of the American Institute of Planners*, Vol. XXXI, No. 1, February, 1965, copyright by The American Institute of Planners.

comprehensiveness. Many have succeeded. Federal policies added the "workable program" and the General Neighborhood Renewal Plan in 1954, the Community Renewal Program in 1959, and the progressive relaxation of limitations on nonresidential renewal.

How does design fare in this drive for comprehensiveness? Directly the impact seems small, but indirectly this focus probably has had large effects. It means city planning becomes less and less concerned with the day-to-day processes of design. Yet planners cannot give up their grip on initiating layouts. Architect Theo Crosby writes: "The usual planning method using block models is very much open to question, for the planner fixes the position and form of the building without being in any way responsible for the architecture. The architect fills in the pattern the way a child colors a drawing book. In this discrepancy the quality of wholeness is lost."[5]

Urban renewal superimposes this split between planner and architect on the dichotomy between public control and private initiative which, for example, divides land use determinations from investment decisions. Nowhere is this split more damaging than in the urban design process. When "wholeness" is lost, only partial solutions are possible. This is not to say a single hand must shape everything; on the contrary, many hands are always needed. But when they work at cross purposes, results are inevitably diminished. Urban renewal shows this over and over: improved neighborhood street layouts get built in the most banal municipal vernacular, and the streets get lined with bizarre bits of get-rich-quick building. A redeveloper and his designer may come up with a brilliant solution to high-density housing only to have it buried by the mindless repetition of ancient planning errors.

These, and problems like them, have been the everyday experience of renewal managers. Of more than 1400 projects on the books, some 400 have been completed or are in an advanced stage of development.[6] Most of these have been executed with slight concern for design; a few have sought to achieve something more. This experience has led to new insights into the connections between project plans and project design. Recent cases suggest that a sophisticated "process comprehensiveness" may hold the key to improved results. This paper will examine some of this experience.

Early Experience in Detroit

Detroit stands among the first American cities to attempt urban renewal. Before World War II, the city began slum clearance and redevelopment through public housing under PWA and the Housing Act of 1937. During and immediately after World War II, faced with the overpowering extent of slums and blight, and stymied by ideological reservations about government-subsidized housing, the city, in concert with private homebuilding leaders, formulated the "Detroit Plan." This plan provided for municipal slum clearance, using eminent domain if necessary, with private redevelopment on land purchased at a write-down from the city.[7]

Although the Gratiot area had been marked for clearance in the late 1930's, nothing happened for ten years until planning began in 1947 within the framework of the Detroit Plan.[8] The first tentative scheme resembled the preliminary design stage or "development plan" of a public housing project. In this totally unprecedented situation, tentativeness can be easily understood. The uncertainties of planning are illustrated by the variety of viewpoints on the controls to be placed on private development. Detroit Housing Director Charles F. Edgecomb described the alternatives to ASPO:

> For instance, there is one school of thought that says the city should make the site and building plans and keep complete control of the home development. I would think that this would be about as much private enterprise as the welfare or the fire departments.
>
> There is the middle of the road group which believes that the city should prepare the site plans and make available to interested capital basic drawings of utilities, streets, etc., and then set up a committee composed of representatives of the building department, city plan commission and the housing commission to check the proposals of potential builders in the area to see that they conform with broad specifications as to density, architecture and land coverage. I, personally, go along with this group.
>
> The other extremists in the picture believe that the city

should take out the property needed for its municipal improvements and auction off the rest of the property to the highest bidder. This would leave the area wide open to exploitation by speculators.[9]

Before Detroit could resolve its dilemma among these approaches, the United States Housing Act of 1949 was passed. Detroit converted Gratiot to a federally aided effort, and Congress and the Housing and Home Finance Agency settled the issue. Federal urban redevelopment statutes permitted no construction with renewal money other than site improvements and streets, and required renewal to give maximum opportunity to private enterprise. HHFA held that these provisions prohibited architectural and site designs in project plans. Plans would state "proposed land uses and building requirements" to control private development.[10]

For two years after the Housing Act of 1949 became law, Detroit's planners, housing officials (the Detroit Housing Commission was designated as the official renewal agency in 1950), city council, mayor, HHFA staff, and local homebuilders debated the pros and cons of various land use, street, and density patterns. A plan jelled in the spring of 1952. It followed neighborhood unit-superblock theory and aimed at housing former slum dwellers in the project area. The scheme set forth a land use map and a zoning-like declaration of restrictions covering use, density, and building layout. These, backed up by City Planning Commission reviews of site plans and architecture, would, it was hoped, insure an adequate redevelopment design.

In the summer of 1952, an auction was held to select redevelopers. Not a single bidder came forth. After nearly a decade of working with residential developers, the city faced a staggering fact: cleared land in Gratiot was unmarketable. Despite the incentive of land cost write-down, other factors including "gray area" location, Negro clientele, and forbidding housing costs formed obstacles which defeated the planners' heroic labors.

Since costs were presumed a major factor, the planners responded to the impasse by amending the plan to permit higher densities and other concessions to reduce the builder's

Improving the Design Process in Urban Renewal 223

unit costs and improve marketability. This effort to attract private redevelopers was tested the following year in another auction. Two bids were received. Six months later, when the high bidder revealed his construction plans, the planners were stunned. He proposed a scheme drawn for a project "in the East" crudely superimposed on the Gratiot tract.[11] Attempts to achieve a better design were fruitless. The plan commission would not approve the plans offered. After more than a year, in the early summer of 1954, the city council, stimulated by the bidder's implication in recent FHA scandals, cancelled the sale contract.

In the meantime land acquisition had been completed; as in most early renewal projects, this was delayed by years of litigation required to establish public purpose for the takings. Clearance, too, was complete. By then Gratiot was known as "Ragweed Acres" (its twin in St. Louis was "Hiroshima Flats"). Relocation, prior to clearance, produced characteristically violent upheavels. Evidence suggests that administrative brutality characterized relocation in Gratiot as it did elsewhere through the early fifties. Except for the Wayne University Medical School building, completed in 1953, and the Lafayette Neuropsychiatric Center, completed a little later, nothing had been built in the seven years the project had been actively underway. Pressures built up to move at any cost to get something—anything—built. Ironically, an intensive planning effort, marked by continuous debate over the most abstruse points of neighborhood design, *produced no buildable result*. Planning hopes were stalled by investor disinterest.

Gaps in Design Process

"The urban renewal program," Scott Greer and David W. Minar have observed, "is completely dependent upon the private market for its 'renewal' effects." They find the renewal program limited by "1) the dichotomy of public versus private control, 2) the tension between federal and municipal agencies, 3) the division of power among different federal agencies, and 4) the fragmentation of power at the local community level. Each is not so much a problem to solve as a powerful constraint to be 'lived with'; one that can distort the program beyond recognition in terms of its stated aims."[12] These constraints separate plans from the process of their realization. They shatter design responsibility into bits and pieces.

Case study evidence can be understood by using a "gap" hypothesis. This idea derives from the seamlessness of urban design processes. Design decisions flow in an uninterrupted stream from the earliest ones about programming and goals to final details of construction and use. One decision builds on the next; all are interrelated. To cut the stream dismembers the design process and cuts off one participant from the others. Each designer's world becomes limited to his separate pool of responsibility. The planner becomes cut off from the social analyst, the street-lights man, the redeveloper's banker and architect.[13]

A fragmented design process is built into urban renewal. Of the many gaps, the most important divides the design continuum into zones of public control at one end and private control at the other. At the public end of the spectrum lies the realm of the comprehensive plan. This is cast in terms of design goals such as "balanced community" and pressures for economic development and tax base increase. On the private side, design responds to different goals. Here individuals and firms seek to maximize income, personal comfort, and status aspirations. They frame these in limited terms bounded by the lot line of a particular redevelopment transaction. Little positive influence flows across the gap from comprehensive plans which outline public hopes for neighborhood units, superblocks, industrial parks, shopping centers, and civic centers.[14]

The "gap" hypothesis suggests that successful accomplishment in urban renewal design results from building bridges across public-private, federal-local, federal interagency and local interagency splits. It sets a theoretical framework for understanding attempts to improve renewal design by viewing them as gap-closing or bridge-building efforts.

Planning and design efforts at Gratiot after the 1954 collapse can be seen in this light. Within the month, a public-spirited pair of businessmen unveiled a new plan. While couched in rudimentary design terms, it clearly aimed at

Improving the Design Process in Urban Renewal 225

building a bridge between public plans and private investors. This proposal stimulated the creation of a new vehicle which could both plan and redevelop: the Citizens Redevelopment Committee, which was a "power structure group" charged by the city council with getting Gratiot moving. CRC began simultaneous planning, design, and marketing efforts.

This time there was a functional connection between redevelopment investor, building designer (and cost calculator), and planner. Changes occurred at all levels, new social goals were adopted, and with them, higher potential rent schedules. A distinguished team of designers was enlisted to plan and design the project. In late 1954, Oscar Stonorov, Minoru Yamasaki, and Victor Gruen (through his associate Carl Van Leuven) unveiled the new scheme for Gratiot. It was neither a public housing site plan, nor a land use diagram, but an architectural layout for a quilt-like pattern of various residential buildings, supported by detailed architectural study of prototypes.[15]

An intensive marketing campaign began. Meanwhile the renewal agency, plan commission, and HHFA made the necessary amendments and approved the new plan. This process drew a sharp issue between the city planning people and the Citizens Redevelopment Committee designers. Neighborhood unit-superblock ideas dominated the thinking of the planning staff. The new CRC group sought to form a grand central avenue along which housing clusters were fastened. The outcome would not be determined by debate of planning theories, however, though much of this went on. Ironically, the success of CRC's marketing campaign led to a neighborhood unit-superblock victory. CRC wanted to find a single developer for the project.[16] At least one committee member predicted that any developer of the requisite size would insist on building his own design, using his own architect, and would show little interest in a ready-made CRC scheme. This was exactly what happened. In the summer of 1955, just a few months after the CRC plan was unveiled, it was abandoned when the committee joined forces with Herbert Greenwald of Chicago to purchase the Gratiot land.

Greenwald had distinguished himself internationally as the patron of the famous German-born, Chicago architect, Ludwig Mies van der Rohe. Mies set to work on Gratiot. By the fall of 1955 he had produced a new plan in association with his long time collaborator, town-planner Ludwig Hilberseimer.[17] This plan was a detailed site design with some generalized architectural indications. Following the settlement unit-superblock precepts of Hilberseimer, it rejected the grand avenue. The design received approval from CRC and the city planners: CRC reluctant to scrap its costly plan, the city planners delighted to return to earlier principles.[18]

Aside from the design and layout of buildings, there was much similarity between the Mies and S-Y-G proposals. Both accepted a changed social and economic program. While CRC member Walter Reuther talked of these plans as "integrated communities," actually they were aimed at a limited, upper middle-income market—Negro and white, of course, but economic facts would sharply limit Negro demand. Presumably none of the displaced former residents of the Gratiot area would be able to scrape up the new rents.[19] The two plans also shared a concern with a larger planning universe than the Gratiot area itself. Both included in a single layout coordinated plans for the Lafayette Extension project area contiguous with Gratiot to the south, and Elmwood Park, a former public housing site, across the railroad cut to the east.

It took about a year to complete Mies' plans and get work under way. In the fall of 1958, for the first time in 11 or 12 years, people began moving in, rather than out, of Gratiot. They could choose to live in a high-rise slab, two-story row houses, or one-story atrium houses. Initially there was resistance to paying $100 to $300 per month for downtown apartments. This sluggish response to the apartments, coupled with objections to some disagreeeable functional features of the two-story buildings, led to a new wave of pessimism. In 1960 there were scores of vacancies. By 1964, none were left: there was a waiting list instead.

However, a tragic and far-reaching event had occurred: in February, 1959, Herbert Greenwald died in a plane crash. No one could take over and complete the project, which was less than half finished (500 units of a projected 1800). The rest of the project fell back in the lap of the Detroit Housing Commission. Bit by bit they sold it off: a public school site,

60 one-story row houses, three groups of low apartment buildings, two additional high-rise slabs, designed by Mies, a shopping center, and one other high apartment building. During this time the market improved steadily. Particularly, the one-story row houses or atrium houses seem to have tapped an inexhaustible demand.

But what happened to the Mies design? With eight different developers (plus the park and street departments), each with his own architect and landscape architect, the result was about what might be expected. Plan Commission review, assisted by a voluntary architectural advisory board, prevented absolute chaos. The result is no disaster, but it is less attractive and it functions more awkwardly than the completed part of the earlier scheme. Measuring design quality at Gratiot or anywhere else raises extraordinary difficulties. Objectivity comes hard, and in the minds of some is irrelevant to the subject. Peter Smithson, the British architect and critic, finds "the essence of what one is searching for is missing from all large-scale developments all over the world, but it can be smelt at Lafayette Park (Mies' part of Gratiot)." Yet the American critic Sybil Moholy-Nagy has damned it mercilessly.[20] While such conflicting judgments may never be resolved, time and less iconoclastic norms make useful evaluation possible. Now that people have lived in Mies' settlement for more than five years, their behavior and the waiting lists demonstrate their affection for it. To the outsider, the design is consistent, powerful, and memorable. Its architectonic austerity is softened by Albert Caldwell's verdant landscape. Where else in America can a school without a parking lot hold a happy PTA meeting? Gratiot joins Radburn, that other incomplete monument, as one of the few triumphs of American urban design.

City planning, DHC, and HHFA approval of the Mies design in 1956 necessitated amending the Gratiot Urban Renewal Plan to incorporate the changes in density, street pattern, open space, and parceling of the land. These changes were embodied in a new land use map and set of controls and restrictions patterned along zoning lines. The death of Greenwald, subsequent abandoning of the Mies scheme, and the arrival of a heterogeneous group of redevelopers to finish up Gratiot provided a fine test of the efficacy of the conventional tools of American city planning in "implementing" design. The evidence suggests that they were of little value. The one tool that seemed to have any effect was design review. On one parcel, the review forced a modified version of the original Mies site plan in place of a mindless bit of suburbia; on another it scotched an equally mindless attempt at "Georgian" exterior decor.

The failure of the Gratiot urban renewal plan to guide project design after the patron had died, confirms the general failure of "comprehensive plan implementation tools" to bridge the design gap and positively influence the environmental order of cities. This is no surprise to American planners. What is surprising is the failure of many to recognize that, in urban renewal, the constraints of police power regulation do not obtain. Instead, there are unprecedented opportunities for innovation.

While the Gratiot renewal image petered out in piecemeal constructions, in other cities renewal design accomplishments were even more disappointing.[21] Shaken by this dismal experience, agencies in a number of localities began to experiment with new kinds of plans and processes in the early 1960's. These efforts struck out in two directions. One aimed at using the opportunities for tight control implicit in the urban renewal plan. The other took advantage of renewal's possibilities for control through process. A third effort married aspects of both streams. The innovations which came out of this ferment formed the background for further developments in Detroit. Today, next to Gratiot, the Elmwood Park project is using many of these ideas.

Police power land use controls in city planning are founded on the twin principles of *one,* uniformity of application, and *two,* withholding development rights—and thus influencing land value—only where public health, safety, morals, or general welfare are threatened. Land use controls in urban renewal stem from sharply different premises. The requirement that land be valued for its planned uses automatically recognizes the impact of controls on potential development rights. The appraisal and disposition processes take into account land value effects of controls since disposition is at "fair value for uses in accordance with the urban renewal plan."[22] Thus, the nature and intensity of controls need not be limited by a concern which restricts the exercise of the police power in zoning and subdivision regulation. For the same reason, there is no need for uniform application of controls in renewal. Each parcel may be controlled independently and its value determined accordingly.

These essential differences have gone largely unnoticed.[23] A few planners, particularly those with an interest in architectural form, have sensed the special power of renewal plan land use controls. In an attempt to close the design gap, they have literally written a complete and detailed design into the controls. Set-back lines can be made mandatory building lines; height limits can be made to work as both minima and maxima; entrances and even fenestration patterns can be written into controls. Functional layout may be made completely specific; that is, a drug store here, restaurant there, rather than necessarily broad listings of permitted or prohibited uses. The imagination of the planner —and the market place—are practically the only limits. "Tight" plans emerge. Compared with the typical urban renewal plan based on the usual implementation tools, "tight" plans greatly enlarge the extent of public control over the design continuum. Such plans seek comprehensive regulation of renewal processes.

At Erieview in Cleveland, I. M. Pei fashioned such a tight plan based on an elaborate, highly refined overall design for the project area.[24] In a redevelopment situation where he was backed by a downtown power structure group similar to Detroit's CRC, Pei produced a plan stated in specific architectural terms. Around it he framed the formal controls of the urban renewal plan. The land purchaser or redeveloper and his architect were expected to fill in the pattern, and they are doing so: Erieview is being built as designed.

The Cleveland Development Foundation and its group of downtown business leaders marketed the plan for Erieview very much the way CRC marketed its plan for Gratiot. If their customer in Cleveland had been the patron of Mies van der Rohe, would the Pei plan have held up? Erieview redevelopment designs were subject to an architectural review procedure, with Pei serving as review advisor to the public agency. Imagine Gratiot if Mies had exercised design review authority over the parcels remaining unbuilt at Greenwald's death!

Erieview's tight plan received such powerful, sympathetic support during its execution that it is difficult to determine whether the tight controls or the marketing and review procedures were the more responsible for its success. What if no investor were willing to risk adding several hundred thousand square feet of rental space to Cleveland's central area? What if the more creative architects were in the service of the private developer, not the public agency? These questions suggest defects in the tight plan approach.

When specific building form and site layouts get built into an urban renewal plan, it takes formal action by both local legislature and the federal agency to make any significant change. Plan amendments prove costly in time, energy, and money, and often generate pointless conflicts.

Renewal projects typically take about seven years to move from legislative approval of the urban renewal plan to an advanced stage of redevelopment and rehabilitation. The best market research is shaky under these conditions: over periods of three to ten years, it must predict specific uses at specific intensities on specific sites at the scale of individual buildings and parcels. Theoretical and practical difficulties argue powerfully for deferring detailed design decisions until a time much nearer actual redevelopment.[25] Since tight plans risk swimming against the current of investment decision, they may be risky and hard to execute. Does a local renewal administrator have the political power to enforce a tight plan in the absence of market support? To what extent should an architectural image be subjected to such pressures?

An equally problematical objection to tight plans derives from functionalist architectural theory, which holds that design is a response to real conditions. Can good urban renewal design emerge from a make-believe world based on chancy predictions about land markets in place of informed builder-clients? In the absence of more pressing determinants architectural form and site layout may tend toward empty formalism.

"Open" Plans

An alternative to both tight plans and conventional ones emerged in Hartford, Connecticut's Bushnell Plaza project. Here an "open" plan put the emphasis on *process*. Its land use controls did not locate uses on a map. Spatial arrangement of the required high-density housing, public park, parking, and landscaped areas, and the inclusion and arrangement of the permitted theater, office, and commercial space were left to the redeveloper and his site planners.[26] To assure a well designed result, the urban renewal plan set forth a design process. This included a procedure for the design of public spaces (site improvements) which insured that they would dovetail with the private redevelopment design. Most important, it established a process for land disposition which made design quality a principal factor. It required active, formal collaboration between public planner and private architect during design development. Land disposition was handled in two stages: first, a prequalification of prospective redevelopers on the basis of business and financial criteria; second, a design competition. The plan provided that the chosen redeveloper would be given a year in which to complete "the final design plans"—their scope was defined—during which time "he will be required to work in close cooperation and coordination with the staff of the agency...."

In support of its "open" controls and its carefully defined design process, the Bushnell Plaza plan contained a formal statement of renewal objectives. Federal regulations require no such statement. Since it is rare for a locality to see beyond bureaucratic requirements, it is rare to find a renewal plan with a stated purpose. It is rarer still to find any indication of design goals. In an open plan such statements of purpose are crucial. Hopes for realizing fine project design depend on the design process as set forth in the plan. To guide this process, to meet requirements for adequate public notice of public action, to avoid arbitrary action, the goals toward which action and process are directed must be spelled out. The open plan is not a miniature comprehensive city plan; it is a miniature "constitution" which guides and legitimatizes public actions.[27]

Seen in terms of the gap hypothesis and the public-private control dichotomy, the open plan establishes a zone of shared control within the design continuum. Public interest in good design gets more effective representation than in the land use map—zoning controls of the typical urban renewal plan. In contrast to the tight plan, the open approach accepts the primary role of private entrepreneur in redevelopment investment decisions. The seven-year interval between plan approval and active redevelopment cannot cripple open plans to the same extent that it injures tight ones. Not the least of their virtues, open plans provide room for architectural—and entrepreneurial—creativity at points where tight plans shut it out.

With all their advantages, such plans have defects. For instance, trouble arises from the limited American experience with procedural or administrative land use control in place of statutory standards. At Bushnell Plaza, this kind of difficulty occurred when the agency became stalled during the second stage of land disposition and was unable to act swiftly in selecting a redeveloper.

One of the points that held up this disposition reveals another aspect of land use control having a special relevance to urban renewal planning. The plan contained a height limit which served no purpose because there were no issues of shading adjoining properties, or need for an indirect control of the intensity of use, or threat to an esthetically pleasing skyline. It probably appeared because a strictly bureaucratic reading of HHFA's *Urban Renewal Manual* seemed to require it. Its effect was also to limit architectural opportunity. Its arbitrariness was confirmed when the redevelopment proposal which was judged best on many criteria violated the height limit. There was no reason for keeping the height limit except that the proposal had to conform to the controls of the plan. And in terms of planning goals, the control was meaningless; yet it inhibited selection of the best design.

This experience indicates the importance of distinguishing planning controls from design or development controls. Because planning concerns, such as overall land use intensity or residential density, have so long been controlled indirectly through restrictions on lot size, building height, or yard sizes, confusing the two has become a conditioned response. *Planning controls* deal with those factors of community interest affecting the world outside the tract in question. *Development controls* are concerned with the specific layout and organization of an actual development design. Development controls are relevant only in terms of a real design. When development controls are based on "standards" and irresponsible "illustrative designs"—irresponsible because not really to be financed and built—they only inhibit urban design.

Another defect of open plans lies in their tendency to circumscribe public initiative. A considerable body of design theory recommends use of public works as catalytic agents to stimulate and direct private action.[28] In Bushnell Plaza, the delegation of responsibility for public works design to the redeveloper left little room for appropriate public leadership. In other situations, experience shows that functional complexity or market softness may be overcome by public leadership in preparing detailed overall designs. Edmund Bacon has described this process at Penn Center, where governmental initiative crystallized a design concept to be taken up by the private investors. Charles Center in Baltimore exhibits this situation in a recent renewal project where the functional and market situations were inappropriate for an open plan.

Design Process Controls

The most recent wave of innovation in relating renewal planning to design has sought to draw on the advantages of tight and open plans while avoiding the defects of both approaches. A series of projects on the West Coast articulated these ideas, beginning with an experiment in land disposition methods in San Francisco's Diamond Heights project. To overcome the inadequate and uncertain effect of a routine land use map and zoning ordinance plan, the redevelopment agency commissioned a special study of the neighborhood shopping center in this project. A preliminary design plan was prepared by architect Lawrence Lackey in collaboration with the landscape architects, Royston, Hanamoto and

Mays.[29] This plan was embodied in the invitation for redevelopment proposals, which stated that the winning bidders would be expected to follow the plan, or they might submit an alternative design of their own which would be gauged by the agency against the yardstick of the Lackey-Royston scheme.[30]

In this modest event lay the seeds of an approach holding the advantages of flexible, open project plans, yet retaining every opportunity for appropriate public leadership in design decisions. In quick succession Sacramento, Fresno, Vallejo, and Oakland, California, picked up the idea and elaborated it. These cities worked out a "comprehensive process" method with three main components:

1. *Preliminary work and the Urban Renewal Plan* Studies are undertaken to explore design potentials and to establish a strategy for design actions. From these studies come the *design objectives and controls* set forth in the urban renewal plan and the *actions and procedures* devised to accomplish the objectives. The plan follows the open or flexible mode rather than building in a tight design. (Note that this is just the beginning of project planning work, not the end. Conventional planning—and urban design—have ended in the survey and planning phase before renewal action gets under way.)

2. *Design Plan* At the beginning of renewal operations, the public agency prepares design plans in incremental but continuous fashion. These plans may become detailed: they may include the actual design of the site improvements and other public construction, advisory material and designs for owners who are rehabilitating their properties, and design plans to serve as a basis for land disposition and redevelopment. The degree of detail and refinement will vary from time to time during the years of project execution, and from place to place within the project, in order to meet real situations as they occur. In terms of modern planning theory, this permits *loss cutting* as well as *goal seeking* behavior on the part of the planners and designers.[31]

3. *Design Action* Each renewal action—site improvement, rehabilitation, land disposition, redevelopment—either follows the design plans or the design plans are used as yardsticks against which alternatives are measured. Processes for

reviewing redevelopment proposals, effecting design coordination, organizing land disposition, and so on, are detailed, enunciated, and put into operation.

In this approach, the public agency works with reliable market information since it need not freeze designs years in advance of renewal action. An unpredictable new development need not force a long bureaucratic hassle over amending the official urban renewal plan. This approach permits powerful public leadership in design without sacrificing flexibility.

In the Gratiot case, imagine the ease with which the Mies design could have been completed had it been an agency design plan rather than a private one dependent upon a patron, and had the public agency more powerful tools in its hands than land use maps and zoning regulations. Imagine, too, the reduction in costly, repeated, and overly detailed site layouts and building type studies initiated too far ahead of actual investment decision. Think of the reduction in pointless bureaucratic infighting if amendment of the official plan were not needed each time a Stonorov or Mies appeared.

Some comprehensive process planning components appear in most renewal projects where distinguished design occurs. Edmund Bacon, for instance, has made the role of process explicit in achieving the elegant architecture and articulate overall design structure of Washington Square East in Philadelphia.[32] New Haven uses a ramified, comprehensive process approach: in Wooster Square and Dixwell it intentionally stretched out design and planning over all the years of project operation. David Crane has also emphasized the importance of process; his influence evidently appears in the Boston Redevelopment Authority's sophisticated set of procedures for insuring high quality design.[33]

Federal policy has been slow to catch up. No significant changes in the *Urban Renewal Manual* and federal review criteria reflect the importance of process over plan. However, a change may be on the way since a series of recent advisory statements have emphasized new ideas in renewal design and planning.[34]

At Elmwood Park, Detroit has turned to a comprehensive process to overcome some of the problems which caused so much trouble at Gratiot. The urban renewal plan for this project was completed in 1961.[35] It is no model of totally open planning, but neither is it a tightly constructed attempt to build in a design. Various factors held up action until 1963, when the housing commission engaged a team to prepare a design plan. Crane and Gorwic, architect-planners; Meethe and Kessler, architects; Irving Grossman, architect; and Johnson, Johnson, Roy, landscape architects made up the group. Their plan provided a variety of different owner-occupied house types and elevator apartments, plus a system of public space and land parceling geared to the design. In 1964 DHC began work using the design plan as a basis for site improvements, and as the yardstick for a fixed-price, competitive land disposition covering the first six of eleven parcels. Sixteen prospective redevelopers submitted proposals. Four were selected: one to develop three parcels. Of the successful bidders, one elected to follow exactly the design plan, and the others submitted alternatives judged equal to or better than the yardstick design. The four developers, with their architects and site planners, are now collaborating with the plan commission group on design. Every indication on the Detroit scene, and from precedent elsewhere, suggests that the outcome will be a stunning demonstration of fine urban renewal design.

In comparison with the land use map-zoning plan and open-plan approaches Elmwood Park and the other process approaches to renewal designs register clear benefits in relevant public control and in decisive public leadership. These benefits rest in part on the value of the design plan in making procedural controls work smoothly. Contrasted with tight plans, design plans and process controls cope with the unpredictability of market and talent. They help, too, by forcing planning out of its fixation on plans and into an active, continuous participation in the process of renewal. The new comprehensiveness can bridge the gap between public renewal intentions and the private entrepreneurs through whom these hopes must be realized.

Author's Note

The author wishes to acknowledge the support of the Rockefeller Foundation and Washington University for making possible the field studies on which this paper is based, the help of the Urban Renewal Administration in making data available, and the help of Michael Lowe in researching and redrawing plans.

Notes

1. G. Thomas Kingsley has stated the case for studying the process rather than the product of urban renewal design in his "The Design Process in Urban Renewal: An Analysis of the San Francisco Experience" (unpublished M.C.P. thesis, University of California, 1963).

2. "Report of the Committee on Urban Redevelopment," Alfred Bettman, chairman, in American Society of Planning Officials, *Planning 1943: Proceedings of the Annual Meeting* (Chicago: the Society, 1943), p. 94. American Institute of Planners, "A Statement of Policy on Urban Renewal," adopted July 1959, brings this view nearly up to date.

3. Housing Act of 1949, Public Law 171, 81st Congress, Title 1—Slum Clearance and Community Development and Redevelopment, section 110 (5) (1).

4. No plan in the *Urban Renewal Manual* sense existed for the Gateway project. Its place was taken by the *Redevelopment Contract* between the Urban Redevelopment Authority of Pittsburgh and the Equitable Life Assurance Society of the United States, February 14, 1950.

5. Theo Crosby, "Contributions to CIAM 10," *Architects Yearbook 7*, ed. Trevor Dannatt (New York: Philosophical Library, 1956), p. 39.

6. Housing and Home Finance Agency, Urban Renewal Administration, *Report of Urban Renewal Operations*, July, 1964. Data on project status from URA redevelopment data files.

7. The Detroit Plan is described in Charles F. Edgecomb, "Detroit," *Planning 1947: Proceedings of the Annual Meeting, American Society of Planning Officials* (Chicago: A.S.P.O., 1947), pp. 152-57.

8. Detroit City Plan Commission, "Revised Narrative Report on Redevelopment Plan: Gratiot Redevelopment Project," D.M.-I (mimeographed, the Commission, December 1951), pp. 30-31. An account of the Gratiot Project from 1946 through 1958 can be found in Robert J. Mowitz and Dell S. Wright, *Profile of a Metropolis* (Detroit: Wayne State University Press, 1962), pp. 1-79. Design aspects of the Detroit Plan proposals for Gratiot are illustrated in Detroit Housing Commission, *Detroit Plan* (Detroit: the Commission, 1950).

9. Edgecomb, *op. cit.*, p. 157.

10. Housing Act of 1949, *op. cit.*, sections 105 (a) ii, 110 (c), and 110 (b)(2).

11. Interview report. This interpretation conflicts with the Mowitz-Wright account, but the meaning is not changed.

12. Scott Greer and David W. Minar, "The Political Side of Urban Development and Redevelopment," *The Annals of the American Academy of Political and Social Science*, vol. 352 (March, 1964), 66.

13. The interdependence of design decisions, from programming to construction, is recognized in the formation of the Development Groups responsible for much large-scale planning and building in Britain. These units bring together in a single team the planners, administrators, fiscal experts, engineers, social scientists, architects, and builders charged with making the project. A seamless responsibility corresponds to a seamless task. Intention at Harlow and Cumbernauld finds precise realization in brick and mortar. See Roger Walters, "Purpose and Organization of Development Groups," *Royal Institute of British Architects Journal*, LXVIII (May, 1961), 273-79.

14. The gap hypothesis corresponds to ideas advanced in more general form by Meyerson and Banfield to explain the failure of planning in Chicago housing site selection. See Martin Meyerson and Edward C. Banfield, *Politics, Planning and the Public Interest* (Glencoe, Ill.: The Free Press, 1955), pp. 274-75.

15. "Redevelopment f.o.b. Detroit," *Architectural Forum*, CII (March, 1955), 116-25.

16. My interview data disagree in some details with the account by Mowitz and Wright, *op. cit.*, pp. 66-72.

17. "Detroit Redevelopment," *Architectural Forum*, CIV (April, 1956), 122-23, compares the Mies plan with the Stonorov-Yamasaki-Gruen plan. "The Miesian Superblock," *Architectural Forum*, CVI (March, 1957), 128-33 and "A Tower Plus Row Houses in Detroit," *Architectural Forum*, CXII (May, 1960), 104-13, are representative of the many articles dealing with the architecture of Mies' plan as proposed and as built.

18. On practically the same day as Mies' plan was approved, the S-Y-G plan national recognition for design excellence in the annual awards program of *Progressive Architecture*. Such is the hazard of making awards to unbuilt projects. *Progressive Architecture*, XXXVII (January, 1956), 76.

19. The "gap" problem seems just as damaging to social and economic intentions as to design. The public-private split is particularly crippling. Greer and Minar write that "the local public authority must either gamble on its knowledge of the private land market or prenegotiate sales. In either event, renewal occurs not where it might benefit the community directly but where it must do so *indirectly through benefiting the private investors.*" Greer and Minar, *op. cit.*, p. 66 (italics added). The heavy critcism renewal has received for building luxury apartments on the ruins of slums seems pointless as long as ideological considerations place renewal at the mercy of the private market. Rehousing slum dwellers requires socialist solutions.

20. A. and P. Smithson, "Postscript: Philadelphia and the London roads," *Architectural Design*, XXXII (August, 1962), 401. Sybil Moholy-Nagy, "Villas in the Slums," *Canadian Architect*, September, 1960, 39-46.

21. Results of the author's field surveys of more than 200 projects will be published. They substantiate the dismal general level of design accomplishment.

22. Housing Act of 1949, *op. cit.*, section 110 (c)(4).

23. John Delafons notes the differences between zoning and renewal plan controls in *Land-Use Controls in the United States* (Cambridge, Mass.: Joint Center for Urban Studies of M.I.T. and Harvard University, 1962), pp. 71-77.

24. I. M. Pei and Associates, *Erieview Cleveland Ohio: An Urban Renewal Plan for Downtown Cleveland* (New York: I. M. Pei and Associates, October, 1961).

25. Land market prediction difficulties and their impact on renewal programs need careful examination. David A. Wallace's "Renaissancemanship," *Journal of the American Institute of Planners*, XXVI (August, 1960), 157-76, suggests this problem may justify a return from "comprehensive" urban renewal planning to "projectitis."

26. Hartford Redevelopment Agency, "Redevelopment Plan for Bushnell-Plaza Project, Conn. R-51" (mimeographed, the Agency, September, 1961); and interview data.

The Bushnell Plaza plan exhibits a particularly clear understanding of the special nature of urban renewal plan controls. Residential density was controlled simply by stating, "the residential structure or structures shall contain not less than 275 units nor more than 325 units . . ."; the public park was required to be "not less than 40,000 square feet nor more than 60,000 . . ."; the controls on the park precisely stated the function it was to serve.

27. This view of the urban renewal plan is to be articulated in a forthcoming article by Herbert M. Franklin.

28. Among the theories propounding a network of catalytic public works in urban renewal design are the "design structure" concepts put forth by Edmund N. Bacon in "Architecture and Planning," *Journal of the American Institute of Architects*, XXV (June, 1961), 68-90; and "capital design" or "capital web" by David A. Crane, in "The City Symbolic," *Journal of the American Institute of Planners*, XXVI (November, 1960), 280-92.

29. Lawrence Lackey, Royston, Hanamoto and Mayes, "Diamond Heights Neighborhood Center: An Urban Design Report to the San Francisco Redevelopment Agency," December 1961. San Francisco Redevelopment Agency, *Two Commercial Sites: Diamond Heights, San Francisco* (San Francisco: the Agency, March 19, 1962).

30. Design plans used in land disposition must be viewed as an articulation of the approved urban renewal plan if this process is to meet the test that land must be sold for fair value for the uses according to the urban renewal plan. This point was clarified by URA in *Local Public Agency Letter No. 267*, "Design in Urban Renewal: Supplement No. 1 to LPA Letter No. 249," May 23, 1963. Design plans move in the direction of increased governmental involvement in design details. This move by URA indicates a partial reversal of early interpretations of statutory requirements limiting construction and providing maximum opportunity for private enterprise.

31. See Albert O. Hirschman and Charles E. Lindblom, "Economic Development, Research and Development, Policy Making: Some Convergent Views," *Behavioral Science*, VII (April, 1962), 215-16.

32. Edmund N. Bacon provides a convincing account of the use of design in this yardstick role in "A Case Study in Urban Design," *Journal of the American Institute of Planners*, XXVI (August, 1960), 224-35.

33. David Crane, "The Public Art of City Building," *The Annals of the American Academy of Political and Social Science*, vol. 332 (March, 1964), 84-94. He recommends a six-step process ranging from design consideration in the master plan to design review of private building.

Boston Redevelopment Authority, *Design and Urban Renewal* (Boston: The Authority, 1964?).

34. Housing and Home Finance Agency, Urban Renewal Administration, *Local Public Agency Letter No. 249*, "Design in Urban Renewal," August 20, 1962. Urban Renewal Administration, *Urban Renewal Notes: Design in Urban Renewal*, July-August, 1963. William L. Slayton, Urban Renewal Administration Commissioner from 1961 to the present, has made numerous speeches and published various articles on behalf of increased attention to renewal design processes. See, for instance, "Design Goals for Urban Renewal," *Architectural Record*, CXXXIV (November, 1963), 149-52.

35. Detroit City Plan Commission, "Elmwood Park Rehabilitation Project No. 1, Urban Renewal Plan" (mimeographed, January, 1961).

Urban Sociology as an Aid to Urban Physical Development: Some Research Strategies

William Michelson

There has been a lot of talk lately about interdisciplinary cooperation in urban physical design. Social scientists seriously turn out research that they feel should aid planners, and planners on their part, when not undertaking the same research themselves, state what kinds of knowledge they should have handed to them.

One crucial problem always seems to bog down these discussions: How can research conducted on *contemporary* social phenomena be useful to the physical building of the *future* metropolis?[1] How can the designer prepare for a modern, more efficient future, yet successfully anticipate public reaction to his brainchild? By physical, I mean the various components of urban form: housing types, siting, distribution of land uses, and so forth. By social phenomena, I am thinking of the types of data open to social scientists—in particular, urban sociologists. The answer, I submit, is beguilingly simple: The urban sociologist may study the basic variables linking men and buildings that are not only present now, but which will also appear throughout the future.

This task is easier said than done. Nonetheless, I should like to outline here my conception of the sociologists' contribution to the building of the future city and point to some strategic approaches that I feel will facilitate this task. These approaches are not new to the sociological repertoire, but

Reprinted by permission from *The Journal of the American Institute of Planners*, March, 1968, copyright by The American Institute of Planners.

they depart from research strategies commonly used these days within urban sociology and ecology.[2]

Current Research and Future Cities

How do you progress from current studies that show meaningful ties between social and physical phenomena in cities to the design of future cities? There are finite elements in the physical environment at present which also will be part of future cities—*specific arrangements of space separating people from other people and from all the various kinds of activities.* People and activities are separated at least by sight, by sound, and by touch. People can see each other, hear each other, and come in contact with each other in potentially measurable degrees. These types of spatial separation imply meaningful physical units—the end process of design. They specify the potential degree of impingement that other people and land uses may have on a person, depending on the person's culturally derived receptivity to these stimuli.[3] Every place in the man-made environment should be open to characterization in these spatial terms, since they represent the fundamental components of design.

If spatial units are the ends of design, then technology is the means. At any given time, the ways in which people know how to create spatial separations are limited. For example, most people can conceive of freedom from many kinds of unwanted impingements only in terms of a single-family home on a large lot in an all-residential neighborhood. Yet, there is no saying that this is the only means of producing spatial separation. At a future time, the same kind of spatial unit may be created by a vastly changed technology. Moshe Safdie claims to have created it by quite different means in Habitat 67 in Montreal. Hence, while arrangements of space are created by particular technologies, they exist independent of any one technology—present or future.

The phenomenon that I believe urban sociologists could study productively is how various kinds of people adjust to the various kinds of spatial separations that abound today. This will carry meaning for the planning of future cities because a huge variety of spatial separations, including some very promising ones, are to be found in bits and pieces throughout the world today. It is likely, therefore, that the overwhelming majority of spatial separations that future technologies will create can be found *somewhere* today.

What the future *will* bring is a multiplicity of new ways of creating spatial separations. For, even if the apparent promise of unlimited technological progress is only minimally fulfilled, we can expect great changes in the way designers shape space in cities. New building techniques abound. New types of transportation make fairly recent science fiction seem outmoded. There is certainly no basis for suggesting that our current stock of buildings should remain in toto the yardstick for future policies.

Thus, our ends are predominantly with us now, but our means will change. Urban sociologists can aid the development of housing by identifying the spatial separations that current research shows most easily accommodate various subsectors of the population. They can and should study the success with which physically different homes and neighborhoods accommodate different social groups. Then, unless physical surroundings make no difference at all as a limiting or encouraging factor in the lives people lead,[4] a product of this work, as applied to any city in particular, would be a distribution of types of desirable spatial separations for the city's residents, which designers could use as a starting point for their plans.

Note that the sociologists are not determining the design or construction of homes, neighborhoods, or cities from their research. They are, rather, offering suggestions for optimal spatial arrangements with consideration for stated criteria of mental health, family and community organization, and the like. The physical designer, on his part, must now come forward with the most efficient physical means to produce the requisite spatial units. He is no longer required to play amateur sociologist, psychologist, or the like; but he is taxed with the challenge of creating a given spatial structure by means that he or his city can afford and which are politically acceptable. In making his role explicit, the division of labor I suggest puts a greater—not a lesser—burden of innovation on the designer than he has now.

In short, urban sociologists can produce informed estimates of the spatial needs of future construction as a result of their present studies, providing that they study human behavior in conjunction with the most basic concepts of space. This will aid experts in design by enabling them to concentrate on the most desirable means to the spatial ends.

Such a concentration of the sociologists' efforts will change the usual conception of their role in the design field from conservative to more neutral researcher. Sociological studies relating to design commonly demonstrate, among other things, attachment of people to their present environment, be it urban ghetto or suburban home. The sociologist, therefore, appears to be defending the continued existence of a physical situation that many designers don't happen to like. It is a much happier service for the sociologist to be able to point to spatial components of a ghetto or an estate which, created by more "acceptable" means, could accommodate the same people as well or better.[5]

There are, however, some formidable obstacles to the realization of this goal. One of them is the extreme difficulty involved in precisely conceptualizing the crucial spatial arrangements. Some fruitful attempts have been made in the past by planners,[6] as well as by other interested parties.[7] Yet, we lack both a terminology for discussing basic spatial separations, and an understanding of just *how* great a variation of spatial arrangements now exists. Work in this area is greatly needed. Nonetheless, despite the difficulty involved, conceptual clarification and codification of spatial arrangements are prerequisites to the research that can aid future planning.

A second obstacle to the immediate realization of the basic goal is the virtual lack of precedent for the kinds of social research needed to link social with physical variables. Here, I can be a bit more positive, and I shall suggest a few approaches and techniques that appear potentially fruitful for study in this area.

Some Approaches to Research

Man, as a thinking being, relates to his spatial environment both in his mind and in his actual presence. This gives rise to two approaches to research, both necessary: *mental congruence* and *experiential congruence* between people and their environment. While fundamentally different, they complement each other.

Mental congruence exists if an individual thinks that particular spatial patterns will successfully accommodate his personal characteristics, values, and style of life. If a great number of people in a society believes that families can best be raised in suburban space, for example, then there is a state of mental congruence between "familism" and "suburbanism";[8] this relationship between a physical phenomenon and a social end is a social fact[9] worth noting, even if the relationship is not empirically substantiated.

All studies that set out to discover what people want and why they want it are concerned with mental congruence. If people regularly expect the same social situation to result from the creation or maintenance of a particular physical environment, then a state of mental congruence between the two can be said to exist. Congruence also implies its opposite, which occurs whenever people regularly dissociate certain physical and social phenomena. Among many people, for example, there is mental *in*congruence between privacy and multiple dwellings.

People cannot be expected to be consistently rational in their preferences. Even though their feelings about environment are usually based to some degree on observation and experience, most people haven't seen or lived in various types of physical environments. Therefore, what is involved in mental congruence is in the nature of hearsay evidence. Yet it is important evidence, since people's beliefs about these relationships affect the objectives they demand. For example, an urban renewal proposal meets with considerable opposition if people feel that the replacement housing will not accommodate them appropriately.[10] Another phenomenon is the so-called self-fulfilling prophecy,[11] whereby the belief in the existence of something often makes it come true. If a man believes that handyman activities are impossible in high density residential situations, for example, then he probably won't undertake this kind of activity while living in such housing.

Experiential congruence, on the other hand, deals with how well the environment *actually* accommodates the characteristics and behavior of people. Thus, to study experiential congruence, one would not ask a person his preference for environment; one would study people living in a specific environment. Although people may not be aware of the existence of experiential congruence, their daily experience, if properly studied, can point out the constraining or enabling power of their environment. Thus in the case of the apartment-bound handyman, we could demonstrate the experiential incongruence of handyman activities and dwellings that feature minimal separations between individuals, if it could be shown how formerly active handymen *unexpectedly* find it impossible to continue this pastime after their move to a multiple dwelling.

Experiential congruence of people and environment is the research approach that is basically needed to form specific physical plans for the future. Nonetheless, a knowledge of mental congruence is necessary to assess the public's predisposition to accept and make successful whatever may be proposed; to ignore this factor is to invite failure, no matter how objectively correct future plans may be. I shall outline three research strategies that I believe are particularly well suited to the empirical study of the interrelations of social and physical phenomena.

Studying Mental Congruence

Research on the mental congruence between people and their urban environment has centered around survey research. What do people *think* about aspects of their housing and cities? What are their preferences? Past surveys have shown both the problems and the promise of this approach.

The problems stem from the difficulty of obtaining information through a finite series of questions which shows how a respondent rates many variables in a complex substantive area vis-à-vis each other. In one study, for example, respondents were asked to rate the importance they attached to specific elements of the environment on a three-point scale (1 = unimportant, 2 = somewhat important, and 3 = very important); every element suggested was rated on the average at least somewhat important, and most of them received a plurality or ratings as very important.[12] How should one establish "real" importance? Or comparative importance?

The semiprojective game situation offers a fruitful approach to mental congruence. Within the context of the intensive interview it is possible to set up hypothetical situations in which people can get involved. When playing the game, people are forced to make a limited number of choices among elements whose relative importance the researcher is attempting to judge; the reasons given for the decisions made are of interest to the researcher, who wants to see if many people make the same choices in order to gain the same goal.

Wilson, for example, conducted a game in studying two southern cities in which respondents were supplied with a limited amount of play money and were forced to spend it judiciously among a variety of elements which constituted the nature of a neighborhood and were present or absent, distant or close, as determined by the respondent's expenditure.[13] He forced people, through a familiar medium, to declare the relative importance to themselves of various aspects of the environment. In this game, they couldn't declare themselves in favor of everything; they had to weigh the elements carefully in order to demonstrate their preferences.

In my own research, as a part of intensive interviews, I had each respondent draw a sketch map of his ideal environment—from housing type to lot size to block and on outwards to the placement of activities in appropriate places through what they later designated as their neighborhood and the rest of the city. One question that I set out to answer was the relative importance to people of these different *levels* of environment. Hence, I asked the respondents to rank aspects of the sketch (home, block, neighborhood, and city), in which they had invested time and thought, with respect to the relative values of them. But rather than to ask for simple rankings, which are difficult for an honest respondent if the alternatives are many or complex, I had them choose between pairs of all the dichotomous combinations of the four levels ("If you could have *either* the (e.g. *home*) you want *or* the (e.g. *neighborhood*), which would you choose?"). By this technique the continuing importance of the neighborhood (though not any single conception of it) in urban areas was brought out, a finding that agrees with Wilson's.

In short, in a realm where opinion is important but where traditionally straightforward questions may be inadequate, the semiprojective game situation may be a source of needed data.

Studying Experiential Congruence

The study of experiential congruence by its definition involves activity and not opinion. Hence, research into this aspect demands straightforward but comprehensive accounting of behavior asserted to be congruent with particular types of spatial arrangements under conditions of exposure to those environments. Research design and techniques are both critical in this context.

The design of the research must specify that the systematic relationships recorded are related to the environment and not to some spurious factor. Thus, people in the process of moving to housing which contrasts to that previously inhabited are natural subjects for study, and it is not surprising that some of the most suggestive research in this area comes from before-and-after studies of urban renewal "victims."[14] Yet, in determining relations and interrelations, one intervening variable has shown up consistently in the literature, although the extent to which it intervenes in the relationship between housing and life style is as yet uncertain; this variable is *time*.[15]

Time is relevant here in several contexts. First, *length of residence* may be an explanatory factor in understanding the behavior of people in specific settings. To what extent is a person's behavior a function of change and the newness of an environment, as opposed to the environment itself?

Many authors who studied suburbia in the 1950's, for example, based their comments on one-time observations immediately after the first wave of settlement.[16] It has been argued more recently that they would have formed a different picture of suburban life if they had returned five years later.[17] The settlement would have "matured," and the pace of life would have changed greatly.

Longitudinal studies of movers can potentially answer a number of questions crucial to planners and sociologists alike:

1. To what extent does a particular residential environment tend to attract a particular type of resident? When selecting a new home, do people envisage how they will lead their lives after moving?

2. To what extent do people carry out the lives they intended to lead in their new environments? What factors prevent the execution of preconceived plans? Could these factors be modified by the provision of appropriate facilities or services?

3. To what extent does a particular way of life become pronounced in a particular physical setting? Do aspects of the environment influence what people do, with whom they do it, and where they do it; or, all else being equal, do they merely repeat the round of life that they formerly pursued in a physically different environment? What consequences do answers to the foregoing questions have for the differential provision of facilities and activities?

4. If a typical way of life emerges in a particular setting, what happens to the new resident who fails to adopt it? Does he tend to move? Does he tend to develop problems of varying degrees of seriousness? Or, on the other hand, are typical patterns only a statistical phenomenon, unrelated to successful adjustment to the residential environment? Is there any way to identify the potential malcontent before his move?

5. Does it take longer for people to adjust to some settings than to others? What problems typically emerge in specific settings during particular time periods after settlement, and could they be remedied if anticipated?

A focus on time is helpful in still another context. A second research strategy for experiential congruence I think worthy of singling out is the *time and activity budget*. It is a technique for eliciting accurate descriptions of behavior, not opinion. The researcher asks his respondents for an account of *what* they did on the weekday before and in finely divided periods of time, *where*, and *with whom* the activity took place. By such relatively straightforward means, the researcher can ascertain the qualitative *and* quantitative aspects of social activity as well as its spatial distribution, together with the necessary information to construct interaction networks and other aspects of social structure.[18] While participant observation and poll-type interviewing can give *glimpses* of the same data, time and activity budgets can serve as the basis for extremely fine environmental comparisons in time and space which can be greatly aided by contemporary computer technology. Diaries, such as have been used in traffic studies, are similarly helpful; but cooperation may be more difficult to obtain in their use, particularly if longer periods of time are covered or if they are used on repeated occasions.

Conclusions

Research as described can serve an instrumental role in designing future cities through imaginative use of strategies and techniques present in the larger field of sociology. It must study people's mental and experiential relations to basic arrangements of space which exist today and which may be recreated more effectively in the future by different design technologies. Some strategies that appear fruitful toward that end are the semiprojective game in interviewing for opinions, the longitudinal factor in the design of studies to assess the effects of spatial arrangements, and the use of time and activity budgets to account for relevant behavior and structural variables.

Notes

1. A recent contribution to the *Journal of the American Institute of Planners* points up this problem. Constance Perin's interpretation, "Some Interests of the City Planner in Social Science Research," Vol. XXXIII (March 1967), 114-16, states that the researchers must: (1) refer to specific transportation types to be considered in surveys on desired urban spatial distribution and utilization and, at the same time, (2) make their findings

applicable to the future rather than the present; but it does not indicate how results based on current technology can then be useful for avowedly futuristic plans. It is this confusing situation that I should like to approach constructively in this piece.

2. See, for example, Jack P. Gibbs, *Urban Research Methods* (Princeton, N.J.: Van Nostrand, 1961), and Philip Hauser (ed.), *Handbook for Social Research in Urban Areas* (Paris: UNESCO, 1965).

3. On the effect of culture, see Edward T. Hall, *The Hidden Dimension* (Garden City, N.Y.: Doubleday & Co., Inc., 1966).

4. This claim has been made, but a large number of studies would indicate the opposite.

5. This, of course, would not solve all possible social problems connected with the rehousing of groups of people. Change of residence is itself a major factor. See, for example, the various publications of the West End study in Boston, of which the most recent relevant report was by Marc Fried, "Functions of the Working Class Community in Modern Urban Society: Implications for Forced Relocation," *Journal of the American Institute of Planners*, Vol. XXXIII (March 1967), 90-103.

6. See, for example, Hans Blumenfeld, "A Theory of City Form Past and Present," *Journal of the Society of Architectural Historians*, Vol. VIII (No. 3-4, 1949), 7-16; Kevin Lynch and Lloyd Rodwin, "A Theory of Urban Form," *Journal of the American Institute of Planners*, XXIV (Fall, 1958), 201-14; and Kevin Lynch, "The Pattern of the Metropolis," *Daedalus*, XC (Winter, 1961), 79-98.

7. See my partial attempt at this, "An Empirical Analysis of Urban Environmental Preferences," *Journal of the American Institute of Planners*, Vol. XXXII (November 1966), 355-60.

8. Wendell Bell, "Social Choice, Life Styles, and Suburban Residence," in William M. Dobrinier (ed.), *The Suburban Community* (N.Y.: G. P. Putnam's Sons, 1958), pp. 225-47.

9. A classic discussion of social facts as a phenomenon is Emile Durkheim's *The Rules of the Sociological Methods* (N.Y.: The Free Press of Glencoe, Inc., 1958, original ed. 1938).

10. An appropriate example from Cambridge, Mass., was described by Ronald Nuttal, Erwin K. Scheuch, and Chad Gordon, "Sanctions Resources and a Typology of Power Holders," paper presented to the 1965 meeting of the Eastern Sociological Society, New York City.

11. For a full discussion of the self-fulfilling prophecy, see Robert K. Merton, *Social Theory and Social Structure* (N.Y.: The Free Press of Glencoe, Inc., 1957), pp. 179-95.

12. Richard A. Lamanna, "Value Consensus Among Urban Residents," *Journal of the American Institute of Planners*, Vol. XXX (November 1964), 317-23.

13. Robert L. Wilson, "Livability of the City: Attitudes and Urban Development," in F. Stuart Chapin, Jr., and Shirley Wein (eds.), *Urban Growth Dynamics* (N.Y.: John Wiley & Sons, Inc., 1962), pp. 359-99. See also Chapin's game on allocation of time, in F. Stuart Chapin, Jr., *Urban Land Use Planning* (2nd ed.; Urbana: University of Illinois Press, 1965), pp. 250-52.

14. See, for example, Chester Hartman, "The Consequences of Relocation for Housing Welfare," in James Q. Wilson (ed.), *Urban Renewal: The Record and the Controversy* (Cambridge, Mass.: M.I.T., 1966), pp. 293-335; Marc Fried, "Grieving for a Lost Home," in Leonard Duhl (ed.), *The Urban Condition* (N.Y.: Basic Books, Inc., 1963), pp. 151-71; Michael Young and Peter Willmott, *Family and Kinship in East London* (London: Routledge and Kegan Paul, Ltd., 1957); and Daniel M. Wilner and Rosabelle P. Walkley, "Effects of Housing on Health and Performance," in Duhl (ed.), pp. 215-28.

15. Herbert J. Gans, "Planning and Social Life: Friendship and Neighbor Relations in Suburban Communities," *Journal of the American Institute of Planners*, Vol. XXVII (May 1961), 134-40, S. D. Clark, *The Suburban*

Society (Toronto: University of Toronto Press, 1966); and Peter Willmott, *The Evolution of a Community* (N.Y.: Humanities Press, 1963).

16. See, for example, "The Busy Busy Citizen," *Fortune*, Vol. 43 February 1951), 96-99, 129; Harry Henderson, "The Mass Produced Suburbs," *Harper's*, Vol. 207 (November 1953), 25-32, (December 1953), 80-86.

17. Clark develops this thesis extensively in *The Suburban Society*.

18. See, for example, Chapin, *Urabn Land Use Planning*, and some examples of the use of this tool in Albert J. Reiss, "Rural-Urban and Status Differences in Interpersonal Contacts," *American Journal of Sociology*, Vol. 65 (1959), 182-95, and F. Stuart Chapin, Jr., and Henry C. Hightower, *Household Activity Systems—A Pilot Investigation* (Chapel Hill: University of North Carolina, Center for Urban and Regional Studies, 1966). In this study, the authors apply fruitfully the concept of activity systems to physical planning, but in a different context than the above suggestion, namely that it could be used to compare the "effects" of contemporary physical environments which differ physically. An expert implementation of this tool can be found in the current "Boston Housing Study" of Charles Tilly. This technique has recently been accorded increased interest, as evidenced by the worldwide studies of time coordinated by Dr. Alexander Szalai of UNITAR which were presented at the 1966 meeting of the International Sociological Association at Evion, France.

Social Research and New Communities

Peter Willmott

This paper, about the application of social research to the planning of new communities, is in two parts. The first examines some of the social aspects of the creation of new communities, particularly aspects in which social research has produced data; the second reports an attempt to associate social research more closely with city planning.

Since the term "new communities" can cover a variety of different kinds of development, it may be helpful to summarize briefly the main types in Britain. First, the *new towns;* under the New Towns Acts (1946 and 1965) these are developed and managed by development corporations specially created for each town. Secondly, *expanding towns,* which are developed under the Town Development Act (1952) and are usually smaller than new towns; they involve the enlarging of a small country town by adding population from London or another large city. The development is carried out by the exporting city authority, the local town council, or a combination of the two. Thirdly, *peripheral projects,* which are developed by the city authority on the edge of the city, sometimes (by agreement) on land outside its own direct jurisdiction; these are mainly small projects, though some have been large, for example, Wythenshawe near Manchester (population 100,000), and Becontree near London (population 100,000).

In addition to these three types of development, much larger *expanding towns* are now in prospect. The Government plans to expand a number of large towns to about

Reprinted by permission from *The Journal of the American Institute of Planners*, November, 1967, copyright by the American Institute of Planners.

Social Research and New Communities 253

double their present size, to link up other towns in major developments, and to create some *new cities* of half a million population. One of the proposed new expansions is of Ipswich (present population 120,000), the subject of the applied research described in the second part of this paper; it is likely to have a population of over 200,000 by 1981.

I Social Problems of New Communities

Peripheral developments have received most attention from social researchers. British studies of these date from the early 1930's, though it was not until more recently that research began to be solidly based upon interviews with representative samples of residents. A number of studies have compared social life in the old "slum" districts with the new suburban projects.[1] These have found that, whereas in the old district people were members of "close-knit" networks of kin and neighbors, in the housing project the immediate family was more isolated. Shops and public houses, which were close at hand and served as local "social centers" in the old area, were nonexistent or more distant in the new, and were thus not able to serve the same social functions. People had difficulty making friends with their fellow residents. They felt more lonely and their lives were in general more strained; one study reported noticeably more mental illness in the new project than the national average.[2]

A number of these studies appeared in the first few years after the new towns had started, and many people assumed that the findings from the peripheral housing projects applied to the new towns as well. The danger in generalizing from such studies was twofold. First, the peripheral developments were different from new or expanding towns in some important respects: for example, their residents were, unlike new town residents,[3] predominantly drawn from "slum" districts; large-scale commuting imposed extra financial and other burdens; and the general standards of shopping and other services were lower in these projects. The second mistake in interpretation was that virtually all the studies of suburban projects were made at an early stage and were based mainly on interviews with residents who had moved relatively recently; nobody knew to what extent the problems were temporary. A study of the Becontree project, published in 1963,[4] suggested that they were largely temporary. This inquiry, carried out some forty years after the project was built, indicated that, though the new way of life was somewhat different from that in the old slum areas, it was one to which most residents—and even more so, their children—had successfully adapted.

The general impression from such research as has been undertaken in new and expanding towns, is that there, too, many of the new residents' difficulties are transitory. Studies among residents of some years' standing in the new towns of Stevenage[5] and Basildon[6] in England, East Kilbride[7] and Cumbernauld[8] in Scotland, and in the expanding town of Swindon[9] portray relatively stable and contented populations. The proportion of families who return to the city is low—something like 1 or 2 percent per year.[10] When people are asked if they are, in general, "glad" they have moved, over four-fifths say they are.[11] This attitude is particularly true where the towns have modern pedestrian shopping centers, as has Stevenage; evidently these are much prized by the citizens.[12] The new and expanding towns, in general, contain a high proportion of skilled manual workers, and they are apparently relatively prosperous compared with manual workers in Britain as a whole; they live in more modern homes and more often own cars and items of household equipment like washing machines and refrigerators.[13]

The proportions of people who are active members of social clubs and organizations are similar to those in more established areas where studies have been made.[14] With regard to friends and neighbors, an inquiry in Stevenage has indicated that though the social patterns are different from those in urban working-class districts, still "there was little isolation or loneliness . . . everyone had some local friends and some had many."[5] To sum up, as far as one can judge, the new towns in particular have now developed into fairly successful communities. This is probably less true of the smaller expanded towns and the peripheral projects, though they can be expected to settle down in time.

It does not follow from this that the new communities have no problems, nor that future developments of this kind need only to emulate what has been done already. The new communities so far created have certainly not been without their difficulties, despite the eventual relative contentment of the residents. As has been pointed out, in British policy the creation of new towns is giving way to larger town expansions and to new cities which, being more ambitious and more complex projects, raise greater problems. Still, the experience of the new towns already in existence has relevance for future city planning.

Apart from social surveys of the kind already referred to, there are two other sources of data about the problems of new communities. First, there have been some general reviews of the social aspects of new communities, drawing largely upon observation and discussions with, for instance, Development Corporation staff; examples are Nicholson's inquiry for the National Council of Social Service[16] and two reports from subcommittees of the Ministry of Housing's Central Housing Advisory Committee.[17] Secondly, there have been some studies, more demographic and economic than sociological, undertaken in preparation for new proposals, in particular the report of the team working for what was then the London County Council on the proposed new town at Hook.[18] These inquiries have revealed a variety of problems associated with new communities. Three issues will serve as illustrations: the problem of the age structure of a new community, the experience of neighborhood planning, and the problems that some residents face in adjusting to the new life.

Age Structure of Population

Every new settlement attracts young people. Those who move to new towns in Britain are predominantly young couples with young children,[19] as are those, for instance, who go to the Levittowns of the United States.[20] This age bias has a number of important consequences. The first is that the rapid growth of the population is accelerated and continued because of the high birth rate of the migrant population. This can be particularly serious if the new community is conceived as a finite development. A population projection for one peripheral development, on a site of limited size, showed that the population growth likely to be generated would far exceed the capacity of the housing project.[21] Thus not only did the residents from East London have to move away from their parents and other kin in order to get a new home; frequently their children, in their turn, would have to move on again because the new project did not allow room for those to stay who wanted to. The study of the Becontree project found that this was exactly what had happened there: the "unbalanced" population of 1931 generated a population by 1961 about 30 percent larger and some of the second generation who wanted to stay had been unable to do so.[22] The British new towns have come to recognize this problem, and have now allowed sites for the expected population increase, though this has sometimes meant using for housing land formerly allocated for open space or other use.[23]

The "unbalanced" age structure of new communities has other consequences. As well as the danger of physical monotony—the result of building large areas of similar-sized dwellings for similar-sized families—there is also the danger of social monotony—the lack of variety in age composition leading to a lack of diversity in social activities. It also creates major problems for the public authorities which have to provide social services and facilities. A bulge in the demand for maternity and child welfare centers in the first years gives way later to a demand for infant schools, then junior schools, then secondary schools. The bulge then comes in the demand for further education and for jobs for graduates. And so the cycle goes on, until it results in an inordinately large need for old people's services. Not only does this impose problems on the local authority each time it has to switch its resources to meet new needs; but in providing services that are adequate for early stages of the cycle, it may find these same devices to be over-generous for later decades.

Neighborhood Planning

When the first round of new towns was being designed, British planning was strongly influenced by theories of neighborhood planning, and the towns were all divided into "neighborhood units," usually of from 5,000 to 10,000 population. But after Cumbernauld was started in 1957 neighborhood planning figured much less.

It seems that the swing in planning opinion had some justification. Such research as has been done suggests that some of the social claims made for the "neighborhood unit" were exaggerated. The suggestion sometimes made was not only that it was a useful way of "structuring" the new community for the provision of schools, shops and other services but also that it could generate something of the "community life" of the pre-industrial village.[24] This implies that residents would strongly identify with "their" own neighborhood and that it would be the locus of most of their informal social relationships and of the formal organizations to which they would belong.

None of these assumptions seems borne out by the research. The evidence on people's identification with their neighborhood is somewhat contradictory; the extent of Development Corporation emphasis on the name of the neighborhood, or of smaller residential areas within it, seems the main determinant of whether people even know which neighborhood they live in.[25] As for friendship patterns, a study in Stevenage showed that, though most "friends" were local, the neighborhood in itself was not a significant area.[26] The addresses of friends visiting were plotted. Of these visitors, 24 percent lived next door, 35 percent elsewhere on the same road, and 18 percent somewhere in a quarter-mile radius. Thus altogether more than three-quarters came from within an area about a fifth of the size of a Stevenage neighborhood. Outside this local area, about a third of the visitors came from elsewhere in the neighborhood, a third from other neighborhoods, and a third from outside Stevenage altogether. Nor is the neighborhood the significant area for other forms of social activity. A study in Basildon of the leisure activities of 100 boys found that:

> The majority of all activities (43%) occurred in the home . . . . The neighborhood was the place for only 8% of all reported activities, while the town centre and other neighborhood units in the town were the setting for 19%. Areas outside the town were the location for 20% of all activities.[27]

A traffic survey in Stevenage, carried out by Birmingham University, found that, of all "social and recreational trips" (including those on foot), 40 percent occurred within the neighborhood, 40 percent elsewhere in Stevenage, including the center, and 20 percent outside Stevenage altogether.[28]

All this suggests that too much was expected of the "neighborhood unit." The concept was applied too inflexibly, emphasizing too strongly each neighborhood's separateness from the rest of the town. Perhaps, too, the "neighborhood unit" is rather too large a locality for most people. But it does not follow that neighborhood planning has no role. Neighborhood shops, schools, and churches are obviously used by local residents. And most people, in old towns and new, perceive their own locality as something distinct and different. Even in Cumbernauld there are recognized local areas—people describe themselves as living in "Kildrum" or "Carbrain," and these districts have some meaning for them.[29] The research reported in the second part of this paper suggested that this was also true of Ipswich. It seems that the reaction against neighborhood planning went too far, and that most people tend to think of themselves as living in some sort of "neighborhood," whether city planners call it that or not.[30]

The Problem of Settling In

Reference was made earlier to the differences in social life in old and new communities and to residents' responses to the move. The generally favorable impression now has to be somewhat qualified by further research findings. People respond individually to moving to a new community, varying greatly in their capacity to resettle. Since in general middle-class people move more often and are able to make friends more readily than manual workers and their families, they settle more easily in new communities.[31] The character of people's social networks in the former district, affected by such factors as the length of residence in the old area and the proximity of relatives, is also influential.[32] As reported earlier, few migrants move back and something like four-fifths of those who stay in new towns say they are "glad" they made the move; but the remaining one-fifth should not be ignored, nor their difficulties and criticisms which are shared by others.[33]

Most people move for a house. In return, they often feel they have given up some qualities of their old life. There is a close correspondence between what was found in surveys in Stevenage and East Kilbride, and what the LCC found in 175 interviews in the small "expanding towns" of Haverhill, Huntingdon, and Thetford.[34] The main things that people "disliked" about their new environment or "missed" about their old were shopping, entertainment, or other amenities (mentioned by about half). The other main criticisms were of infrequent or expensive bus services (about a fifth or a quarter) and relatives or friends left behind (again about a quarter). With some people—wives more than husbands—the sense of loneliness is acute. The "quietness," the relative absence of other people that results from low density and from rigid land-use "zoning," the sense of loss from leaving relatives and friends—all this can lead, in a minority of wives, to what has been described as "transitional neurosis."[35] The questions raised are: first, is it possible to reduce the problems of transition; second, how could the new communities incorporate some of the particularly valued features of the old?

Social Problems and Research

There are many other social issues besides those to which this review has drawn attention. One should certainly point out that a major concern is the long-term future of the new community. In addition to the already mentioned question of age structure, there is the issue of "balance" in the social structure, and, where an existing town is to be substantially expanded, the "integration" of the newcomers with the old residents. Nor should the personal difficulties of the people who move to planned communities be ignored. Another set of problems, closely connected to the above, concerns the physical design of the town; it involves the location of industry and shops, as well as the issues of neighborhood planning and mixing social groups in residential areas.

The general impression so far may be that there is now a substantial body of social research data on British new communities. This is not so. There have been hardly more than a handful of studies on new towns and there is still extraordinarily little solidly based information about their experience. The changes in planning thought from one "generation" of new towns to the next reflect much more the shifts of fashion than a response to firm evidence. But at least there is growing awareness among British planners of the importance of social questions and the potential contribution of social research.

II Participation in the Planning Process

Most of the research referred to in the first part of this paper was undertaken by social scientists working independently. They looked at what city planners had done and reported what was wrong with it. In recent years the relationship has been slowly changing; sociologists have been drawn into partnership with planners. The Ministry of Housing itself now employs a number of sociologists; one has, for example, undertaken research on the leisure needs of new towns,[36] others have worked with architects in the Research and Development Group,[37] and still others have carried out a social survey as part of a study of the prospects of rehabilitation in a declining area in Lancashire.[38] Some city authorities, like those of London and Liverpool, now have sociologists on the staff of their planning departments.

The author of this paper and some of his colleagues at the Institute of Community Studies have similarly become more directly involved in planning, acting as sociological consultants to two teams working on major town expansions—Shankland, Cox, and Associates on Ipswich, Wilson and Womersley on Northampton. With both towns the planners' tasks were the same, and the "terms of reference" from the Minister of Housing almost identically worded.[39] Each town had been mentioned in the *South East Study*[40] as suitable for expansion and both town councils were agreeable. The preparatory planning work fell into two parts. In the first year, the team would study the town and its subregion, see whether the proposed expansion was feasible, suggest what general form it should take, and propose the area for "designation" under the New Towns Act. In the second, they would prepare a "basic plan" for the guidance of the new developing authority and the town council.

This work started in mid-1965 and finished in mid-1967. In this paper the purpose is not to discuss the proposals of the respective teams but only the contribution made to their work by the sociologists. To simplify presentation, the work discussed is that done for one town, Ipswich, but that in Northampton was similar.

From the beginning the sociologists' contribution was seen as something more than simply carrying out relevant social research. They prepared papers setting out some "sociological criteria" for expansion and suggesting appropriate policies. Quasi-literary techniques were sometimes used to convey the human aspects of development. For example, the social research findings referred to earlier were drawn upon to create hypothetical "profiles" of three contrasted families before and after the move. Here are some extracts from one such "profile":

> Mr. A. is 35 and lives in a rented Victorian terraced house in the Islington district of London; with his wife and two children (aged four and seven), he occupies the whole house —two small rooms up and two down, an outside toilet, no bath. Mr. A. opted to move with the firm, not only because he has a good job, but also because he wants something better, above all 'for the kiddies.' He wants more space, a modern bathroom and toilet, a modern kitchen for his wife, and a garden for the children, He also wants fresh air, the countryside nearby, and a 'better district.' His own life is already largely 'home-centred': he has a drink with some workmates on Friday night (he works about a mile away) and visits his parents once a fortnight, but otherwise when not at work he is at home. Most evenings he watches television, though about one night a fortnight his wife's unmarried sister babysits and the couple go to the cinema, or sometimes to the West End for a 'show' or a Chinese meal. Mrs. A. grew up about half a mile away, where her parents still live. She sees her mother three or four times during the week and a married sister who lives locally nearly as frequently. The women shop for each other and help out, for example when anyone is ill. Apart from the circle of relatives, Mrs. A. knows many other people in her part of Islington;

while out she often meets former schoolfriends or workmates, or friends of her mother or sisters, and she is known to many of the shopkeepers. Mr. A. is not quite so much at home in the district, but by now he knows a good many people—other men living in the same street, his wife's relatives and friends, some local shopkeepers and publicans, The nearest shops are a few minutes walk away, as are the bus routes to the local cinema, the street market and the West End. Their main local shopping centre is about 15 minutes walk, five minutes on the bus . . . .

After the move Mr. A.'s journey to work will probably be shorter. He will, in the main, still be working with the same people—which will help make the move less strange for him than for his wife. They will have a much pleasanter house—more spacious, better equipped, newly decorated and sparkling—and both of them will appreciate this for themselves and their children. But Mrs. A. feels 'lost' and lonely, at least at first. She is, for the first time in her life, among a whole community of strangers. She neither has relatives within reach nor knows any of the other people, though she may get to know some through their being workmates of her husband. For between six months and two years, she feels unsettled and lonely. The mud, the unmade-up roads, the absence of shops and telephone boxes or pillar boxes make it all seem worse. She is not able to go out much with her husband—since most of the neighbors also have young children, babysitters are scarce. She will, however, almost certainly 'settle' in time: she will get to know other wives, particularly through her children; she will begin to feel more at home, less nostalgic for relatives, friends and the old district. But it will probably still be, in many ways, a very different life: even more 'home-centred' than back in London, partly because of the problem of babysitting, already mentioned, partly because the new home is a joy to stay in, partly because there is 'not much to do' close at hand. She will also have a longer walk to the shops, to the clinic or the doctor's office, and bus services will be infrequent. She will find, unless she goes into the town centre to shop, that prices are higher, the choice narrower, than in her local market in Islington. She will probably notice too that there are 'less people around' in the district where she lives and those there are will be more like each other; the place is empty of men in the daytime, dominated by children and prams and pregnant mums . . . .

The sociologists also played a full part in the team's deliberations and shared in its decision. In doing so, they inevitably had at times to desert the usual standards of scholarly detachment and be prepared to express an opinion insupportable by firm data. Because time and money were limited, even such interview surveys as were carried out were small scale. The main sets of interviews, in Ipswich and London, were with relatively small samples—about four hundred in Ispwich and two samples of one hundred and fifty in London. These surveys were supplemented by small numbers of interviews in Ipswich with some "opinion leaders" and in London with key officials and employers considering moving their firms out of the city. In addition, four small expanding towns were briefly visited and the officials there asked about their experience. The sociologists drew also on earlier sociological studies (their own and other people's) and on the general body of sociological knowledge.

The objectives of the sociological studies, formulated at the outset, naturally reflected the issues referred to in the first part of this paper. One purpose was to suggest policies which would attract a more balanced age structure than is usual with new communities, and a population which included all occupational strata. Another was to suggest how the "integration" of newcomers and existing residents might be assisted. The sociologists also agreed to contribute to thinking about neighborhood planning and in particular about the mixture of different standards of housing—and thus different types of residents—and to suggest how the problems of "settling in" might be eased.

There were some other specific tasks. One was to investigate the opinions of existing Ipswich residents about their town and about the proposed expansion—these were obviously related to the issue of "integration." Another was to form a view about the likely demand for different kinds of housing both from Ipswich people and from potential migrants from London—and about the likely demand for houses to buy instead of rent. The contribution of the research on some of these questions is now briefly discussed.

Ipswich Survey

The main survey in Ipswich was based upon 390 interviews with a randomly selected sample of adults. Various background information was collected about their households, housing, occupation, income, journey to work, shopping, leisure patterns, etc. People were asked about their opinions of the proposed expansion. The survey also tried to discover what elements in the existing town were valued. One question was designed to show what physical features particularly "symbolized" the town; there was strong emphasis on the medieval core and particular sections of it.[41] Similarly, a majority of people, in answer to a general question on what they "liked" about the town spoke of the center or of the "country-town atmosphere" that characterizes it. Thus local opinion tallied with the town planning judgment that it was important to preserve and enhance the center and its distinctive character.

For neighborhood planning purposes informants were asked to indicate on a map "where your neighborhood begins and ends." All but a handful were able to do so, and their boundaries were plotted on a plan of the town. On the plan, the thickness of particular lines indicated the extent of agreement about them as boundaries. Though there was great variation in the sizes of neighborhoods and in the boundaries, there was also a high degree of consensus about certain major boundaries. These were mainly physical features—a major road, a railway line, the river. This exercise showed that people in Ipswich (and in Northampton) thought of themselves in some sense as belonging to "neighborhoods" and that, despite the individual variations, there were some recognized boundaries. The map showing these was taken into account in considering planning proposals, particularly on new roads, for the existing town.

Regarding housing preferences, owner-occupiers wanted to move "nearer to the country," the direction in which many others had already moved. Some tenants of public housing desired to buy their home and others would be prepared to pay more rent for a larger or more modern one, or one with a garage. These findings were hopeful because they indicated that some existing Ipswich residents would move to the new expansion areas; this could assist "integration" in two ways—the new areas could include Ipswich people as well as Londoners and, if the management problems could be overcome, vacant houses in existing public housing schemes in the town could be made available to those newcomers who wanted an older property at a lower rent and nearer to central Ipswich.

London Surveys

There are two main sources of recruits from London to new and expanding towns. Some move with their employers, the proportion varying between one town and another from about half to three-quarters. Most of the rest go through what is called the Industrial Selection Scheme; this is a register, administered by the Greater London Council and the Ministry of Labour, of people living in London who are in housing need and are willing to move to a new or expanding town. They are classified according to their occupations, so that they can be selected to fill job vacancies in new communities. In December 1966, the Register covered about forty thousand people, and the main survey in London was a series of ninety-nine interviews from which a sample of married men was drawn.

The objectives of the survey were to find out something about these potential migrants, to study their attitudes to moving, and to gather data on specific policy suggestions that had previously been formulated. Because we could not know how far the occupational needs of the town would reflect the occupational structure of the Register, we could not generalize from the sample to the people likely to move to Ipswich via this channel. But we could draw some general conclusions about the people on the Register. Predictably, they were predominantly young couples with young children. They were badly housed—overcrowded, sharing toilets with other families, often lacking bathrooms altogether. But they were not all poor by English standards. More than half had a net household income of over £20 a week (about $56). A majority had skilled blue-collar jobs and only 6 percent were unskilled.

Not surprisingly, the thing that people most disliked about their present life in London was their housing; and "to get a house" was the overwhelming reason for moving. The features about their present life that people said they "liked" corresponded to the criticisms of new communities cited earlier. The most valued feature was the accessibility and variety of shops and other amenities. The second most important was a set of "social" qualities, mainly the presence of relatives, friends, or neighbors.

Like the earlier research in new communities, these interviews suggested that there would be advantages to some residents if relatives moved as well. Another series of questions explicitly asked about this. People were asked if they thought their parents or their spouse's parents would like to go to the same new town as themselves. Some, of course, did not have parents alive. Of the rest, fourteen said parents or parents-in-law would like to go and another twenty said they might, amounting to a third of the sample altogether. People were also asked about other relatives and friends who "might like" to go. The answers suggested that such migrants, if free to do so, might take with them about half as many other households (as well as the parents already referred to). There is the problem of work; there would need to be arrangements for such people to be considered for job vacancies in the new community. If this were done, and if the scheme were selective toward middle-aged relatives and friends, it would have a double advantage. Together with provision for parents, it would both help to create a more balanced age structure and allow some of the new residents to maintain social ties they valued.

The interviews with this London sample also provided some guidance about the kind of housing such people might need. Overwhelmingly, they would prefer a house to an apartment, though a large proportion of small households, when asked, said they would be willing to start in an apartment if they could transfer to a house later when their family grew. This had some obvious implications for the balance of different building types, suggesting that more apartment blocks might be built than has been usual with new towns. (In most English new towns apartments have accounted for about 10 percent of all dwellings; in Ipswich the proportion is likely to be about 30 percent.) On the issue of promoting intermixture of old and new residents by offering older and cheaper public housing inside Ipswich to new residents from London, a fifth of those in the sample (mainly less skilled and lower paid workers) said they would choose this.

A further set of fifty-three interviews was carried out in London, with employees intending to move with one particular firm to the expanded town of Swindon. The sample was not only small but also could not be considered representative of people moving with their employers; it could, however, give another perspective. The sample was certainly different from that drawn from the Register. The people were older and, though not generally better paid, were in better housing; nearly half owned their home, whereas none of the Register sample did. The attitude toward moving was also different, with the main reason for going not to get a house but to continue working for the company. Again, though, many were concerned about leaving relatives or friends behind and others thought they would miss the variety and choice offered in London.

One issue on which it was hoped the two sets of London interviews might give some guidance was the proportion of houses that should be built for sale. Of the Register sample, about a quarter wanted to buy and were likely to be able to afford to do so. Of those moving with their firm, well over half were actually arranging to buy. The obvious lesson from this was that the demand for houses for sale would largely depend on the proportions recruited in the two different ways and on what kind of employees moved with their firm. On the basis of the available evidence, the sociologists suggested that the initial proportion of new homes for sale should be about a third, with the opportunity of increasing this later if the demand grew, as it probably would. Obviously these sets of interviews, though modest, produced other suggestions. Those mentioned give an indication of the kinds of information collected and of their relevance to the planners' tasks.

Implications

It should be emphasized that the collaboration described was experimental. Furthermore, this was a particular kind of planning exercise—a proposal for designation of a new town, followed by a "basic plan"—and the experience of cooperation in other kinds of planning work would inevitably be different. The exercise does, however, suggest a number of conclusions.

The first is a general one about the role of the sociologist in the formulation of planning policy. In both parts of this paper, the discussion has inevitably been oversimplified; the case for a better age balance, for instance, has been put without discussion of its possible disadvantages. This issue and many of the others raised are complex and involve conflicts of values. There may well be conflicts between desirable objectives—for example, between allowing relatives to move together and rehousing those in bad housing in London, or between attracting the firms with the largest proportion of middle-aged workers and attracting those with the greatest potential for economic growth. In such conflicts, though the sociologist is not necessarily committed to any one standpoint, he frequently finds himself speaking in support of what he sees as the needs and preferences of the people being planned for—partly because their case has in the past so often gone by default. Thus one way of describing the sociologist's role is to say that, as well as contributing information about the social aspects of planning, he also adds a different voice, largely informed by different criteria, to the team's deliberations.

The second point is about the importance of management in city planning. The more planning tries to take account of social considerations, of people and their needs, the more critical is management. One example of the interrelationship between design and management policies is population structure; the design proposals must be influenced by the likely age structure of the population, including the distribution of types and sizes of dwelling, but getting a more balanced structure itself depends on pursuing particular management policies. If city planning is to respect social criteria, therefore, it must increasingly concern itself not only with physical design but also with the policies that will enable the design to work. The planner's report must include management recommendations as well as land use maps and development timetables.

This reciprocity of design and policy should ideally be followed through the processes of development, which, with a major project like a new town, could take 10 or 15 years.

The cooperative venture described here was for a specific contract; the relationship could clearly be more fruitful if the same planning team continued to work on the actual development and if the sociologists continued to be associated with the work. This would make it possible for social research to study the responses of residents moving into the first areas developed, feed back the results of the research, and thus influence both the design and management of later stages.

At a more specific level, the cooperation suggests some lessons about the kinds of questions that are most useful. Opinion questions—for example those put to the Ipswich sample about the town and the proposed expansion—can, despite their limitations, provide a useful guide, if only on how to present planning proposals. Hypothetical questions about what people "want" are of doubtful value, unless they are posed fairly precisely, and, as with the questions about house purchase, can be supplemented by reference to objective determinants like income. In general, questions about what people actually do or what they think of something they have experienced are much better. As in all research—a familiar lesson, though often ignored—the social investigator needs to have a clear idea of what he wants to find out and why. A specific question, to help resolve a specific planning or management issue, is likely to provide more useful data and to be applied more fully by the planning team than the rather vague idea that it might be useful to carry out a social survey.

All this underlines the main conclusion. The important thing about the experience was that it brought together, as partners, sociologists and other members of the planning team. There were of course difficulties in the collaboration. For a start, there was the familiar problem of communication across disciplines. Some members of the team, furthermore, found it difficult to fit what the sociologists were doing into their conception of planning. The sociologists for their part could not always collect the information needed, present it in the most useful form or translate it into helpful policy suggestions. But as the work proceeded both sides increasingly came to see the other's point of view, and even began in some measure to think like each other. This growth of mutual respect and understanding was perhaps the most hopeful pointer for the future.

Notes

1. See Hilda Jennings, *Societies in the Making* (London: Routledge and Kegan Paul, 1962); John M. Mogey, *Family and Neighbourhood* (London: Oxford University Press, 1956); Tom Brennan, *Reshaping a City* (Glasgow: House of Grant, 1959); Vere Hole, "Social Effects of Planned Rehousing," *Town Planning Review*, XXX (July 1959), 161-173; Michael Young and Peter Willmott, *Family and Kinship in East London* (Glencoe: Free Press, 1957).
2. F. M. Martin, J. H. F. Brotherston, and S. P. W. Chave, "Incidence of Neurosis on a New Housing Estate," *British Journal of Preventive and Social Medicine*, XI (October 1957), 196-202.
3. A recent study showed that among new town residents from London little more than a third were from the inner London districts where the housing is, in general, worst. See B. J. Heraud, "The New Towns and London's Housing Problem," *Urban Studies*, III (February 1966), 11-12.
4. Peter Willmott, *The Evolution of a Community* (London: Routledge and Kegan Paul, 1963).
5. Peter Willmott, "Housing Density and Town Design in a New Town," *Town Planning Review*, XXXIII (July 1962), 115-127.
6. Nick Reid, "Housing in Basildon," *Journal of the Town Planning Institute*, forthcoming.
7. Peter Willmott, "East Kilbride and Stevenage," *Town Planning Review*, XXXIV (January 1964), 307-316.
8. Peter Willmott, "Housing in Cumbernauld," *Journal of the Town Planning Institute*, L (May 1964), 195-200.
9. Kenneth Hudson, *An Awkward Size for a Town* (Newton Abbot: David and Charles, 1967).
10. See for example, J. H. Nicholson, *New Communities in Britain* (London: National Council of Social Service, 1961), pp. 79-80.
11. See Willmott, "East Kilbride and Steventage," p. 310; P. Sainsbury and Joyce Collins, "Some Factors Relating to Mental Illness in a New Town," *Journal of Psychosomatic Research*, X (July 1966), 48.
12. Willmott, "Housing Density and Town Design in a New Town," p. 124. See also J. H. Nicholson, pp. 140-141.
13. Willmott, "East Kilbride and Stevenage," pp. 312-313.
14. *Ibid.*, pp. 314-315. This compares East Kilbride with studies reported in T. Cauter and J. S. Downham, *The Communication of Ideas* (London: Chatto and Windus, 1954), pp. 64-65, and Peter Willmott and Michael Young, *Family and Class in a London Suburb* (London: Routledge and Kegan Paul, 1960), p. 91.
15. Richard MacCormac and Peter Willmott, "A Radburn Estate Revisited," *Architects Journal*, CXXXIX (March 1964), 691-695.
16. Nicholson, *loc. cit.*
17. Ministry of Housing and Local Government/Welsh Office, *The First Hundred Families* (London: Her Majesty's Stationery Office, 1965); Ministry of Housing and Local Government/Welsh Office, *The Needs of New Communities* (London: Her Majesty's Stationery Office, 1967).
18. London County Council, *The Planning of a New Town* (London: London County Council, 1961).
19. See for example, Nicholson, pp. 130-132, and Willmott, "East Kilbride and Stevenage," p. 308.
20. See for example, Herbert J. Gans, *The Levittowners* (New York: Pantheon, 1967), p. 22.

Social Research and New Communities 271

21. Young and Willmott, *Family and Kinship in East London*, pp. 212-214.

22. Willmott, *The Evolution of a Community*, p. 37.

23. See Nicholson, pp. 63-64.

24. See for example, G. Brooke Taylor, Lewis Keeble, and Wyndham Thomas, "New Towns and Neighbourhood Planning," *Architecture and Building*, XXXV (April 1960), 138-139; and the *Report of the Ministry of Housing and Local Government 1960* (London: Her Majesty's Stationery Office, 1961), p. 87.

25. Willmott, "Housing Density and Town Design in a New Town," pp. 124-125, and Dan Waldorf, "Neighbourhood Unit Assessments—Simple or Complex?," *Official Architecture and Planning*, XXX (March 1967), 373-374.

26. Willmott, "Housing Density and Town Design in a New Town," p. 125.

27. Waldorf, p. 377.

28. Raymond C. Bunker, *Travel and Land Use in Stevenage* (Birmingham: Department of Transportation and Environmental Planning, University of Birmingham, 1966), pp. 64-65.

29. Personal observation by the author, while interviewing residents of Cumbernauld.

30. In recent British reports on new towns, a great variety of synonyms for "neighborhood" have been advanced; for example the "residential areas" of 5,000 for a new town in Wales, Economic Associates Ltd., *A New Town in Mid-Wales* (London: Her Majesty's Stationery Office, 1966), p. 51; the "villages" of about 4,500 people in Washington, Llewelyn-Davies, Weeks, and Partners, *Washington New Town Master Town Report* (London: Her Majesty's Stationery Office, 1966); the "super-block residential units" of 4,000-5,000 people in Hook, *The Planning of a New Town*, p. 37.

31. See Peter Willmott and Michael Young, *Family and Class in a London Suburb*, p. 104, and William H. Whyte, *The Organisation Man* (London: Jonathan Cape, 1957), p. 289.

32. See Marc Fried, "Functions of the Working-Class Community in Modern Urban Society: Implications for Forced Relocation," *Journal of the American Institute of Planners*, XXXIII (March 1967), 91-98.

33. Despite the fact that, as Gans points out, most people who move to the Levittowns of the United States are not disturbed by the move, a minority are, and the difficulties they describe are broadly similar to those found in British studies; see Herbert J. Gans, pp. 225-241 and 255-259.

34. London County Council, *Survey into Design Aspects of Expanding Towns at Huntingdon, Haverhill and Thetford* (mimeographed) (London: London County Council, 1964).

35. The Phrase is used in the report of a study by a physician in East Kilbride, S. D. Coleman, *Mental Health and Social Adjustment in a New Town* (Glasgow: University of Glasgow, undated), p. 79. It should be explained that the findings on mental illness in new communities are contradictory. Since the study by Martin, Brotherston, and Chave, a number of other inquiries have suggested that the incidence of mental ill health is in general no higher in new towns or peripheral developments than in other kinds of districts. See Lord Taylor and Sidney Chave, *Mental Health and Environment* (London: Longmans, 1964); E. H. Hare and G. K. Shaw, *Mental Health on a New Housing Estate* (London: Oxford University Press, 1965); P. Hall, "Some Aspects of Moving House as an Apparent Precipitant of Psychiatric Symptoms," *Journal of Psychosomatic Research*, X (July 1966), 59-70. But there is also evidence that a minority of housewives pass through a temporary neurotic spell after their arrival in the new community; apart from Coleman, see Sainsbury and Collins, p. 51.

36. Margaret Willis, "Meeting Places for Hire in New Towns" (un-

published paper) (Ministry of Housing and Local Government, January 1966).

37. For a review of some of this work, see Research and Development Group, Ministry of Housing and Local Government, "Housing Research and Development," *Architectural Design* (August 1966), 378-400.

38. Ministry of Housing and Local Government, *The Deeplish Study* (London: Her Majesty's Stationery Office, 1966).

39. See for example, Shankland, Cox, and Associates, *Expansion of Ipswich: Designation Proposals* (London: Her Majesty's Stationery Office, 1966), Appendix A.

40. Ministry of Housing and Local Government, *The South East Study 1961-1981* (London: Her Majesty's Stationery Office, 1964), pp. 72-75.

41. People in Ipswich were asked, "When I say the word 'Ipswich' what particular place or building comes into your mind?" We were trying to explore what Lynch has called "imageability"; see Kevin Lynch, *The Image of the City* (Cambridge: The Technology Press and Harvard University Press, 1960), pp. 9 and 140-141.

WALDEN EDITIONS
from Ballantine Books

THE FUTURE OF TREASON, Peter Dreyer $1.50
In this firsthand account, Dreyer, an expatriate by choice, discusses what leads a man, necessarily, to oppose the government or governments under which he lives.

THE ONE QUEST, Claudio Naranjo $1.50
An innovative psychologist illuminates the factors common to the many and varied ways in which people seek personal growth—religion, education, and psychotherapy. "The first scientific treatment of meditation that is really good."
—*Whole Earth Catalog*

STEPS TO AN ECOLOGY OF MIND,
   Gregory Bateson $1.95
One of the most respected figures in anthropology uses the findings of his field, cybernetics, and ecology to build a new understanding of man as part of nature.

THE MARVELOUS ADVENTURE OF CABEZA DE
  VACA/MALINCHE, Haniel Long $1.25
The unique story of a Conquistadore who made a great discovery—that of the brotherhood of all men, and of the power within each man. "This story is a bright spot in the history of man."
—Henry Miller

SINGING FOR POWER: The Song Magic of the
  Papago Indians, Ruth Murray Underhill $1.25
A fascinating collection of songs and speeches reflecting the whole range of Papago life from the great yearly rain ceremony, through planting, harvesting and wild plant gathering to the dry-season activities of games and hunting.

THE OLD STRAIGHT TRACK, Alfred Watkins $1.95
First published in 1925, this important book reveals the extraordinary network of tracks left throughout Britain by an ancient race. A fascinating study of a branch of prehistoric scientific knowledge now all but lost.

To order by mail, send price of book(s) plus 25¢ per order for handling to Ballantine Cash Sales, P.O. Box 505, Westminster, Maryland 21157. Please allow three weeks for delivery.